# THE
# RHODODENDRON
## STORY

# THE RHODODENDRON STORY

*200 Years of Plant Hunting and Garden Cultivation*

*Edited by*
*Cynthia Postan*

THE ROYAL HORTICULTURAL SOCIETY

*Published in 1996 by*
*The Royal Horticultural Society,*
*80 Vincent Square, London SW1P 2PE*

*ISBN 1 874431 42 6*

*Edited for the RHS by Karen Wilson and Pat Pierce*

*Honorary Editor for the Rhododendron Group*
*Cynthia Postan*

*Editorial Board*
*Bruce Archibold*

*Front cover photographs:* Rhododendron *'Fastuosum Flore Pleno,* R. falconeri, R. *'Sappho',*
R. javanicum, *all © Harry Smith Collection. Back cover: the frontispiece from Joseph Hooker's*
Rhododendrons of Sikkim-Himalaya *© George Hooker*

*Designed and typeset by Grahame Dudley Associates, Hanworth, Middlesex*

*Printed by The KPC Group, London and Ashford, Kent*

# CONTENTS

# EDITOR'S PREFACE

This book tells the story of how the rhododendron was discovered and introduced into the West over a period of nearly 350 years. It is dedicated to all those who have devoted themselves to the task, including some who will for ever remain nameless and others whose lives were forfeit to the quest. They have left us a priceless legacy that each spring renews the wonder of bud, leaf and flower. They include collectors, solitary men, exposed to loneliness and danger; amateur gardeners who sought to enhance their woodlands and parterres with exotic novelties; professional gardeners whose working life was spent cajoling seedlings and plants to thrive in unfamiliar surroundings; nurserymen who helped to create, popularize and disseminate the hybrid clones; botanists who classified and named the species.

They are too many to mention by name, but we remember them, and perhaps the logo at the top of this page will stand as a symbol of what the Rhododendron fraternity has come to represent.

The Greek word signifies *Rhododendronphilloi*, or Rhododendron lovers. The central truss was designed by Sir Herbert Maxwell, an early member of the Rhododendron Society founded in 1915. The Greek word was devised by Dr M R James, later Provost of King's College, Cambridge. It was made as the die for a medal, and was presented to the Society by Gerald Loder, later Lord Wakehurst, in memory of his brother Sir Edmund Loder, the breeder of that unique hybrid which bears his name.

There are also those who have helped me with the book. Some, like the small editorial committee of the Rhododendron Group, encouraged me to pursue an apparently unattainable goal; others whose expertise and knowledge is distilled in the various chapters; more who lent, gave or searched for pictures to illustrate the story and offered practical suggestions for improvements, compiled the index, translated, typed the text and supported me when self-doubt intervened. They will all know of the debt I owe them. There are also my pen friends from overseas whose correspondence has widened my horizons. I would like to meet them one day. Nor should I forget my mentor, the late Walter Magor, soldier, civil servant, botanist, gardener, Great Cornishman, who watched over my efforts as editor with kindly forebearance.

If any are not mentioned by name in the following list I apologise and assure them that their generosity has not been in vain – for here is the book itself!

To the President and Council of the Royal Horticultural Society I owe special thanks for their faith in the project.

Susanne Mitchell, Pat Pierce and Karen Wilson, my editors, know how much I needed their guidance and friendly advice.

Lastly, I would like to express my personal thanks to our generous sponsor, His Highness Sheikh Zayed bin Sultan al-Nahyan, President of the United Arab Emirates, whose material help and deep interest in the cultivation of the genus in his historic garden at Tittenhurst Park tipped the balance in our favour at a moment when I feared all was lost.

Cynthia Postan.

# FOREWORD

❦

*'Perhaps with the exception of the Rose, the queen of flowers, no plants have excited more interest throughout Europe than the several species of the genus* Rhododendron.*'*

These words are attributed to Sir William Hooker when he was introducing the first part of his son's work, *Rhododendrons of Sikkim-Himalaya*. For my own part, full awareness of the beauty of the genus has come only in recent years.

I came to Tittenhurst Park, my family home in England, for the first time in 1989. The rhododendron 'Mrs Tom Lowinsky', seen in full glory at that time, stands out very clearly in my mind. At the Chelsea Flower Show in 1995 I was particularly thrilled with the knowledge that on our exhibit we were able to give pride of place to the progeny of perhaps the mother-plant of 'Mrs Tom Lowinsky', still growing strongly at Tittenhurst.

The contributors to this history of *Rhododendron* clearly reflect the enthusiasm of kindred spirits who are growing or studying such a diversity of species over a widely distributed area of the world. I am told that this is the first time that an account of the last 200 years of rhododendron culture in the West has been attempted. The Society has every right to be proud of celebrating with this special book edition. I am privileged to have been associated with its production.

H.H. Sheikh Zayed bin Sultan al-Nahyan

# INTRODUCTION

## CHRIS BRICKELL

Many plant genera have excited botanists and gardeners during the last 200 or more years but, apart perhaps from *Rosa,* none has gained quite such an admiring and devoted following worldwide as the genus *Rhododendron.* In their multitudinous variation of colour, form and habit the species demand immediate attention whether cosseted in gardens or gracing Himalayan forests or moorlands; and as a result of their wide-ranging, and often arranged, marriages when brought into gardens, and their profligacy in the production of offspring, the already wide choice has been vastly expanded by the introduction of numerous, often complex, hybrids to suit all sizes of gardens and all tastes.

As a result of such enthusiasm gardeners wanting to glean more knowledge and information inevitably come together to form specialist societies, associations or groups where like-minded people can discuss, argue about, eulogize over, and write about all aspects of their favourite genus.

In Britain the wealth of new species being introduced early this century by great plant collectors, like George Forrest, Ernest Wilson, Frank Kingdon-Ward, Reginald Farrer and others, acted as the stimulus for the formation of the Rhododendron Society in 1916 which was succeeded by the Rhododendron Association in 1928. Much very useful information was published during the period up to the Second World War, but thereafter the Rhododendron Association faded to be replaced by the Rhododendron Group formed under the aegis of the Royal Horticultural Society, already housing under its broad wings similar groups devoted to lilies and daffodils. In 1946 the production of a slim, elegant *Rhododendron Year Book* marked the birth of this specialist Group and the current volume has been published to celebrate the 50th year of its publication.

It might be thought that so much has already been written about rhododendrons that there was little ground still to cover, but the aim of this volume is to draw together a number of aspects of rhododendron history and work on the genus that is either poorly recorded or is scarcely known at all. It is a review of more than two centuries of different areas of history and lore by acknowledged authorities on the genus, assembled by Cynthia Postan without whose enthusiasm and dedication it would not have seen the light of day, and who also contributes valuable chapters on the national and international rhododendron societies and other organizations.

Since Linnaeus' day botanists have been studying, and often puzzling over, the taxonomic status and relationships of the vast collections of dried herbarium material and seed-raised plants received from plant collectors. These topics have been expanded on by Professor and Dr Philipson covering the history of the taxonomy of rhododendrons, by Dr James Cullen from the herbarium viewpoint and by Robert Mitchell on the habitat and environment. Historically, the introduction of rhododendrons into Britain and the gardens, gardeners and nurserymen associated with them is described by Ken Hulme and, as an example of the achievements of one of the earliest collectors, Mary Forrest presents a chapter on Sir Joseph Hooker's rhododendron introductions from Sikkim and their survival nearly 150 years later.

Peter Cox, with many recent introductions of *Rhododendron* to his credit, comments on changing techniques of collecting, while the history and aims of hybridization during the last century are set out by Walter Schmalscheidt, Lionel de Rothschild, Pat Halligan, Renaud de Kerchove and Jozef Heursel, to provide an

overall survey of the achievements of enthusiasts both before and after the Asian flood gates opened and so many species were made available to gardeners, particularly in the West.

Dr George Argent contributes a history of Vireya rhododendrons, scarcely known or grown in Britain, but of immense horticultural value both as species and hybrids, many among the most attractive of all members of this very beautiful genus. And to capture and record the names and descriptions of the cultivars, Dr Alan Leslie explains the system of International Registration for rhododendrons administered by the RHS. Dr Brent Elliott covers an area seldom touched upon, the changing role of the rhododendron in the fashion for garden design.

Not all topics can be fully covered in this one volume of course, but the contents of the 50 years of the Year Book since it was first published in 1946 have contributed so much to the knowledge and enjoyment of its readers that it is an appropriate time to reflect upon and review the work that has been done on the genus. It is also, perhaps, a time to look at international co-operation more closely and to collaborate worldwide with other enthusiasts to ensure that the study, cultivation and knowledge of rhododendrons is maintained and extended. Much better co-operation is certainly needed in relation to habitat conservation and studies of species distribution, taking into account the views of, and collaboration with, the people of those countries where rhododendrons grow naturally. Exploitation and destruction of habitats are well-known problems still waiting to be solved. Less well known or understood, but of equal importance, is the exploitation of the natural resources of individual countries, and as we approach the 21st century the need to work together globally becomes more and more essential if an expansion of interest in, and knowledge of, the genus *Rhododendron* is to be promoted further and maintained to provide additional pleasure and enjoyment for gardeners throughout the world.

CHRISTOPHER BRICKELL *was Director General of the Royal Horticultural Society from 1985 until 1993; before that he was Director of the RHS Garden, Wisley, for 16 years. He is a prolific writer on horticultural and botanic matters and has been on many plant collecting expeditions to China and other parts of the world*

# CHAPTER 1

# HABITAT AND ECOLOGY: CHANGES OVER 200 YEARS

## BOB MITCHELL

Rhododendrons are among the top five garden favourites and there is a multi-million pound industry focused round them. They are now grown on every continent by enthusiasts who enjoy their flower and foliage display. There are species and cultivars for every taste and climate, for not only do we have the choice of dwarf species from the mountain tops for the drier areas but also the rainforest giants which flourish best in the milder, high rainfall parts of the world. Rhododendrons are grown on the fringe of Rannoch Moor in Scotland at an altitude of 365m (1,200ft). As a contrast there are many tropical Vireya species grown in warmer countries like Australia. Many enthusiasts in colder climes grow the Vireyas in heated glasshouses or as pot plants in homes.

Rhododendrons have been known since Roman times but the first to be introduced into cultivation was probably *Rhododendron hirsutum* in 1656, followed by species from eastern North America, before the flood from South-East Asia.

The collector's description of the habitat, associations, climate, topography and altitude has been of great value to growers, giving an indication of conditions needed for successful cultivation. Research on the distribution of rhododendrons growing in their native habitat and their dependence on a host of other plants, can best be carried out through field research by trained botanists, studying their variability and ecosystems. It is essential for the determination of species.

The species of rhododendrons in cultivation in Britain flower from January with *R. mucronulatum* and *R. dauricum* through to July with *R. keysii* and *R. ungernii* and into August with *R. auriculatum* and its hybrids; so the flowering season is long. The stunning foliage, especially the young growth, provides the visual value for the rest of the year. Rhododendrons associate well with the genera *Magnolia, Primula, Meconopsis, Lilium, Nomocharis, Notholirion* and a host of Ericaceous plants which form part of their natural ecosystem in the wild.

Rhododendrons grown in cultivation,

demand a moist but well-drained acid soil. Accounts of them growing on limestone ranges are well documented by all the collectors in South-East Asia and are certainly true. Soil samples from the Cangshan Range recorded a range of pH values from 3.71 to 8.14. The low pH relates to samples registering the huge build-up of leaf litter over the centuries in a stable environment and overlying the limestone rock; in a similar manner to the peat build-up on the limestone pavement in the Burren in County Clare. The high pH sample was taken from soil and rubble with little humus among the roots of a very healthy *R. cephalanthum,* well above the tree line. The soil analysis records low levels of exchangeable calcium and sodium. So the elements which damage growth were not available to the plant, thus resolving the limestone question. Interestingly, phosphate and potash levels were also generally low, although moderately high in the 8.14 pH sample.

## Phytogeography

About 130 million years ago when the Indian plate broke away from Gondwanaland and drifted north to collide with Laurasia about 53 million years ago, it pushed up the mountain ranges to produce the land outline we know today. It is recognised that the western Chinese mountains, which contain coral fossils from the Triassic period, were formed before the Himalayan ranges. Frank Kingdon-Ward described south-west China as 'the land of the great corrosions' to reflect the concertina effect of the land surface with its four great river systems – the Yangtse, Mekong, Salween and Irrawaddy – and their towering mountains, 3,050m (10,000ft), above. The area consisting of the Himalayan mountain ranges, south-east Tibet (Xizang), south-west China and the Malaysian land mass never suffered the dramatic consequences of several Ice Ages, but permanent ice and snow are present about the 5,200m (17,000ft) altitude.

The flora of South-East Asia dates from Tertiary times, therefore many primitive plants grow here and have survived millions of years. At the same time the plant kingdom has evolved to cope with the changing climate and its habitat. This is certainly reflected in the great wealth of plants. So we find the early angiosperms such as *Magnolia, Paeonia* and *Camellia* intermixing with *Rhododendron,* also of ancient origin, in its highest concentration of species. In similar manner *Primula, Omphalogramma, Meconopsis, Nomocharis, Notholirion, Incarvillea,* and endless other genera we could name, are found here in what has been acclaimed to be their centre of diversity. In the Sino-Himalayan area we find several floral kingdoms coming together to make this one of the richest areas of temperate plants.

With such a large area and with seemingly endless habitats, it is not surprising that there is considerable diversity and form within a genus. And so it is with *Rhododendron* which occupies a huge range of climatic situations from subtropical rainforest to rugged mountain tops and displays the genus in all its diversity.

Rhododendrons in the wild are predominantly northern hemisphere plants although their distribution dips south of the Equator in South-East Asia with the exciting and brilliantly coloured Vireya species of Malaysia, Indonesia and New Guinea. Only one species, *R. lochae*, is found in Australasia, in the mountains of north Queensland in Australia. The geographical distribution of *Rhododendron* extends north to Korea and Japan into circumpolar regions and eastward into North America where species are found in both eastern and western areas, generally in the mountains. Rhododendrons extend westward from the Sino-Himalayan region to Afghanistan and in the Caucasus mountains, through Turkey and into Europe. There are no rhododendrons in Central and South America, Africa, Polynesia, or Australasia (apart from *R. lochae*) although Ericaceae or Epacridaceae, a closely related family, are found in every continent.

**South-East Asia**

In South-East Asia three floral areas are recognised – the Himalayan, the Indo-Malaysian and the Chinese Regions. All have very rich flora and rhododendrons are present at different altitudes in each of these areas. It is appropriate to look at them all to see where rhododendrons are found and to detail the habitats to enable growers to have a better understanding of their cultural needs and problems.

The most ancient are the tree species which grow in the temperate rainforest where they can attain 25 to 30m (80-100ft). Where they grow, there is little respite from the rains and high humidity. The monsoon simply brings more rain to encourage growth. In these humid conditions many of the epiphytic species are found, securing a niche in the moss and lichens on the limbs of trees or on mossy banks with their scent pervading the air.

The Himalayan Region stretches from Bhutan to Kashmir where we find a host of rhododendrons. It was the collections of Wallich and Griffith in Nepal and particularly Joseph Hooker's introductions from Sikkim in 1848 which started the great enthusiasm for rhododendron cultivation on the large scale. Many of Hooker's plants are still growing in Britain's west coast gardens. In the Himalayan mountain chain the rainfall decreases from the heavy monsoon in the east, to much lighter rainfall in the west. Naturally, so does the proportion and abundance of species.

Stainton, in *Forests of Nepal* published in 1972, outlined many distinct forest types. From the tropical and subtropical foothills, ten distinct tree associations are recognised but it is not until we reach the 1,830m (6,000ft) level that we find *R. arboreum* present in the *Schima-Castanopsis* forest. *Rhododendron arboreum* has the widest distribution of the Himalayan species. Some would argue it is the most primitive of all the rhododendrons and this is reflected in the number of subspecies and varieties. This species was one of the first Himalayan species to be introduced.

In the altitudinal progression this is followed by the Temperate and Alpine Broadleaved Forest of which Stainton recognized 11 different associations. Here belong the *Quercus, Castanopsis, Aesculus, Juglans, Acer* and *Rhododendron* forests ranging in altitude from 1,700 to 3,350m (5,500-11,000ft) and here we find the bulk of the Himalayan species such as *R. arboreum, R. falconeri, R. grande* and *R. hodgsonii* with *R. dalhousiae* and *R. lindleyi* in the understorey at the lower elevations. *Rhododendron campanulatum, R. campylocarpum, R. thomsonii* and *R. wallichii* form the next banding while *R. fulgens* and *R. wightii* are found at the higher level in the *Rhododendron* Forest. Above this, and overlapping, is the Birch Forest which contains many of these species but also *R. barbatum* and *R. campanulatum*, while in the upper levels *R. lepidotum* and *R. lowndesii* are dwarf in comparison to withstand the more severe climate.

Contiguous with this group is the Temperate and Conifer Forest also existing at the elevations of 1,800 to 4,000m (6,000-13,000ft) where *Pinus excelsa, Tsuga dumosa,* and *Abies spectabilis* are found in the east and central parts of Nepal, while *Picea smithiana, Abies pindrow* and *Cedrus deodara* are confined to the western areas. Larch, *Abies spectabilis*

and *Juniperus wallichianum* form the highest coniferous forests. However, among these conifers most of the previous rhododendron species are to be found together with *R. cowanianum,* (indigenous with *R. lowndesii* in Nepal), and *R. anthopogon,* the link with the Alpine Associations.

As in all mountain ranges, rainfall significantly affects the flora and where there are rain shadow areas, naturally the flora is less abundant. In the Moist Alpine Scrub associations, from 3,650 to 4,420m (12,000-14,500ft), there is also a definite tier effect with *R. campanulatum, R. wallichii, R. campylocarpum, R. wightii* and *R. fulgens* occurring at the lower elevations and *R. anthopogon, R. lepidotum, R. pumilum* and *R. setosum* growing above them. *Rhododendron anthopogon* and *R. lepidostylum* grow in the Dry Alpine Scrub and above them is *R. nivale,* reaching the highest altitude of the Himalayan species and found at 5,900m (19,000ft).

The extension of rhododendrons in the western Himalayas continues with *R. lepidotum* and *R. anthopogon* subsp. *hypenanthum* into Kashmir, while *R. collettianum* and *R. afghanicum* grow in light forest in north Pakistan and Afghanistan.

The Indo-Malaysian Region covers the eastern Himalayas and Arunachal Pradesh (which used to be called Assam), and here, at its borders with south-east Tibet (Xizang) and Burma the monsoon is at its strongest. The region covers the Ganges delta southward to Sri Lanka (where *R. arboreum* subsp. *zeylanicum* grows in the hills) and eastward to encompass Burma with a rainfall from 200 to 360cm (80-142in). It can be subdivided into four main zones. From sea level to about 1,060m (3,500ft) the Indo-Malaysian Jungle is extremely rich in its trees and lianas, but it is the Temperate Rainforest where we find the epiphytic species including *R. maddenii, R. dendricola, R. megacalyx, R. edgeworthii, R. megeratum* and *R. taggianum*. Tree rhododendrons like *R. arboreum* and *R. grande* extend from Nepal while *R. arboreum* subsp. *delavayi* is more easterly in its distribution and all three overlap here while *R. sidereum* and *R. magnificum* are confined to this region. These giants are also found as the vegetation changes with altitude at about 2,750m (9,000ft) to *Abies* Forest and *Rhododendron* Scrub where the majority of shrubby species are found in this band to 3,350m (11,000ft). Above this the Alpine Zone commencing about 4,600m (15,000ft), hosts its own dwarf and ground hugging species such as *R. campylogynum, R. cephalanthum, R. calostrotum* subsp. *keleticum, R. pumilum,* etc.

To the east, in the China Region, and particularly in the provinces of Yunnan and Sichuan where most of the Chinese rhododendron species are to be found, we find also a layered grouping of species. The land mass of Yunnan Province increases in altitude from south to north and it has been suggested that zones of vegetation align horizontally with latitude. The whole is controlled by the monsoon in differing intensities, but not to the same extent as in the previous region for, here, the rain shadow areas are marked by very dry areas particularly in the river valleys of the Salween, Mekong and Yangtze. This is quite dramatically observed on the west facing slopes where the bulk of the rains fall and lush vegetation is found, while the eastern slopes in this rain shadow get what remains and the vegetation is sparser.

Vegetation zones are described in sequence from the Tropical rainforests in the south, leading into the subtropical zones, Evergreen Broadleaf Forest which can be divided into two types with the gradation of the monsoon rains in its southern range, to the north portion where it is a much drier woodland type. With altitude as well as latitude the transition is into the Cold Temperate Needle Forest leading, at the highest elevations, to the Alpine Meadow on mountain tops and on the high plateau.

In Yunnan, in the areas where rhododendrons grow in more abundance, it is clearly possible to identify altitude by the species. As we ascend from 1,220m (4,000ft) the vegetation changes from predominantly Evergreen Hardwood Forest to Deciduous Forests of *Quercus, Juglans, Chrysobalanopsis* and *Castanopsis* etc. *Rhododendron simsii* extends from Hong Kong through south China into Burma where it grows at less than 305m (1,000ft). In Yunnan Province it grows up to 2,200m (7,220ft) on the Cangshan (Tali) range. Here it associates with another azalea – *Rhododendron microphyton* – in a range of colours and *R. pachypodum*. At 2,500m (8,200ft) *R. maddenii* subsp. *crassum* and *R. virgatum* subsp. *oleifolium* gradually merge with *R. arboreum* subsp. *delavayi* and *R. decorum* to reach the significant altitude of 3,050m (10,000ft) where it is recognised that plants should be hardy in Britain. Here also *R. edgeworthii*, *R. sulfureum* and *R. neriiflorum* are found before reaching the Bamboo Belt which extends for a further 600m (2,000ft) in altitude and it is here where the greatest number of *Rhododendron* species grow. But the sequence of species with altitude continues with *R. cyanocarpum*, *R. dichroanthum*, *R. haematodes* (endemic to the Tali range) *R. rubiginosum*, *R. selense* subsp. *jucundum* and *R. yunnanense* gradually giving way to *R. rex* subsp. *fictolacteum*, *R. heliolepis*, *R. lacteum*, *R. racemosum* and *R. sinogrande* at 3,200m (10,500ft). Above this altitude there is the *Abies* and *Rhododendron* Scrub where almost pure stands of *R. roxieanum* and *R. taliense* with *Abies delavayi* intermix, occurring to 4,000m (13,200ft) above Dali. *Rhododendron balfourianum* also occurs at this height but on the western slopes. In the Alpine Meadow consisting of rock and grassland above 4,000m (13,200ft) *R. fastigiatum*, *R. cephalanthum* and *R. campylogynum* are sometimes found in great swathes.

Other mountains have their own plant associations and endemics and this is repeated throughout the ranges. In the north-west of Yunnan and its borders with south-east Tibet (Xizang), the *Rhododendron* Heathland, with scattered rocks extends between 4,300 to 5,000m (14,100-16,500ft) where the dwarf carpet-forming species (mainly *Lapponicum*) with their aromatic foliage, are to be found.

## The Vireyas

The 300 species of Vireya rhododendrons, which constitute a third of the known wild species, also demand attention and, although requiring protective conditions in Britain, they are equally exciting and as colourful as the hardy species (see Chapter 7). The greater majority are found in the Mossy or Cloud Forest from 1,525 to 2,300m (5,000-7,550ft); in the Elphin Wood to 3,050m (10,000ft); or in the Sub-Alpine Grassland which extends to 3,660m (12,000ft). In many parts of this varied area the rainfall can be as high as 254cm (100in) where the plants grow as normal shrubs in humus-rich soil or as epiphytes in the abundant moss.

## North-East Asia

The distribution of *Rhododendron* extends north through the Pacific island of Taiwan, which boasts about 20 species, while Japan has at least 30 species. Many of these are azaleas, including *R. kaempferi*, *R. obtusum* and *R. kiusianum* from which the Kurume azaleas have been derived. Another wonderful plant is *R. yakushimanum* which itself is attracting so much attention from hybridists for its fine shape, form and floral attributes. There are about six species in Siberia including *R. lapponicum, R. aureum, R. mucronulatum, R. dauricum, R. redowskianum* and *R. camtschaticum* and it is the latter which links Japan to Kamtschatka and the Kuriles Islands where it bridges the Bering strait to the south coast of Alaska.

## North America

*Rhododendron macrophyllum*, discovered by Archibald Menzies in 1792 is the state flower of Washington and is one of the seven species native to western North America. Among them is *R. albiflorum* which does not do well in cultivation, and *R. occidentale*, found by David Douglas in 1830, one of the most important species to be introduced not only for its value in plant breeding but also for its later sweetly scented flowers. I have seen more than 30 different wild forms of this wonderful azalea. This is one of the many problems facing taxonomists when naming plants, for natural variation certainly exists throughout the geographical range of any species.

In central and eastern North America there are a further 20 species, the bulk of them azaleas. Three – *R. canescens, R. periclymenoides* and *R. viscosum* – have been in cultivation in Britain since 1734. The importance of the introduction of *R. catawbiense* in 1809 by John Fraser cannot be over-emphasised for its value as a parent in the breeding of so many of the garden-worthy hardy hybrids we still have today.

## Europe and South-West Asia

The nearest we can get to a rhododendron in Britain is the charming little trailing azalea – *Loiseleuria procumbens* – of the Scottish mountains, yet *Rhododendron ponticum*, in particular, behaves as if it were indeed a native plant. Before the Ice Ages, *R. ponticum, Ginkgo* and *Magnolia* were native to these shores. From these three only *R. ponticum* remains from pre-glacial times in Europe. *Rhododendron hirsutum* was introduced from Europe about 1656. Interestingly, *R. ferrugineum,* known to the ancients, did not arrive in Britain until about 1739. Its close relations *R. myrtifolium* (syn. *R. kotschyi*) is also from central Europe. *Rhododendron lapponicum* is found in north Scandinavia and westward in Iceland and Greenland to link with North America while its geographical distribution extends eastward across Siberia, as a circumpolar species.

*Rhododendron ponticum*, native to south Spain and Portugal, is the European link with south-west Asia, its main centre being Turkey, together with the Pontic azalea, *R. luteum*. Three other rhododendrons extend the range eastward to the Caucasus where *R. caucasicum, R. smirnowii* and *R. ungernii* are found.

## Fragile Ecosystems

The capacity of rhododendron to regenerate is well known. The seed is tiny and is carried some distance in the wind from the parent plants. Visit any rhododendron collection and you will find great swards of young seedlings. Where species grow together and overlap in their flowering, there inevitably will be cross pollination.

In the wild, it is a well established fact that, if there is disturbance of the fragile ecosystem where rhododendrons co-habit and flower at the same time, natural hybrids will be found. Field work can resolve this problem of identification as it did in 1981 when *R. agastum* 'Irrorata' was found to be a natural hybrid between *R. arboreum* subsp. *delavayi* and *R. decorum*, being intermediate in all its characters. This phenomenon was noticed where the natural tree cover had been disturbed, letting in the light. *In situ* only the strongest seedlings will establish themselves and some of them may be hybrids.

Deforestation, leading to the destruction of the natural habitat, is not a new phenomenon, for it was Augustine Henry who, in 1898, wrote about the destruction of the forests in Yunnan Province. This was one of the factors which led to Ernest Wilson being sent out to collect in central-west China in 1899 and to the discovery of over 1,000 species of plants which were new to science, many of them rhododendrons. Deforestation continues today throughout this region. In western China, timber is being extracted from virgin pine forest close to the border with Tibet (Xizang) to meet the demands of the increasing home market. Already 40 per cent of the natural forest has been destroyed in Yangbi County, on the western flank of the Cangshan (Tali) range,

and this loss of forest cover has resulted in a noticeably reduced rainfall. The rain is important for the crops, so here is a catch-22 situation.

Increasing populations throughout the world are placing habitats at great risk. In order to survive people need fuel wood for cooking and heating and more land for cultivation which they are claiming higher up the hillsides to altitudes where there is marginal cropping leading to the inevitable loss of natural vegetation and its flora. As we have noted all species grow only in their own niche in an altitudinal progression on the hillsides.

Equally worrying is the threat of monsoon rains sweeping the soil away or eroding deep gullies through these newly cleared areas. On the high mountain slopes the soil is thin, producing only one crop every two years compared with the two crops in a year on the lower ground. In China, it is recognised that the loss of habitat has put over 3,000 species of plants at risk, or facing extinction.

There is another factor, not generally taken into account, and that is the effect of tourism. While it does bring welcome revenue to countries like Nepal, tourists need to be fed and this certainly takes its toll on the forest. A recent account states the number of annual visitors to Mount Everest National Park is double that of the local population. But the country as a whole is losing 400,000 ha (990,000 acres) of forest a year, much of which is at altitude and therefore includes the

*Rhododendron* Forest. This cannot go on.

The most vulnerable areas are in the mountains where the Broadleaved Forest merges with the Conifer-*Rhododendron* Forest and where we find the highest levels of cultivation. It is imperative that there is a well-established vegetation to prevent flash floods which in recent years seem to be increasing, and with them the disastrous removal of the precious top soil. It is not only the rainforest which is at risk.

## Conservation

In China, the local leaders and elders are embarking on educational programmes to ensure better usage and management of the forests by trying to stop the high altitude burning by the hill tribes in an attempt to procure better grazing. It is also encouraging to note that the Government has designated the Cangshan Range to be a National Nature Reserve, so the legislation is in place. But part of the problem is that, with easier access to higher altitudes, habitats become more vulnerable.

It has been decreed that everyone in China should plant a number of trees each year. While this is a fair statement, these trees need to be tended and allowed to grow to become effective in their habitat. The reality is that most will not survive the ravages of animal grazing and the climate. It is therefore so important to safeguard the stability of the natural vegetation ensuring, through educational programmes, the best way to manage the forest. It is important to initiate and continue the serious tree planting programmes with native species and to make sure that they are a success. An alternative fuel for cooking would help to save many trees. This has been attempted in Nepal. Tree nurseries in Nepal are raising hundreds of thousands of seedling trees for replanting the vulnerable high altitude forests. This is encouraging but. . .

Loss of habitat is not confined to the Sino-Himalaya: it is happening elsewhere throughout the world. The Rio conference was a useful step but it needs the will of Governments throughout the world, the goodwill of the local population and the understanding of visitors to ensure that our natural heritage is secure for future generations to enjoy and to be able to research the plants for the benefit of mankind.

In Bhutan there appears to be the ideal situation, for the Royal Family and the Royal Government are conservation minded; they discourage clear felling and encourage replanting of native species; they control the number of visitors which in itself puts pressure on the environment and the population is still small enough to live in equilibrium with its surroundings.

BOB MITCHELL, *currently Property Manager at Branklyn for the National Trust for Scotland, was Curator of the University Botanic Garden in St Andrews. In 1981 he led the Sino-British Expedition to China, the first joint Sino-European botanical expedition since 1947*

# CHAPTER 2

# THE TAXONOMY
# OF THE GENUS:
# A HISTORY

## WILLIAM AND MELVA PHILIPSON

One morning, in the years before World War II, one of us, arriving as usual at the Botany Department of the British Museum, South Kensington, welcomed a young visitor newly arrived from Berlin to study in the herbarium. This was Dr Hermann Sleumer, whose forthcoming classification of *Rhododendron* was to do so much to influence ideas about the genus during the next 50 years. Much of the history of *Rhododendron* is concentrated in this short span, but before considering it we must first review its long and slow development.

The Near Eastern species of *Rhododendron*, were known in classical times, though the name rhododendron was not applied to them but to the oleander. The early herbalists of western Europe knew the alpine rose, and the name rhododendron was first tentatively extended to it by the Italian Andreas Caesalpino in 1583. A brief review of the early history is given by Cowan (1949). However, the history of the classification of *Rhododendron*, that is

the arrangement of the various species into related groups, began when Linnaeus divided the few species then known into two genera, namely *Rhododendron* and *Azalea*. Two hundred and forty years separate this simple beginning from the present elaborate arrangement of almost 1,000 species into just under 100 categories of subgenera, sections and subsections. Previous reviews are few and mostly concerned with special aspects, as that of Wilson and Rehder (1921) which deals with azaleas. Zabel (1902) and Sleumer (1949) both give much concise information and Philipson and Philipson (1974) review the history up to that time. The present account does not seek to record all the details of the tortuous history, but rather to note the origin of new ideas which have proved significant in the development of our understanding of the genus.

### Linnaeus to G Don, 1753-1834

When Linnaeus published his *Species*

*Plantarum* in 1753 he included nine shrubs that would now be placed in *Rhododendron*, though he treated five of them as members of *Azalea*. This subdivision, which was based on the number of stamens (10 and five respectively), has persisted until the present day, although the characters used to define the two groups have been revised and the groups have rarely been regarded as distinct genera since Salisbury (1805-08) pointed out good reasons for uniting them.

For 80 years after Linnaeus, the classification of rhododendrons made little progress. Several new species arrived in Europe during this period and botanists were often puzzled by their overall resemblance to *Rhododendron,* combined with peculiarities which did not fit with their idea of the genus. It was unfortunate that the genus was first known from peripheral areas where several aberrant species occur. It was much later that the heart of the genus, in the Himalaya and Western China, became known. Only then did it become possible for the relationships between the anomalous forms to be understood. With so many more species available now we can see how all these forms link together, but at that time the readiest solution to these puzzles was to create new genera to accommodate each peculiarity. In the second edition of his *Species Plantarum* (1762), Linnaeus created the genus *Rhodora* for a shrub of the north-eastern United States and Canada, its principal distinguishing feature being its two-lipped flower. Several species became known from the Malayan archipelago and these Blume (1826) placed in a new genus *Vireya*, with the rather slight characters of a small calyx and the stamens scarcely included within the corolla. At the same time Blume proposed another genus, *Hymenanthes,* (for the plant now known as *R. metternichii*), which he compared with *Befaria* rather than *Rhododendron*, although we know it to belong to the same section (*Ponticum*) as a species that had already been described by Linnaeus. The fact that its floral parts are arranged in whorls of seven was given great weight at a time when Linnaeus' largely numerical system was in vogue. The name *Hymenanthes* has proved of importance because it was the first generic name to be applied to a species that is neither lepidote nor an azalea. It therefore serves as a useful label for the non-lepidote rhododendrons, which together form the largest and horticulturally most important part of the whole genus and is now acknowledged as the subgeneric name for them. A Chinese species, *R. farrerae*, was thought by Tate (1831) to provide a link between the azaleas and rhododendrons. He placed it with *R. dauricum* into a section which he named *Brachycalyx*. The existence of this supposed link stimulated him to suggest that the azaleas should be united with *Rhododendron*. He used Kaempfer's name *Tsutsusi* for the azalea section.

These piecemeal changes were co-ordinated and further developed when

George Don wrote his *General History of Dichlamydious Plants* (1834). In view of the great part the Royal Botanic Garden at Edinburgh was to play in the later development of the genus, it is interesting to learn that George Don's father was Superintendent of the Garden. George Don the younger went south to take charge of the Chelsea Physic Garden, to undertake tropical collecting expeditions, and to publish many botanical articles and books.

With the appearance of his *General History* the framework of a system for rhododendrons was established for the first time. One important advance was his formal union of the azaleas and rhododendrons, a step foreshadowed by Salisbury (1805-08) and Tate (1831). He failed to unite the poorly known Malayan Vireyas and the misapprehended *Hymenanthes*.

A second important advance was his subdivision of the genus into sections, a process that affected the azaleas as well as the rhododendrons in the limited sense. His division of the azaleas (a term he does not use, reserving it for *Loiseleuria*) is clearly on a geographical basis, though this is not stated. He reserves the name *Tsutsutsi* (now so spelled) for Asiatic species, though the species he listed are now considered to be of many types (for example sections *Azaleastrum*, *Sciadorhodion*, and *Pentanthera*). He coined the name *Pentanthera* for the North American azaleas, excepting *R. rhodora* (=*R. canadense*) which he left in a section of its own, Section *Rhodora*. The characters used to separate

his two sections *Tsutsutsi* and *Pentanthera* are the small calyx and narrow flowers of the American species contrasted with the foliaceous calyx and campanulate flowers of the Asiatic.

Even more important is his attempt to subdivide the remainder of the genus. His Section *Lepipherum* clearly foreshadowed the all-important distinction between lepidote and non-lepidote species. While scales are mentioned in the definition, the group appears to be defined principally on the nature of the calyx, so that several lepidote species are in fact placed in his section *Ponticum* (which was much more widely conceived than the present *Ponticum* Series). Although he left the aberrant *R. dauricum* in the *Lepipherum* group, Don was astute enough to see that *R. anthopogon* merited a section of its own (*Pogonanthum*). The Vireyas he continued to regard as a distinct genus. His attempt to subdivide the non-lepidote species into two sections, *Ponticum* and *Booram*, was mainly based on the number of cells in the ovary together with features of the calyx. Although this distinction was to influence ideas for a long time, it has not survived into present classifications. It is difficult to understand why he did not include *Hymenanthes* in his section *Booram*.

The section *Chamaecistus* included two very different plants, namely *Rhodothamnus* and *R. camtschaticum*.

In reviewing Don's system it is a remarkable fact that seven out of the eight sections he proposed are still regarded as valid groups, and in addition *Vireya* is still maintained, though as a Section.

## Don to Maximovicz, 1834-70

Very little progress was to be made until the revolutionary system of Maximovicz appeared 26 years later. Don's scheme served as a basis for subsequent publications, though his influence was less than it might have been since some of his ideas were rejected by De Candolle in the very influential *Prodromus* (1839). De Candolle retained *Azalea* as a separate genus to include the deciduous species of both the old and new worlds, while he treated the evergreen azaleas as section *Tsutsutsi* of *Rhododendron*. Inexplicably, he places one deciduous azalea (*R. farrerae*) in *Eurhododendron* and another, North American, species in the evergreen Asiatic *Tsutsutsi*. He reunited Don's *Ponticum* and *Lepipherum* sections and together with *Vireya* formed them into a large amorphous group – *Eurhododendron*. De Candolle retained *Hymenanthes* and *Rhodora* as genera and *Booram, Pogonanthum* and *Chamaecistus* as sections. He created another genus, *Osmothamnus*, to include species now regarded as members of *Pogonanthum*. It was therefore redundant.

During this period, increasing numbers of rhododendrons were reaching Europe from the Himalayas, especially as a result of Joseph Hooker's expedition to Sikkim, and of Booth's to Bhutan and Assam. Hooker (1849) was aware of relationships among the Sikkim species, but

the first attempt to subdivide the main body of the Himalayan species into named groups was made by Thomas Nuttall (1853) when reporting on Booth's collections. These were defined principally on the form of the calyx and the number of cells in the ovary, and while none of Nuttall's names has survived into modern use, it is clear that he was in some instances grouping truly related species. Two years later Nuttall was so impressed with the tubular flowers and pseudo-lateral inflorescences of *R. keysii* (he describes and figures them as overtopped by lateral shoots) that he proposed a sub-genus *Keysia* for this species and this continued to be recognized for some years by later authors. Similarly, Klotzsch (1862) considered the magnificent species, *R. argenteum* Hook. f., to be sufficiently distinctive to require a new genus which he named *Waldemaria* after Prince Waldemar whose collections from Bhutan he was naming.

At this time Jules Emile Planchon was interested in the Chinese azaleas. In an account published in 1854 he recognized sub-genera to include: **1.** the deciduous azaleas of both the old and the new worlds (*Azalea*); **2.** the evergreen 'Indian' azaleas (*Tsutsusi*, in which he mistakenly included *R. molle*); and **3.** a new group which he named *Azaleastrum*. This was the first recognition of one of the most important features of rhododendron classification, namely, that within the azaleas several atypical groups are to be found. It is unfortunate that he did not recognize the peculiarities of *R. championae,* which he placed in his *Tsutsusi* group, or he would have anticipated Adrien René Franchet's *Choniastrum* by 30 years.

The classification of rhododendrons took its greatest step forward with the publication of Maximovicz's *Rhododendreae Asiae Orientalis* by the Imperial Academy of Sciences of St Petersburg in 1870. As curator of the Herbarium of the St Petersburg Botanic Garden, Maximovicz had made collecting expeditions through Siberia, Manchuria and Japan, so that he knew most of the species he was discussing at first hand in the field.

The most important contribution made by Maximovicz was his use of the position of the flower-buds and their relationship with leaf-buds ('innovations') to define the major subdivisions of the genus. He realized that the great majority of the species were characterized by terminal flower-buds with separate leaf-buds below them. Contrasted with these were three other groups. First, there were the 'evergreens' or 'Indian' azaleas, in which the flower-buds are also terminal but whose innovations spring from among the scales of the floral buds. We have seen that the name *Tsutsutsi* had become restricted to these plants; Maximovicz used it in the form *Tsusia.* Secondly, there were those rhododendrons whose flower-buds are borne laterally (in the axils of the foliage leaves) not terminating the twigs. *Azaleastrum* was found to have this type of flower arrangement, and to these Maximovicz added *Keysia* (having misinterpreted Nuttall's description) and also another group which he called *Rhodorastrum,* and which included *R. dauricum* and *R. mucronulatum.* The third group, whose inflorescence-form contrasted with the normal arrangement, he called *Rhododendra Anomala.* This included *R. camtschaticum* and its close relative *R. redowskianum* in which the arrangement of leaves and flowers is unique within the genus. In them the terminal buds produce a shoot which bears leaf-like bracts below the flowers. Maximovicz gave this group the name *Therorhodion,* and some subsequent authors have thought it better to treat this small section as a distinct genus.

For the rest, Maximovicz retained the section *Osmothamnus,* but he redefined it and expanded it from its original usage to include virtually all the lepidote species. By merging Don's *Booram* with his *Eurhododendron,* this Section comes to include all the non-lepidote species (excluding azaleas), together with the lepidote *R. formosum.*

Maximovicz's insight into the shoot-morphology of the genus was the most important event in the history of rhododendron classification. The fact that some of the other features of his arrangement are not so advanced as those of Don is probably attributable to his concentration on the Far Eastern region. His feeling for the azaleas was remarkable, but the other two major groups, represented poorly in that region, were interpreted with less insight.

## Hooker to Wilson and Rehder, 1870-1921

Hooker's treatment of the Ericaceae in the monumental *Genera Plantarum* (Bentham and Hooker, 1876) includes a detailed account of *Rhododendron* that follows Maximovicz very closely, and the few changes are for the better. One change is to correct the application of *Osmothamnus* to the original usage (=*Pogonanthum*) with the consequential employment of another name (*Graveolentes*) for the bulk of the lepidote species. Hooker follows Carl Johann Maximovicz in defining *Eurhododendron* by means of bud-scale characters and consequently includes some lepidote species in this group. They are chiefly species of the *Maddenia* and *Edgeworthia* Sub-sections and of *Vireya*.

Another improvement is the recognition of a series to include *R. schlippenbachii* and its allies, though this is defined on foliage characters and the nature of the inflorescence buds is still misinterpreted. The series is therefore associated with the deciduous azaleas rather than with *Tsutsutsi*. However, Hooker's principal contribution was his attempt to break down the large number of non-lepidote (excluding azaleas) and lepidote species into several subseries. In this he was taking further the work of Nuttall and, like his, Hooker's groups are largely based on the nature of the calyx and the number of loculi in the ovary. However, Hooker does not use Nuttall's names and their respective groups can only be equated very generally.

In 1882 Charles Baron Clarke continued this subdivision by publishing a key to the Indian species, but he proposed no formal classification of groups, at least among the principal lepidote and non-lepidote groups. However, a notable advance was the dependence on the presence or absence of scales for the major cleavage, so that for the first time species of the *Maddenia* Sub-section (see figure 2) appear among their lepidote colleagues and the non-lepidote group emerges uncontaminated (except for *R. edgeworthii*, which Clarke admitted might be better placed with the lepidote species). Also, Clarke divided *Vireya* into the true Vireyas and another group, *Pseudovireya*, characterized by the valves of the capsule not twisting in the manner he considered characteristic of *Vireya*.

When the collecting of the French missionaries began to make known the many species of Yunnan and Sichuan, Franchet rightly remarked that the centre of gravity of the genus had been moved there from the Himalayas. In his treatment of the collections of David and Delavay, Franchet (1886) followed Hooker closely, but found it necessary to make some modifications. In the lateral-flowered subgenus he proposed a new section, *Choniastrum*, to include *R. stamineum*, and he foreshadowed the need to subdivide *Rhodorastrum* by separating *R. racemosum, R. scabrifolium, R. oleifolium* and *R. virgatum* into a section distinct from *R. dauricum*, though he did not formally take this step. It is of

*Sir Joseph Hooker in 1867 after he was appointed*
*Director of the Royal Botanic Gardens Kew*

interest also that he, mistakenly, included *R. lutescens* in *Rhodorastrum* because many of its fascicles of flowers are borne in the axils of the leaves.

Towards the end of the last century German botany was coming into the ascendancy, and Adolf Engler was bringing out his great work, *Die Pflanzenfamilien,* Otto Drude (1891) covered the Ericaceae and included a treatment of *Rhododendron*. This was not as full as that of Hooker, nor so up to date.

There now occurs a long gap in the history which must have been a period of consolidation. Some very good accounts appeared of the species known in cultivation, for example those of Dippel (1889),

Koehne (1893), Zabel (1902) and Schneider (1907), and in their *Genera Siphonogamarum,* Dalla-Torre and Harms (1903) give a very complete generic synonymy of all the groups within *Rhododendron.*

During this time more and more species were becoming known. Not a few of these were discovered by Ernest Henry Wilson on his many plant collecting expeditions to China, first for Veitch's nursery and later for the Arnold Arboretum. When his collections came to be written up the section on *Rhododendron* was contributed by Alfred Rehder in collaboration with Wilson himself (1913). The groups recognized mainly agree with those of Maximovicz, though in a different arrangement and with amended nomenclature. A novel feature is a section *Lepidoto* (= *Triflorum*) which is detached from the main body of the lepidote species. In 1921, the same two authors issued a monograph of azaleas, in which more important innovations appear, and where previous misconceptions and errors are corrected. New features are the introduction of a section, *Sciadorhodion*, to include *R. schlippenbachii* and its allies, and the transfer of the Asiatic species *R. pentaphyllum* and *R. albrechtii* to the North American section *Rhodora*, a move that might have been better left unmade. The even more aberrant species, *R. nipponicum*, was also transferred to *Rhodora*, although Matsumura and Nakai had already (Nakai 1916) placed this species in a section of its own (*Viscidula*). It is interesting to note that Nakai also recognized the need for a section to include the relatives of *R. schlippenbachii* and that his name, *Verticillatae*, was published in the year following Rehder and Wilson's Monograph (Nakai, 1922).

The account of this period may conveniently conclude with reference to Schlechter's work on the New Guinea species (1918) and Copeland's treatment of the Philippine species (1929). Both these authors propose subdivisions of the Vireyas.

## Tagg, Hutchinson and Rehder, 1930

Throughout the previous period the number of species known continued to rise and many were brought into cultivation. The

increase in the size of some sections, especially of *Eurhododendron* (=*Hymenanthes*) and the lepidote species, stimulated attempts to break these down into more manageable units. We have already seen how this process began in Britain with Nuttall, Hooker and Clarke.

A sustained attack on this problem was begun at Edinburgh where Professor Isaac Bayley Balfour began to cluster the many species into Series. These appeared with more or less formal, but often informal mention in a sequence of papers in the Transactions of the Botanical Society of Edinburgh (1919a) and Notes from the Royal Botanic Garden (1916, 1917, 1919b, 1920) together with an account of the *Maddenii* Series by Hutchinson (1919).

These studies culminated in the production of a volume, *The Species of Rhododendron*, by the Rhododendron Society (ed. Stevenson, 1930). It is difficult to assess a book which has been so useful in stimulating interest in and knowledge of the genus, which in several ways advanced knowledge of the genus, and yet at the same time set aside so much of the accumulated knowledge of the best way in which to group the species.

The plan of this work was to place the species into numerous series without in any way grouping these into larger units. One result is that all the azaleas with their wide ranging differences form a single series with no more standing than the smallest series of, say, the lepidote species,

*Professor Sir Isaac Bayley Balfour (1853-1922).*
*Regius Keeper of the Royal Botanic Garden*
*Edinburgh, who made the first attempt to classify*
*the many new species from China*

which may differ from another series by some ill-defined character. Nor is the grouping of non-lepidote (excluding azaleas) and lepidote series retained, nor the presence among the latter of the group *Rhodorastrum.* The occurrence of *Azaleastrum* (in the broad sense) is not recorded, though notes under Series *Ovatum, Semibarbatum, Stamineum* and *Albiflorum* refer to their similarity.

In spite of their failure to present an overall scheme, the three authors, H F Tagg of Edinburgh (elepidote), J Hutchinson of Kew (lepidote) and Alfred Rehder of the Arnold Arboretum (azaleas and their allies), are responsible for several advances. Most of these are concerned with the recognition of the 13 series into which non-lepidote species are grouped and the 23 series of the lepidote species.

Interesting new subdivisions are also proposed among the groups with lateral flowers and among the azaleas. In the former, the authors took up a suggestion that we have seen was made by Franchet 40 years before, and divided (i) *R. virgatum,* and (ii) *R. racemosum, R. scabrifolium* and their allies, as groups separate from *R. dauricum.* Among the azaleas they separated *R. albiflorum* and *R. semibarbatum* each into a series of its own, and they also separated *R. tashiroi* as a sub-series of azalea.

The work on the series which was initiated at Edinburgh by Balfour and continued there by Tagg was carried further by a sequence of articles by JM Cowan and HH Davidian in which several series were revised (Cowan & Davidian, 1947; 1948; 1949; 1951; Davidian 1954; 1963; 1964; Davidian & Cowan, 1956).

## Sleumer: Ein System der Gattung Rhododendron – 1949

With the publication of *The Species of Rhododendron* there were virtually two systems of classification in use. Outside Britain the slowly developed botanical system largely prevailed, but in Britain, especially among horticulturists, the simplicity of many series, all equivalent in rank (though some were divided into sub-series) was irresistible, especially as no good account of the botanical system had been published in Britain. In any event, the series provided a more extensive range of pigeon-holes for the many known species. All that was lacking was the grouping of the series into classes of higher rank. That this should be attempted was suggested by Cowan (1949).

In that year Hermann Sleumer, a life-long research worker on the family Ericaceae, provided the necessary link between the two systems in his 'Ein System der Gattung Rhododendron' which appeared in the *Botanische Jahrbuch* (1949). In this comprehensive treatment he sets out the full botanical hierarchy of groupings as we have seen it develop from the time of Don and provided a key.

Apart from this synthesis of the two classifications, Sleumer continued the long process of refining the recognized groups within the genus. First, he adopted the view of Small (1914), Hutchinson (1921) and Copeland (1943) that *R. camtschaticum* and its allies should form a genus of their own, *Therorhodion.* Secondly, he divided *R. trichocladum* and its allies from the remainder of the lepidote groups as a new sub-genus (*Pseudazalea*) on the basis of more or less deciduous foliage and precocious flowers. Thirdly, Sleumer took even further the subdivision of the lateral-flowered lepidote species by separating *R. racemosum* from *R. virgatum* and *R. oleifolium.* Finally, he brought together the scattered work on *Vireya,* from Clarke to Schlechter and Copeland, into an orderly system. The nomenclature used in 1949 was subsequently slightly amended (Sleumer 1958; 1964).

For some decades after the publication of Sleumer's system, horticulturists debated the relative merits of the Balfourian system versus that of Sleumer. It was commonly believed that the two systems were unrelated, whereas Sleumer had skilfully united the two existing treatments into one. The old system, whose long history we have been tracing, and whose basis remained unshakeable, was nevertheless very weak in subdividing the many species in each of the two major parts of the genus. This was the strength of the Balfourian treatment, with its multitude of series and sub-series, but that system virtually ignored the well-established botanical subdivisions of the genus. The intention of the authors was to present their empirical groups (series) in as simple a manner as possible. To achieve this the old hierarchies were deliberately omitted although the authors firmly believed in them. Rehder, especially, had used the botanical classification extensively in his writings and had even introduced improvements to it, as noted above. In a sense, the treatment in *The Species of Rhododendron* is not a classification, but a careful avoidance of classification. This is hardly too sweeping a statement for a treatment that divides a multitude of species into 42 groups of equal rank. The human mind calls for an hierarchical arrangement and this was already present, though, until Sleumer, it had made little provision for the huge increase in the number of species that became known about 1900.

However this may be, the availability of *The Species of Rhododendron* resulted in British horticulturists thinking almost exclusively in terms of series, while their counterparts on the Continent and in the United States mostly continued to refer to the subgenera and sections of the older botanical arrangement, though the series were making some ground in the United States. As we have seen, it was Dr Sleumer who, in 1949, provided a synthesis of these two approaches by distributing the various series into appropriate pigeon-holes of the older system and giving them the more formal status of sections. In this way the advantages of both systems were combined. In spite of this, his proposals were slow to be adopted generally, no doubt because for long they were not available in an English version. A full translation finally appeared in the *Proceedings of the New York International Rhododendron Conference* (Luteyn and O'Brien, 1980).

The subject was extensively discussed at that Conference in 1978, when a resolution was adopted that the system of Sleumer, as modified by later work not yet considered here, provided a useful framework for the taxonomic organization of *Rhododendron* at the level of sections and subgenera. It also was acknowledged that this system built upon and incorporated much of the well-known scheme of Balfour.

Some adherents of Balfour's treatment have not been able to acknowledge the advances made by Sleumer and his successors. In particular, in his book *The Rhododendron Species* vol.I, H H Davidian (1982) states that he cannot accept

Sleumer's classification, nor that of Cullen, Chamberlain nor ourselves. He insists that the heart of rhododendron classification is the recognition of two groups, lepidote and non-lepidote (or elepidote). The importance of the presence or absence of scales is, of course, acknow-ledged by all recent botanists who have worked on the genus. However, there is a crucial difference in Davidian's classification: for him all rhododendrons which lack scales are lumped together in one heterogeneous group. This means that *Hymenanthes* is combined with the deciduous and evergreen azaleas, together with the azaleastrums and smaller subgenera, to form one immense group, the elepidote species, which is defined by the absence of scales and are not linked by the possession of some common characteristic. Davidian, therefore, neglects features found in all classifications since Don, 160 years ago, and especially since Maximovicz gave the genus its modern look over 100 years ago.

It must be emphasized that the term elepidote has been used in different senses: to some it includes all members of the genus which have no scales, but to others it is restricted to all rhododendrons which have no scales in this case using rhododendron in the narrow sense as opposed to azaleas. That is to say, for them elepidote is equivalent to *Hymenanthes*. In view of this confusion and since species without scales do not form a natural group, the term elepidote serves no useful function and would be better abandoned.

## Some Recent Modifications

From the preceding account it is evident that progress has been made when some new feature of the plant has been brought into use in classification. Since Sleumer's system was published much new evidence has become available and some modifications to his system have been proposed. The study of hairs by Seithe (1960) resulted in her proposing three major subdivisions of the genus. Two of these virtually correspond to Sleumer's subgenera *Rhododendron* and *Hymenanthes,* while the third comprised the remainder of the genus. Since this includes several rather dissimilar subgenera, united only by the possession of simple hair types, it has not been adopted by later taxonomists. James Sinclair (1937) had discovered interesting variations in the folding of leaves within the winter buds. In all lepidote species (except Subsection *Edgeworthia*) the young leaf-blades lie flat, whereas in all other species they are rolled back. Frank Kingdon-Ward (1935, 1947) demonstrated the value in classification of seed characters and of flower shape, and Cowan (1950) drew attention to the value of the number of hypodermal layers in the leaf.

We studied the pattern of veins entering the leaf from the stem and found variations which corresponded with the major subdivisions (Philipson & Philipson, 1968). One of us demonstrated that the cotyledons also show variations, mainly of pubescence and venations, which also correspond with the major groupings (M N

Philipson, 1970). These seed-leaf characters were used to refine the placing of some asiatic members of Subgenus *Pentanthera*, *R. pentaphyllum* and *R. albrechtii*, were seen to be more correctly linked with *R. quinquefolium* and *R. schlippenbachii* so these four species were united by us into a section, *Sciadorhodion* (Philipson & Philipson, 1982). A series of studies comparing the embryology of the subdivisions of the genus carried out by us in collaboration with Dr Barbara Palser (1971, 1985, 1991) emphasized the distinctness of Section *Vireya* from other lepidote groups.

These anatomical characters greatly stengthen belief in the existing system. We have discussed their implications (Philipson & Philipson, 1970) and conclude that the Subgenera *Rhododendron* and *Hymenanthes* are coherent and natural, each representing a single evolutionary line, whereas the azaleas are too diverse to be other than several separate lines. Consequently we raised two monotypic sections, *Candidastrum* and *Mumeazalea* to the status of subgenera, and restored *Therorhodion* to the genus (Philipson & Philipson, 1982). Cullen (1980) restored the subgenera *Pseudorhodorastrum, Rhodorastrum* and *Pseudazalea* to Subgenus *Rhododendron*, and Chamberlain & Rae (1990) placed Sleumer's monotypic Section *Tsusiopsis* in the much larger Section *Tsutsusi*. Kathleen Kron and Walter Judd (1990) modified the limits of the genus by adding *Ledum* and again removing *Therorhodion*.

A completely new set of evidence is afforded by chemo-taxonomy. Harborne and Williams (1971) studied the flavonoids and phenols of *Rhododendron* and Dr Spethmann (1987) investigated the flavonoids and carotencids of most of the major sections of the genus and proposed some modifications to the classification.

**The Revisions**

This history has been concerned, so far, with the gradual improvement of an arrangement of the various subdivisions of the genus. A recent trend has been a careful reconsideration of the species contained within these subdivisions. It was becoming evident that the differences between many of the species were trifling, and that a reduction in their number was overdue. At the suggestion of Harold Fletcher, the Director at Edinburgh, we undertook a revision of the Lapponicum rhododendrons in which 53 species previously listed were reduced by half to 26 (Philipson & Philipson, 1975). Dr James Cullen (1980) revised the lepidote species (adopting our Lapponicum revision and excluding Section *Vireya*. He recognized 162 species, reducing the synonymy one third of those in Mr Davidian's first volume. Dr David Chamberlain (1982) treated Subgenus *Hymenanthes*. He recognized 225 species, reducing to synonymy nearly one third of those in Davidian's second and third volume. To this series of revisions we contributed a treatment of Subgenus Azaleastrum and the three small subgenera *Mumeazalea, Candidastrum* and *Therorhodion* (Philipson & Philipson, 1986). David Chamberlain and Sally Rae (1990) have revised the species in Subgenus *Tsutsusi* and Kathleen Kron those in Section *Pentanthera*. The revision of the species will be completed with treatments of Sections *Rhodora, Sciadorhodion, Viscidula* and *Vireya*

## References

ADANSON, M (1763) *Familles des Plantes,* 2. Paris.

ARGENT, G C G (1988). Vireya taxonomy in field and laboratory. *Proc. 4th International Rhododendron Conf. Wollongong,* N.S.W. 124-26.

BALFOUR, I B (1916). New species of Rhododendron, 1. *Notes RBG Edinb.* **9**: 207-320.

(1917). New species of Rhododendron, 2. *Notes RBG.Edinb.* **10**: 79-165.

(1919a). Rhododendron trichocladum Franch. and its allies. *Trans. Bot. Soc. Edinb.* **27**: 79-88; Rhododendron laetum Franch. *l.c.:* 97-104; Rhododendrons of the Irroratum Series, *l.c.:* 157-220.

(1919b). New species of Rhododendron, 3. *Notes RBG Edinb.* **11**: 19-153.

(1920). New species of Rhododendron, 4. *Notes RBG Edinb.* **12**: 85-184.

BLUME, C L (1826). *Bijdragen tot de Flora van Nederlandsch Indie.* Batavia.

CANDOLLE, A P de (1839). *Prodromus Systematis naturalis Regni Vegetabilis* VII (2). Paris.

CHAMBERLAIN, D F (1982). A revision of Rhododendron II. Subgenus Hymenanthes. *Notes RBG Edinb.* **39**: 209-486.

CLARKE, C B (1882) in Hooker, JD. *Flora of British India,* 3. London.

COPELAND, H F (1929). Philippine Ericaceae, I: The species of Rhododendron. *Philipp.J.Sci.Bot.* **40**: 133-79.

COWAN, J M (1949). A Survey of the Genus Rhododendron. *The Rhododendron Year Book,* 4: 29-58. London.

(1950) *The Rhododendron leaf, a study of the epidermal structures.* Edinburgh

& DAVIDIAN, H H (1947). A Review of Rhododendrons in their Series, I. The Anthopogon Alliance. *The Rhododendron Year Book* **2**: 55-86. London.

(1948). A review of Rhododendrons in their Series, 2: The Boothii, Glaucum, Lepidotum Alliance. *The Rhododendron Year Book,* **3**: 51-112. London.

(1949). A review of Rhododendrons in their Series, 3. The Campanulatum and Fulvum Series. *The Rhododendron Year Book,* **4**: 159-82. London.

(1951). A review of Rhododendrons in their Series, 4. The Thomsonii Series. *The Rhododendron Year Book,* **6**: 116-183. London.

CULLEN, J (1980). A revision of Rhododendron I. Subgenus Rhododendron sections Rhododendron and Pogonanthum. *Notes RBG Edinb.* **39**: 1-207.

DALLA TORRE, K W von & HARMS, H (1903) *Genera Siphonogamarum ad Systema Engleriana conscripta.* Leipzig.

DAVIDIAN, H H (1954). A review of Rhododendrons in their Series, 5. The Campylogynum and Saluenense Series. *The Rhododendron and Camellia Year Book,* **8**: 75-98. London.

(1963). A review of Rhododendrons in their Series, 7. The Triflorum Series. *The Rhododendron and Camellia Year Book,* **17**: 156-222. London.

(1964). A review of *Rhododendrons* in their series, 8. The Auriculatum, Edgeworthii, Scabrifolium and Virgatum Series, with a new series Griersonianum. *The Rhododendron and Camellia Year Book,* **18**: 104-133. London.

(1982). *The Rhododendron Species I. Lepidotes.* Portland.

(1989). *The Rhododendron Species II. Elepidotes (i) Arboreum-Lacteum.* Portland.

(1992). *The Rhododendron Species III Elepidotes (ii) Neriiflorum, Thomsonii, Azaleastrum* and *Camtschaticum.* Portland.

& COWAN, J M (1956). A review of Rhododendrons in their Series, 6. The Lacteum Series. *The Rhododendron and Camellia Year Book*, **10**: 122-155. London.

DIPPEL, L (1889). *Handbuch der Laubholzkunde*, I. Berlin.

DON, G (1834). *A General History of Dichlamy dious Plants*, III, *Calyciflorae*. London.

DRUDE, O (1891). Ericaceae in Engler, A & Prantl, K *Die natürlichen Pflanzenfamilien* 4 (I). Leipzig.

FRANCHET, A (1886). Rhododendron du Tibet Oriental et du Yun-nan. *Bull. Soc. Bot. Fr.*, 33: 223-36.

HARBOURNE, J B & WILLIAMS,. C A (1971). Leaf survey of flavenoids and simple phenols in the genus Rhododendron. *Phytochem.*, **10**: 2727-44.

HOOKER, J D (1849). *Rhododendrons of Sikkim-Himalaya*. London.

(1876). in Bentham, G & Hooker, JD *Genera Plantarum*, 2. London.

HUTCHINSON, J (1919). The Maddenii Series of Rhododendron. *Notes RBG Edinb.* 121-84.

(1921). The Genus Therorhodion. *Kew Bull.*: 201-05.

KINGDON-WARD, F (1935). Rhododendron Seeds, with special reference to their classification. *Journ. Bot.*,. 73: 241-47.

(1947). Observations on the classification of the genus Rhododendron. *The Rhododendron Year Book*, 2: 99-114. London.

KLOTZSCH, J F & GARCKE, F A (1862). *Die botanischen Ergebnisse der Reise des Prinzen Waldemar von Preussen in 1845-46*. Berlin.

KOEHNE, B A E (1893). *Deutsche Dendrologie*. Stuttgart.

KRON, K A (1993). A Revision of Rhododendron Section Pentanthera. *Edin. J. Bot.*, 50: 249-364.

& JUDD, W S (1990). Phylogenetic Relationships within the Rhodoraea (Ericaceae) with specific comments on the placement of Ledum. *Syst. Bot.*, 15: 157-68

LINNAEUS, C (1753). *Species Plantarum*, ed. 1 Stockholm.

(1762). *Species Plantarum*, ed. 2. Stockholm.

LUTEYN, J L & O'BRIEN, M E (1980). Contributions toward a classification of Rhododendron. *Proc. International Rhododendron Conf. New York Bot. Gard.* Bronx.

MAXIMOVICZ, C J (1870). Rhododendreae Asiae Orientalis. *Mem. Acad. Sci.St. Pet.* ser. 7, **16**: 1-53.

NAKAI, T (1916). Notulae ad plantae Japoniae et Coreae 12. *Tokyo Bot. Mag.* 30: 274-90.

(1922) *Trees and shrubs indigenous in Japan proper.* Tokyo.

NUTTALL, T (1853). Descriptions of and observations on some species of Rhododendron collected in Assam and Bootan by Thomas J. Booth. *Hook. J. Bot. Kew Gard. Misc.* 5: 353.

PALSER, B F, PHILIPSON, W R, & PHILIPSON, M N (1971). Embryology of Rhododendron, 1. Introduction and ovule, megagametophyte and early endosperm development of R. yunnanense. *J. Ind. Bot. Soc.* 50A: 172-88.

(1989). Development of ovule, megagametophyte and early endosperm in representative species of Rhododendron (Ericaceae). *Bot. J. Linn. Soc.* 101: 363-93

(1991). Characteristics of ovary, ovule and mature megagametophyte in Rhododendron L. (Ericaceae) and their taxonomic significance. *Bot. J. Linn. Soc.* 105: 289-390.

PHILIPSON, M N (1970). Cotyledons and the Taxonomy of Rhododendron. *Notes RBG Edinb.*, 30: 55-77.

& PHILIPSON, W R (1970). The Classification of Rhododendron. *The Rhododendron and Camellia Year Book*, 25: 1-8. London.

(1975) A Revision of Rhododendron Section Lapponicum. *Notes RBG.Edinb.*, 34: 1-72.

(1974). A History of Rhododendron Classification. *Notes RBG.Edinb.*, 32: 223-38.

(1986). A Revision of Rhododendron III. Subgenera Azaleastrum, Mumeazalea, Candidastrum and Therorhodion. *Notes RBG.Edinb.* 44: 1-23.

PLANCHON, J E (1854). Sur l'histoire botanique et horticole des plantes dites Azalées de l'Inde. *Rev. hort.* ser. 4, **3**: 42-68.

REHDER, A & WILSON, E H (1913). in SARGENT, CS. *Plantae Wilsonianae* I. Cambridge, Mass.

REICHENBACH, H G L (1827), in MOSSLER, J C *Handbuch der Gewächskunde*, ed. 2. Altona.

SALISBURY, R A (1805-08). *Paradisus Londinensis.* London.

SCHLÈCHTER, R (1918). Die Ericaceae von Deutsch.-Neu-Guinea. *Bot. Jahrb.* 55: 137-94.

SCHNEIDER, C C (1907). *Handbuch der Laub-holzkunde.* Jena.

SEITHE, A geb. v. Hoff (1960). Die Haarformen der Gattung Rhododendron L. und die Möglichkeit ihrer taxonomischen Verwertung. *Bot. Jahrb.,* 79: 297-393.

SLEUMER, H (1949). Ein System der Gattung Rhododendron L. *Bot. Jahrb.,* 74: 511-53.

(1958). The genus Rhododendron L. in Indochina and Siam. *Blumea,* suppl. 4: 39-59.

(1964). Ericaceae of Malesia, suppl. 2. *Blumea,* 12: 339-47.

SMALL, J K (1914). Ericales in *North American Flora,* 29: 1-102.

SPETHMANN, W (1987).A new infragenreic classificationand phylogenetic trends in the genus Rhododendron (Ericaceae) Pl. Syst. Evol., 157: 9-31

STEVENSON, J B (ed) (1930). *The Species of Rhododendron.* London.

SYNGE, P M (ed) 1967. *Rhododendron Handbook, 1967 part 1. Rhododendron species in general cultivation.* Royal Horticultural Society, London.

TATE (1831). in Sweet, R, *British Flower Garden,* ser. 2, I: t.95.

WILSON, E H & REHDER, A (1921). *A monograph of Azaleas.* Cambridge, Mass.

ZABEL, H (1902). Uber unsere Freiland-Azaleen. *Mitt. Deutsch. Dendrol. Ges.,* 11: 23-39.

DR MELVA PHILIPSON *was formerly a botanist in the Department of Scientific and Industrial Research New Zealand.* PROFESSOR WILLIAM PHILIPSON *is Emeritus Professor of Botany of Canterbury University. Jointly they have published many articles on rhododendrons including revisions of Subsection Lapponica and of four of the smaller genera*

# CHAPTER 3

# THE IMPORTANCE
# OF THE
# HERBARIUM

## JAMES CULLEN

Gardeners are often bemused when told that most plant classification is based on dried and pressed specimens. It is, indeed, hard to believe that these desiccated fragments of plant, mounted on sheets of white cardboard and kept in cupboards, can reveal anything of the structure of plants, compared with the living plants themselves. Because of this, taxonomists have something of a bad reputation among gardeners as people who shuffle about 'heaps of hay', and, on the basis of these miserable objects, change plant names and classifications to the general confusion of everyone.

Since the late 18th century rhododendrons collected in the wild before modern techniques of preservation or air transport were usually sent back to botanic gardens for study in the form of dried specimens. A great deal of skill was needed by the collectors to dry woody plants like rhododendrons and to display their individual parts – leaves, flowers and so on in a suitable way. Peter Cox in Chapter 8 tells us about some of the problems collectors had to overcome.

Herbaria formed from these early conditions are still to be found in the great botanic gardens of the world and when properly used, are an invaluable and permanent resource of plant information.

## The Herbarium

Herbarium specimens consist of parts of plants, generally including flowers or fruits, collected in the native habitat of the plants concerned, placed between sheets of absorbent paper and pressed by various means, so that the plant parts are slowly dried and flattened. Some plants (for example many annuals and small herbaceous plants) can be dried and pressed whole, and the process is easy and relatively quick. With other, larger plants, only parts can be pressed, and the process may be quite long, the absorbent papers requiring changing on a regular basis, to produce a properly dried and flattened specimen. With yet others (for example, cacti and mesembryanthemums, palms), this method of preservation is not really appropriate.

Along with the plant parts, a set of notes is also generally provided by the collector. These notes should contain all the information about where the plant was collected (country, province, exact location, sometimes including latitude and longitude references, altitude), notes on the type of habitat, and notes on features that may be lost in the drying and pressing process, such as the colour of flowers. Collectors vary in the amount and quality of such notes; some merely give the location details, others provide short essays on the plant and its surroundings. The notes are an integral part of the specimen, and can convey much information about the plant to the user which is not directly available from the plant material itself. A few collectors also include photographs with their specimens, or hold slides, cross-referenced by the collector's number (see below)

Most collectors collect sufficient material of each plant to make more than one actual specimen; these duplicate collections can be distributed to different herbaria around the world. Once collected, dried, brought back and distributed, the specimens are mounted (stuck down, either with glue, strips of glued paper or with blobs of adhesive material,

on to standard-sized sheets of cardboard). Mounting like this means that the specimens are protected from accidental damage, and can be stacked one above the other within folders in the herbarium cupboards. The notes are copied in sufficient number for the duplicate specimens, and these are also stuck to the sheet, so that plant material and notes can be conveniently studied together. Once mounted in this manner, the sheets can be stored very conveniently, so that thousands of plant specimens can be kept together in a relatively small space, and are easily available for comparison in large numbers (not possible with living plants).

Most collectors number their collections, so that each specimen (and its duplicates) bears the same unique number; this makes reference to the specimens easy and convenient. It also has enormous value where both dried and living plants are collected together, so that the dried specimens and the living specimens (or seeds from them) bear the same number. This facilitates the checking of living plants against the permanent herbarium specimen (a record of what was actually collected); if they clearly belong to different species, then something has gone wrong during the career of the living plant in cultivation: it may well have been mislabelled during the propagation process. Such cross-checking is an absolutely vital part of the maintenance of wild-origin living collections. Because rhododendrons in gardens hybridize so widely and easily, collector's numbers should only be given to seed collections from plants which genuinely bear the number.

Once mounted, kept in a suitable dry and insect-free environment and handled with care, the specimens form a permanent, always available record of what was collected in the wild. The pressing flattens various plant parts (especially flowers), so that these can look unappealing on the sheet, but they can generally be reconstituted by taking them off the specimen and boiling them gently in water to which some detergent has been added. This restores their general shape (though not their colour), and allows the interior structures (stamens, ovary, cells of the ovary, ovules, and so on) to be studied just as they would be in a living plant. Pressing does not destroy the structures, or, indeed, the chemical constituents of the plant, and even DNA can be extracted from herbarium specimens of at least some species. Similarly, though some shrinkage occurs in the drying process, measurements made on herbarium specimens are generally comparable to those of the original, unpressed plant, or a simple correction can be made to account for the shrinkage.

Such specimens can be used in taxonomic work, for comparison, measurement, study of distribution, and so on. Because so many of them can be studied together, comparison of a wide range of plants is possible, and it is on this basis that taxonomists carry out their work. Of course, living plants (if available) are important as well, especially if they are of known wild origin (that is, their origin from plants in the wild is recorded) as they often show features that are not available from the dried specimens – the overall habit of the plant, colour of flowers, various organs that tend not to be present when flowering herbarium specimens are collected (for example in the case of rhododendrons, the scales of both vegetative and inflorescence buds). Such information plays an important part in classification, but as living plants cannot be assembled together in such numbers, wide comparisons are not possible.

Some herbarium specimens gain particular importance by being those studied by the original describer of the species, subspecies or variety to which they belong. In general terms, the describer chooses one particular specimen to govern the use of the name he gives. These specimens are called type-specimens, and are often especially protected in herbaria with coloured folders (so that they are easy to pick out). It is important to remember that these type-specimens are not necessarily intended to be typical of the species; they are merely the specimens which form points of reference for the use of the names. Thus, when Adrien Franchet described *R. sulfureum* as a new species, he chose the specimen *Delavay* 2212 as the type. Because he worked in the herbarium in Paris, the specimen held there is considered to be the one he described, and this is known as the holotype; duplicates of this collection, such as the one held in Edinburgh, are known as isotypes.

When a taxonomist is working at a classification he compares and sorts the specimens, accumulating heaps (either literally or metaphorically) which he considers belong to the various species he wishes to recognize. He then looks through each heap to see which type-specimens it contains. When I did this for Subsection *Boothia,* I ended up with one heap which contained the type-specimens of four previously described species: *sulfureum, theiochroum, cerinum* and *commodum.* After checking that all these names had been validly published according to the internationally agreed rules of nomenclature, I was obliged to choose, as the proper name for the species, the oldest available; this was *R. sulfureum* of Franchet (1887). The other names, published by Bayley Balfour and his colleagues, date from 1916 and 1922. Hence, the correct name for this heap (species) is *R. sulfureum* Franchet, and the other names become synonyms of that.

The discovery that plant parts could be dried, flattened and stored for future investigation was made during the 15th century. The idea spread rapidly across Europe, and by the beginning of the 17th century, numerous private collections were in existence. By the end of the century, various 'national' collections were coming into being.

There are now herbaria in most countries of the world. The current index of herbaria (Holmgren, P K, Holmgren, N H, and Barnett, L C, *Index Herbariorum Part I: The Herbaria of the World,* 8th edition, 1990), lists 2,639 herbaria in 147 countries, containing over 200 million specimens. Of these, 15 countries (USA, France, former USSR, UK, Sweden, Germany, Switzerland, China, Italy, former Czechoslovakia, Austria, Japan, Canada, Australia and Holland) hold about 75 per cent of the total. Because the specimens are of reasonable size and can be easily packed, it is possible for experts who work in one herbarium to borrow specimens from other herbaria. Such loans form an integral part of the business of plant classification, and this aspect, again, contrasts with living plants.

**Rhododendrons in the Herbarium**

So much for herbarium specimens in general. As regards *Rhododendron,* all that has been stated above applies to them. The remarks that follow will be restricted to the classic collections made in the main hardy 'Rhododendron' area (western China and adjacent north-east. Burma and north-east India), but the same principles apply to collections made anywhere in the vast range of the genus.

The collection of rhododendrons for the herbarium goes back to the time before Linnaeus (second half of the 18th century), when the European species were being collected. Then, increased exploration of the world led to the collection of species from Caucasus, North America,

South-East Asia generally, the Himalayas, and ultimately, by about 1880, China and Japan. A vast number of specimens has been collected, some of them by collectors who collected only dried material, others by collectors who were taking not only dried plants, but living plants or seed as well. A few collectors have collected only living plants or seed.

Because of its central position in the study of the genus, the greatest accumulation of specimens (both herbarium and living) is at the Royal Botanic Garden, Edinburgh (RBGE). Specimens were either collected by collectors sent out under Edinburgh's auspices (for example Forrest) or by others who realized that if they wanted their specimens critically studied, it was necessary that they should be there (Farrer, Kingdon-Ward, Rock and so on). Yet others were acquired as duplicates from other herbaria (for example David's and Delavay's, from Paris). The collection there is still increasing, as modern expeditions send their plants for identification and incorporation in the collections; this expansion is enhanced by specimen exchange with other herbaria (for example Kunming, Beijing)

Other large and important collections of herbarium material of *Rhododendron* are in Kew, the British Museum (especially Ludlow, Sherriff and their co-collectors, Kingdon-Ward), Paris (the French missionaries and material from the more tropical parts of South-East Asia, especially Indo- China), Leningrad (Caucasian and East Asiatic collections), Leiden (mainly, collections from tropical South-East Asia), the Arnold Arboretum, Boston (Wilson's collections, Kingdon-Ward's last Burmese collections, many American collections), and numerous American, Indian, Chinese, Japanese and Australian herbaria.

## The Collections

The stories of the main collectors of rhododendrons are well known, and will not be elaborated here, but some remarks on their herbarium collections are appropriate.

### French missionaries

The French missionary collections during the late 19th and early 20th centuries (see Lennon, J, 'J M Delavay in Yunnan [1882-95] and his relationship with David, Franchet and others', *Rhododendrons 1985/86 with Magnolias and Camellias*, pp. 20-25). The earliest Chinese rhododendrons were collected by a group of French Jesuit missionaries – David, Delavay, Fargés, Bodinier, Maire, and so on. They sent back both herbarium specimens and living material (seed) to Paris – the dried plants to the Museum d'Histoire Naturelle, the living plants to the Jardin des Plantes. Some of these collectors (for example Delavay) numbered their specimens, others did not. The dried specimens were studied and described by Adrien Franchet, the first great name in Rhododendron classification. He provided the names and descriptions for many new

*Adrien Franchet, taxonomist at the Museum d'Histoire Naturelle in Paris, who named the dried specimens sent from China by the French missionaries.*

species, most of which are retained today. The living plants suffered a more obscure fate: there is anecdotal evidence that they were treated as stove plants, and succumbed to overheating and waterlogging, but the reliability of this information is uncertain. What is certain is that none of them still exists.

The main sets of these herbarium collections, including many holotypes, remain in the herbarium of the Museum d'Histoire Naturelle in Paris, but duplicates of many of them were acquired early by the herbarium of the RBGE, and, more sporadically, by other herbaria. Franchet published the results of his studies of the important collections in the beautifully illustrated *Plantae Davidianae* (1884-88) and *Plantae Delavayanae* (1889-90).

### Ernest H Wilson

Wilson collected mainly in Sichuan and Hubei, somewhat outside the richest area of rhododendrons in China, as well as in Japan. However, he collected numerous specimens, both living and pressed, using the same numbering system for both. His dried specimens are scattered through many herbaria, though the main set, together with his notes and papers, is at the herbarium of the Arnold Arboretum. They are provided with little label

*One of George Forrest's herbarium specimens of* R. yunnanense. *The label in Forrest's handwriting reads: Forrest 19443, collected in May 1921. China, NW Yunnan. Divide between La-shi-pa and Yangtze valleys, Lat. 26"54'N, Long. 100"06'E, 9000ft. Shrub of 4-7ft. Flowers pale rose with crimson markings. On cliffs and the crown of the ravine*

information, and, in fact, are best used in connection with C S Sargent's *Plantae Wilsonianae* (3 volumes, 1911-17) and Wilson's own travel books (for example *A Naturalist in Western China,* 1913), to obtain the maximum information on where they were from and the conditions in which they grew.

### George Forrest

Forrest is the premier collector of Chinese rhododendrons and his nine journeys have been well covered in: anon., for the Scottish Rock Garden Club, *George Forrest, VMH* (1873-1932) and Cowan, J M, *The Journeys and Plant Introductions of George Forrest,* VMH (1952). The importance of Forrest from the present viewpoint is two-fold. First, the field notes to his herbarium specimens are extensive and informative; secondly, he collected many of the same plants both in flower and in fruit, marking the plants when in flower, and revisiting them (either in person, or using his Chinese assistants) in the autumn, giving the collections different numbers, but cross-referencing these on his labels. These specimens cross-relate to the seed he introduced (under the numbers of the fruiting specimens) so it is possible to check the identity of almost every living (cultivated) Forrest specimen. Experience has shown that, during the 60 to 90 years that these plants have been grown in gardens, many have acquired, by one means or other, the wrong number and identification. It is noticeable that this applies

particularly to those species that are easily propagated and/or small (for example plants of Sub-section *Lapponica*).

Forrest's collections, both seed and dried, were sent back to RBGE, where both were studied first by Sir Isaac Bayley Balfour and his co-workers (Forrest himself, Tagg, William Wright Smith) and then by William Wright Smith and his co-workers (Tagg, Hutchinson, Cowan, Davidian). Many hundreds of new species were described (mainly in the journal *Notes from the Royal Botanical Garden Edinburgh*), and the type-specimens of all of them remain in the Edinburgh herbarium. Many of the collections are also still growing in the living collections. Most of these new species have later been reduced to synonyms of others, but their description was important at a time when new plants were coming in at regular intervals – attention was drawn to the plants' variation, so that it could be conveniently studied. Only later did a wider comparison of specimens make consolidation possible.

Duplicates of Forrest's collections are to be found in several herbaria, as he collected most plants in quite large numbers.

### Reginald Farrer

Farrer collected in Hubei, Gansu and north-east Burma. His herbarium material is quite well labelled and was worked on by Bayley Balfour and his colleagues and distributed by RBGE (where most of the type-specimens are to be found). As with Wilson and Kingdon-Ward, reference to his travel books (for example, *On the Eaves of the World,* 1917, and *The Rainbow Bridge,* 1921) is often helpful in providing further information on the plants he collected, as are Cox, E H M (ed.), *The Plant Introductions of Reginald Farrer* (1930), and Illingworth, J, and Routh, J (eds), *Reginald Farrer, Dalesman, Plant hunter, Gardener* (1991).

### Frank Kingdon-Ward

Kingdon-Ward was an indefatigable explorer, and collected numerous dried and living plant specimens on his travels. The dried specimens are mainly in the herbarium of the Natural History Museum, London, though those of his last expedition (to north-east Burma) are at the Arnold Arboretum. His specimens are well annotated and duplicates are quite widely distributed. Kingdon-Ward wrote many popular books on his travels and these provide a great deal of additional information about his plants (both living and dried). Considerable details about his travel and collections are given in Schweinfurth, U, and Schweinfurth-Marbey, H, *Exploration in the Eastern Himalaya and the River Gorge Country of SE Tibet – Francis (Frank) Kingdon-Ward (1885-1958) – an annotated bibliography with a map of the area of his expeditions* (1975).

### Joseph Rock

Rock was a polymath, andcollecting plants was only one of his many activities in China and Tibet. He collected numerous specimens, both dried and living; the dried specimens are well labelled. Rock's main herbarium eventually came to rest in Edinburgh, together with a large archive of diaries, notes and photographs, but duplicate specimens are quite widely distributed in herbaria. His specimens use mainly one single number sequence, but one set of seed collections was distributed by the United States Department of Agriculture under USDA numbers (mostly five-figure numbers beginning with the digit '5'). A rather rare publication (Anon., *Field Notes of the Rhododendrons collected by Rock in 1923/24,* privately printed and distributed, undated) provides a cross-reference between these numbers and the herbarium numbers. Rock lived for many years in Lijiang (Yunnan), right in the centre of the main rhododendron area. He was forced out by the approach of Mao tse-Tung's army in 1949, and his last collections bear numbers from 1 to about 250.

### Frank Ludlow, and George Sherriff and their co-collectors.

Ludlow and Sherriff made several expeditions to areas to the west of the main rhododendron area, including Bhutan and south-east Tibet. With their co-collectors (who included Sir George Taylor, Colonel H Elliot and Dr G H Hicks), they collected numerous *Rhododendron* specimens, both living and pressed. The main set of their well-annotated herbarium specimens is in the collections of the Natural History Museum but duplicates are quite widely distributed. The museum collections also contain an archive of fine black and white photographs of plants taken on these expeditions. A very full description of their travels is provided in H R Fletcher *A Quest of Flowers: The Plant Explorations of Frank Ludlow and George Sherriff* (1976).

### *TT Yü*

This distinguished Chinese botanist collected many *Rhododendron* specimens, which, in 1938, he brought to Edinburgh for study in collaboration with William Wright Smith and others. At the outbreak of World War II, he returned to China, but left an extensive collection of living and dried plants at Edinburgh. These are well labelled and include numerous type-specimens. They are not widely distributed in western herbaria, but presumably there are sets in herbaria in China.

### *Modern collections*

Between 1939 and 1980 very little collecting of rhododendrons was done in the main Chinese area (except by Chinese botanists, whose specimens were unavailable to taxonomists in the West). Since 1980, however, many western expeditions have been to Yunnan and Sichuan, and many new well-labelled, dried and living specimens have been collected. On the whole these are still being studied and so details will not be included here. As part of this reopening of China, exchanges between western and Chinese herbaria became possible – in fact, a set of Forrest's specimens, prepared and packed for sending to Beijing from Edinburgh in 1949 was eventually dispatched in 1982.

To reiterate: herbarium specimens are thus basic to the business of plant classification, both in terms of defining the various groups of plants (genera, species, subspecies, varieties, formae) and in controlling the names that are applied to these groups. They have this basic status for the reasons given above: they are, if properly stored, a permanent (if sometimes partial) record of what was collected in the wild, and they can be stored in large numbers for convenient comparison. Living plants are also important in this respect, especially for those characteristics that do not survive on herbarium specimens, but they cannot have the same importance, simply because not enough of them can be accumulated in any one place to make the wide comparison possible. In Edinburgh, for instance, there are some 250 herbarium specimens of *Rhododendron rubiginosum*, covering the whole geographical and structural range of the species, whereas, in the garden collection, there are only 17 examples of known wild origin. They also provide a check on the identity of living plants cultivated under collector's numbers. If the living plant does not belong to the same species (or subspecies or variety) as the matching herbarium specimen, then something has gone wrong with the living plant and the collector's number and the plant's name should be withdrawn from it. What has gone wrong can sometimes be deduced (labelling mistakes during propagation or distribution being the most common cause), but often cannot. It is important that growers are scrupulous about such matters, to prevent incorrectly named and numbered material being distributed. A similar proviso applies to seed collected from numbered plants: as garden seed is so likely to be hybrid, it should not be distributed under the collector's number of the female parent.

DR JAMES CULLEN *was Assistant Regius Keeper at the Royal Botanic Garden Edinburgh from 1972 to 1989, where he worked on the Revision of the Lepidote species of* Rhododendron. *He is now Director of the UK Stanley Smith Horticultural Trust and Chairman of the Editorial Committee of the European Garden Flora*

# CHAPTER 4

# NOMENCLATURE: AN ORDERED UNIVERSE

## ALAN LESLIE

Although in the West we tend to think of ourselves as in the vanguard of those involved in the development and recording of rhododendron and azalea cultivars, the truth is somewhat different. In Japan there was sufficient interest and knowledge as far back as 1692 for Ito Ihei to publish a detailed, illustrated account of a large number of azalea cultivars. Some of these persist to this day and Ito's account too is still available, translated and republished as *A Brocade Pillow* (Weatherhill, 1984). It is an early example of a continuing tradition of fine Japanese works on azaleas, continuing to the present day in the detailed accounts published by the Japanese Satsuki Azalea Society.

It was much later, well into the 19th century, before a similar number of rhododendron or azalea cultivars had been developed in Europe, later still in the USA. But then they came pouring out of British nurseries such as Standish & Noble and the various Waterer establishments at Knap Hill and Bagshot. In continental Europe the establishments of Vervaene and van Houtte launched countless new azaleas and Seidel in Germany developed a steady stream of new rhododendrons (see chapters 9, 10, 12 and 13).

With so much activity in different countries, involving such a wide range of firms, using different languages and even different alphabets, it is not difficult to see why the names used for the plethora of new cultivars became duplicated or confused. Without a single international authority to turn to, raisers of new plants simply had to manage on their own, often in ignorance of what others had done before them. One has to remember too that at this time *Rhododendron* and *Azalea* were still regarded as separate genera, so the use of the same cultivar name within both was quite usual. Standish & Noble, for example, listed an Indian azalea 'Comet' in an 1848 catalogue having already offered a hardy hybrid rhododendron of the same name in 1847. Later James Veitch & Sons also raised an Indian azalea of this name and by 1862 Liebig in Germany was offering a 'Comet' derived from *R. formosum* x *edgeworthii.* Such examples are not uncommon and lead to all manner of confusions.

Trying to introduce some international order and method into this rather haphazard process of naming cultivars is clearly impossible without an agreed set of rules setting out what is and is not acceptable and what procedures need to be followed. The first steps in establishing such a code were taken by Alphonse de Candolle in 1862, and by 1867 the International Botanical Congress in Paris accepted his *Lois de la Nomenclature Botanique.* This incorporated an article indicating that plants of horticultural origin should be given fancy names, that is names in a common language as distinct as possible from the Latin names of species. The inadequacy of this article soon became apparent but attempts to produce expanded rules foundered during World War I. However, by 1930 a collaborative venture involving the Natural History Museum and the Royal Horticultural Society produced a set of rules that were finally incorporated as an Appendix to the Botanical Code of 1935. It is significant for cultivar registration that in discussing these proposals the 1930 International Horticultural Conference suggested that the starting point for nomenclature in horticultural groups should be either a horticultural monograph or an *ad hoc* list of varieties drawn up by a recognized body of specialists. Where such bodies did not exist it was suggested that some recognized

society be charged with the work. Working experience of the new rules dictated further revision. After much international discussion and collaboration articles on the botanical names of hybrids were incorporated as an appendix to the 1952 Botanical Code, leaving the bulk of the cultivated plant regulations for still further discussion. These eventually produced an agreement on the first Cultivated Plant Code, published in 1953. Full details of the historical development of that Code are given by Professor William Stearn in his scholarly introduction to the text. The Code included a section on registration indicating that: 'Adequate and accurate registration of names is of first importance for their stabilization. The aim of registration is to avoid duplication of names and the creation of names which are unnecessary or are likely to produce confusion and controversy'. In a Note it was recommended that for any large group of plants there should be a recognized International Registration Authority. Essentially this all still holds true today

In 1955 the 14th International Horticultural Congress at Scheveningen in The Netherlands appointed the first such International Registration Authorities, IRAs, and it was at this time that the RHS took on the responsibility for *Rhododendron* (including *Azalea*), as well as *Narcissus* and perennial *Delphinium*, with orchids, conifers, dahlias, lilies and dianthus following at a later date. By 1958 the first International Rhododendron Register had been published by the RHS.

Rhododendron and azalea growers in the UK had not however been entirely idle during this long period of gestation that ended with the 1958 Register, and their efforts to a large extent shaped its form and content. In the *Rhododendron Society Notes* for 1926 HD McLaren and EH Wilding published a 'List of Rhododendron hybrids that have flowered and have been named, and of which the parentage can be traced back to species on both sides'. This consisted of just over 100 names, but excluded all vireyas and azaleas. In 1928 the highly exclusive Rhododendron Society expanded its membership to become the Rhododendron Association. While not exactly going out of its way to recruit the common man, it became a rather more accessible organization for the rhododendron and azalea enthusiast. From the issue of its first Year Book in 1929 it carried a 'List of Hybrid Rhododendrons compiled from the lists of principal nursery gardeners' (an euphemism one supposes for, dare one say it, the trade). Some acknowledgement of name duplication was already evident, but the only additional information listed was flower colour and an indication of hardiness. The list contained over 600 names, but again omitted Vireyas and azaleas. It grew steadily over the succeeding years and included some European cultivars.

Significant changes occurred in 1934 with not only the first separate list of azalea cultivars, but the first attempt at a Rhododendron Stud Book. This was intentionally an exclusive list, intended to distinguish only primary hybrids (between two species), hybrids with an Award of Merit (AM) or First Class Certificate (FCC) from the RHS or hybrids involving a 'registered' rhododendron. A committee was available to consider 'application for registration'. The Stud Book differed from the nursery list in giving parentage, raiser/exhibitor and a date, but the entries lacked a description. A second table listed the named progeny of each individual species or hybrid.

All these lists continued in the Association's Year Books, sometimes in a supplementary volume, up to World War II. During the hostilities the Year Book ceased publication, but the RHS published the lists of new rhododendron hybrids in its *Journal.* Of particular note in the 1943 listings was the information that the previously listed cultivars 'Bellona' and 'Jupiter' had had to be re-named as earlier usages had been discovered.

In 1945 the Rhododendron Association transmogrified to become the RHS Rhododendron Group, a designation that happily continues to the present day. The first Year Book from the new Group was published in 1946 and contained a listing and description of newly awarded plants but neither the commercial lists nor Stud Book. These were now contained in the new *Rhododendron Handbook* (1947). This also incorporated many of the other features of the old Association Year Books, such as the systematic account of the species and the lists of collectors' numbers. The cultivar lists continued to appear in later editions (latterly in a separate volume) until 1969. The *Handbook* now concerns itself with species alone.

Examination of these various lists shows that much of this material and the style in which it was presented evolved directly into the Register. This is not to say that Dr Harold Fletcher, the first International Rhododendron Registrar, and his assistants, did not add a tremendous amount of further entries from other sources worldwide to produce a list with *c*.8,000 entries. Annual Register supplements have been published by the Society every year from 1962 onwards. Until 1987 these were incorporated within the Group's Year Book, but subsequently have appeared as a separate publication. Sadly, it is no longer possible for the Supplements to be circulated automatically with the Year Book and the 1994 Supplement (number. 34) had to 'go it alone' for the first time.

Following Dr Fletcher's translation from Wisley to Edinburgh, David Pycraft took over the Registrar's work in 1970 and continued in this role until 1983 when he in turn was relieved by Dr Alan Leslie. The Register continues to be based at Wisley where work on a new edition has been in hand for some time. Progress has sometimes seemed to be (and has been!) at a snail's pace, due to the Registrar being diverted to other responsibilities. However the revision is now going hand-in-hand with computerization of the records so any future editions will be much more readily produced. At the time of writing (January 1995) about one-third of the 20,000 or so records have been entered on the database and a draft of the 'A's has been circulated for comment to a small international panel of advisors.

It might be appropriate here to recognize the continued co-operation the Society enjoys from many individuals and Societies concerned with the genus *Rhododendron* from all over the world. In particular the local Registrars in the USA, Australia, New Zealand and Japan have been an essential element in facilitating the gathering of information and promotion of registration. It would be much more difficult for the Society to function as the International Registration Authority without their help. Like the Society, they are all committed to the Cultivated Code's principles of promoting 'uniformity, accuracy and fixity' in the naming of cultivars. Moreover, a Register which tries to record as much information as it can about each entry provides a valuable source of reference for more than just names: parentages, raisers, descriptions, awards are all included and provide a unique database, one which computerization will make easier to use for a variety of purposes.

Maintaining a Register, even with so much voluntary assistance is a costly exercise and is an essential part of the Society's 'charitable works'. Indeed, although it used to charge a fee, initially of 2*s* 6*d* and rising gradually to £1.00, even this has now been dispensed with and since January 1995 the smart-looking registration Certificate is also issued free of charge, provided it has been requested by the registrant. We feel the Certificate is a small 'thank you' to those who bother to register their new plants.

The Register exists to take account of all named cultivars. It is not a function of the IRA to pontificate on the quality or the distinctness of the plants themselves. The sheer practical difficulties of doing this in such a large, widely dispersed group would make it an impossibly daunting task to do. Such assessment should be undertaken by the raisers before any plant receives a name. Once it has a name and that name is promulgated the Register has to take notice. If you feel too many plants are being named it is up to you to try to influence those involved, preferably through your local Societies, to convince those concerned that the introduction of too many similar cultivars is not in the best interests of the rhododendron growing world.

As will already be evident, International Registration Authorities do not make the rules. Their actions and decisions are determined by the Cultivated Code. It is this Code which determines the maximum number of words (there has to be a limit!), bans the use of new cultivar names in Latin form and recommends a whole series of elements that, ideally, should *not* be used. The Code also indicates how new names should be published and no name is fully legitimate until it has been validly published. The International Commission responsible for the Cultivated Code recently met in Seattle (August 1994) to consider the first revision since the 1980 edition. The results of their labours are expected to be published in 1995 and will ease some of the apparently petty restrictions on the form of cultivar names. Experience will determine whether such relaxations will be beneficial and the results will be carefully monitored.

Naming new plants is a strange business. Some raisers show great originality and, whatever one may think about the vast number of new cultivars produced in the USA in recent years by Mr and Mrs Delp, they show great originality in their nomenclature. Luckily we are now spared the tongue-twisting epithets so beloved by Edward Magor and others in the 1920s and 30s, which gave us Cilkeisk Group, Cilaspis Group, Cilbooth Group and the like, but some registrants can still be very unimaginative and show a remarkable lack of concern for the euphonious quality or commercial potential of their new names.

What of the future? The priority must be to make a new, fully revised International Register available and to make good use of the computerized database it will represent. Versions on compact disc or even direct electronic access will no doubt need to be considered. We need to continue trying to improve our channels of communication, 'spreading the word' and trying to chase up plants that have slipped through the net. Azalea breeders in particular have a very poor record as registrants and more needs to be done to bring them into the fold. Despite the extensive work already undertaken there is also much more historical investigation to undertake, sorting out ancient confusions, providing information about the plants still in cultivation today. The task is endless!

So, if you are likely to be naming new cultivars please make the effort to register the name. All we require now is information. Remember that once duplication occurs the name alone will never again be unambiguous and communication will suffer. The horticultural community as a whole benefits from a flourishing and active registration system. Help us to help you by playing your part in its operation.

DR ALAN LESLIE, *RHS Senior Registrar with overall responsibility for all nine International Registers in the Society's care, has been International Rhododendron Registrar since 1983. As a member of the International Commission for the Nomenclature of Cultivated Plants he has been involved in revising the Cultivated Plant Code*

# CHAPTER 5

# HOOKER'S RHODODENDRONS: THEIR DISTRIBUTION AND SURVIVAL

## MARY FORREST

To paraphrase Sir William Hooker's remark that no plants have excited a more lively interest than the genus *Rhododendron*, one could make a similar remark about his son Joseph's contribution to the collection and subsequent distribution of rhododendrons to gardens in these islands and around the world. Joseph Hooker travelled in the Sikkim-Himalaya for two years from 1848 to 1850. While rhododendrons from India had already been introduced into cultivation by Captain Thomas Hardwicke, the species introduced by Hooker greatly expanded the range available. The enthusiasm for their cultivation that developed among the gardening fraternity continues even to the present day.

Hooker sent seed to the Royal Botanic Gardens, Kew where his father Sir William was Director and the Gardens were 'eminently successful in rearing them'. Commencing in 1850, young rhododendron plants were distributed to individuals, nurserymen and botanic gardens, throughout the world. The distribution of these plants was recorded by Kew at the time and their use in the 19th century gardens and the occurrence of original plants of known provenance today is described in this chapter. Several gardens have reported that their plants were cultivated from seed supplied by the Hookers and there is little doubt about their authenticity.

Of the 43 species collected by Hooker, 30 were illustrated in the *Rhododendrons of Sikkim-Himalaya*[1] published in 1849 and 1851 in two fascicles. The list of species is given in Table 1, together with the current scientific name, the number of plants distributed and the date when the species first flowered in cultivation.

Donation books at Kew, *Plants*

*The young Joseph Hooker from the portrait by George Richmond (1855)*

*Outwards from 1848 to 1859,* record the distribution of plants from the Gardens, the name and address of the recipient and the name and number of species dispatched.

The most commonly distributed species, with 88 plants, was *R. dalhousiae,* described by Hooker as the 'noblest species of the whole race', with the medium-sized shrubs *R. ciliatum* and *R. glaucophyllum* also donated freely. Only one specimen of *R. lanatum* was distributed and this would accord with Millais' comment that seedlings were difficult to raise. Some of the dwarf alpine species described by

Hooker were not distributed from Kew, while others indicated by an asterisk were not included in his book.

Himalayan rhododendrons were sent to individuals in Britain and Ireland (Table 2), to botanic gardens (Table 3), to gardens (Table 4), to nurserymen (Table 5) and to other parts of the world (Table 6). Years later Sir Joseph was to remark that 'the Himalayan Rhododendrons grow better here [Britain] than they do in Sikkim'. Their success in gardens cannot be denied (see Chapter 6).

Many of the individuals and nurseries listed in Tables 2 and 5 had subscribed to

**Table 1. Rhododendrons of the Sikkim-Himalaya and their distribution of plants from Kew**

| Name in Records | Current Name | Number distributed from Kew | Date of First Flowers |
|---|---|---|---|
| R . arboreum | R . arboreum | 10 | |
| •R . campbelliae | R . arboreum | 4 | |
| •R .arboreum rubrum | R . arboreum | 4 | |
| •R . arboreum roseum | R . arboreum | 7 | |
| R . argenteum | R . grande | 8 | 1850 |
| R . aucklandii | R . griffithianum | 25 | 1850 |
| R . barbatum | R . barbatum | 3 | |
| •R . campanulatum | R . campanulatum | 16 | |
| R . aeruginosum | R . campanulatum | | |
| R . campylocarpum | | 34 | 1848 |
| R . aliatum | | 70 | 1850 |
| R . dalhousiae | | 88 | 1854 |
| R . edgeworthii | | 39 | 1851 |
| R . falconeri | | 16 | 1850 |
| R . fulgens | | 49 | |
| R . glaucum | R . glaucophyllum | 66 | |
| R . hodgsonii | | 28 | |
| R . lancifolium | R . barbatum | 51 | |
| R . lanatum | | 1 | |
| R . maddeni | | 49 | 1849 |
| R . niveum | | 51 | |
| R . roylei | R . cinnabarinum roylei | 15 | 1850 |
| R . cinnabarinum | | 51 | 1850 |
| R . thomsonii | | 60 | 1850 |
| R . wallichii | | 16 | |
| R . wightii | | 3 | |
| R . pendulum | | 15 | |
| R . pumilum | | | |
| R . triflorum | | | |
| R . camelliiflorum | | | |
| R . candelabrum | R . x candelabrum | | |
| R . setosum | | | |
| R . salignum | R . lepidotum | | |
| R . elaeagniodes | R . lepidotum | | |
| R . nivale | | | |
| R . virgatum | | | |

**• Species not included in *Rhododendrons of Sikkim-Himalaya***

---

**Table 2. Distribution of Hooker rhododendrons to individuals**

Miss Walker, Drumseugh, Edinburgh, Sept 17th 1851

Mr Fairbairne, April 29th 1851

Mr Harryatt, Wimbledon, 12 Nov 1851

Mr W Cunningham, Liverpool, 13 Nov 1851

W Downing, East India House, March 27, 1852, 1853 June 10th 1859

Nuttall, Esq, May 29th 1852

Miss Gurney, Cromens

Mr Curtis, Jersey

Mr Seeman, Kew, July 31 1852

Rev Medland near Brighton

The Bishop of Exeter

Mrs Th Brighteven

Mr Liddell, Cadogan Place 1853

Mr Bentzien

R H Jenkinson, Norbiton 1853

Mr Hutt, Maddock Street

Mr Darwin 12 Sikkim Rhododendrons and *Berberis darwinii*

Lady Meldrid (*sic*) ,Hope, Oct 20th 1856

Sir C Russell, Bart, Nov 17th 1857

E Morney Esq, Wallinford, 24th Feb 1859

G K (*sic*) Gowan (*sic*) Esq, Highclere, Feb 3 1852

---

the publication of the second edition of *Rhododendrons of Sikkim-Himalaya*. Little is known about the individuals listed in Table 2. Miss Walker of Edinburgh received 11 plants from Kew and in 1863 *R. maddenii, R. dalhousiae, R. glaucophyl-*

---

**Table 3. Distribution of Hooker rhododendrons to Botanic Gardens**

Mr Moore, Glasnevin, Sept 11th 1855 *R. maddenii*

Mr Ferguson, Belfast, Dec 26th 1851, July 18th 1856

Mr James McNab, Edinburgh, Oct 6th 1852

Mr Niven, Hull, April 30th 1853

Dr Goeppert, Botanic Garden Breslau

Mr Moore, Sydney, Nov 13th 1854

RBG Schonberg near Berlin, 1856

Botanic Garden, Dijon, 1853

---

*lum* were in cultivation in her conservatory.[2] It is interesting to note that in 1855 12 Sikkim rhododendrons and *Berberis darwinii* were sent to Mr Darwin. Joseph Hooker and Charles Darwin had been friends and correspondents over many years and Hooker was a pall bearer at Darwin's funeral.

Thomas Nuttall FLS *(Rhododendron nuttalli)*, a naturalist who subscribed to the book and received plants in 1852. Mr Seeman, Kew was probably Seeman of Hannover, a botanist and naturalist. G K Gowan *(sic)* supervised the rhododendron breeding for the Earl of Carnarvon at Highclere, Newbury: his most famous cross being *R.* 'Altaclerense', *(R. arboreum* x [*catawbiense* seedling x *ponticum*]).

In December 1851, *R. cinnabarinum roylei, R. grande, R. ciliatum, R. dalhousiae, R. thomsonii, R. glaucophyllum, R. hodgsonii* and *R. maddenii* were sent to Mr Daniel Ferguson, curator of the Botanic Gardens in Belfast. *Rhododendron ciliatum* was sent to this garden in 1856. In 1875, *R. dalhousiae,* and other Himalayan rhododendrons not listed above, were in cultivation in the Palm House.[3]

Cowan[4], writing about the rhododendrons in the Royal Botanic Garden Edinburgh in 1953, stated that *R. grande, R. campylocarpum, R. falconeri, R. fulgens, R. niveum, R. wallichii, R. lanatum, R. dalhousiae, R. glaucophyllum* and *R. lepidotum* had been received from Kew in 1850. In 1852 *R. hodgsonii* and *R. maddenii* were sent from Kew to Edinburgh, and in 1856

*R. arboreum* var. *campbelliae* was received. *Rhododendron fulgens* was removed in 1950. In 1995 there were no longer any Hooker plants or material propagated from them in the garden.

In 1854, *R. grande* and *R. ciliatum* were sent to Mr Charles Moore, Curator of the Sydney Botanic Gardens, Australia. A year later, *R. maddenii* was sent to the Botanic Gardens, Glasnevin, Dublin where his brother, David Moore, was curator.

Species were also cultivated at Kew. In 1876 a note in *The Gardeners' Chronicle* (5) recorded that *R. barbatum, R. arboreum, R. ciliatum, R. fulvum* and *R. grande* were in flower in the Temperate House. In 1881, *R. arboreum, R. grande, R. glaucophyllum, R. cinnabarinum blandfordiiflorum* and *R. edgeworthii* and *R. niveum* were in flower.[6]

Some properties listed in Table 4 are still maintained as gardens or parks and it has been possible to ascertain whether any plants are still alive.

In May 1852, the following species were sent to Sir Thomas Acland, Killerton, Devon. *R. dalhousiae, R. ciliatum, R. glaucophyllum, R. niveum, R. fulgens, R. campylocarpum, R. thomsonii, R. griffithianum, R. hodgsonii, R. maddenii, R. edgeworthii, R. barbatum* and *R. arboreum.* A second consignment was forwarded to Killerton in July 1853 and included some Hooker species: *R. glaucophyllum, R. cinnabarinum* and *R. edgeworthii.* In 1969, Mr Davidian of RBGE noted the following 'Hooker'

---

**Table 4. Distribution of Hooker rhododendrons to gardens**

HRH Prince Albert, Osborne House, Isle of Wight, Oct 3 1850

Sir Wm Middleton, Bart. Shrubland, Ipswich, Nov 28 1851

Sir Charles Lemon, Carclew, Cornwall, Dec 5th 1851

The Hon. H Liddell, Ravensworth Castle, near Gateshead, Tyne and Wear, Jan 22 1852

J Luscombe, Kingsbridge, Combe Royal, Devon, April 3 1852

Mr Burn, Tottenham Park, near Marlborough, Wilts, April 27th 1852

Charles Barclay Esq. Bury Hill, May 11th 1852

Lord Rutherford, Lauriston Castle, Edinburgh, May 13th 1852

Sir Thomas Acland, Killerton, Devon 1852, later Sir Thomas Auckland (*sic*), 1853

Thomas Cubitt, The Denbies, Dorking

Rev TG Parsons, Selbourne, Alton, Hants, June 26 1852

Lady Foley, Stoke Edith Park, Ledbury, Hereford. Sept 26th 1852, 1856

Mr Counihan, Phoenix Park, Dublin, Ireland, Oct 6th 1852

Viscountess Doneraile, Doneraile, Cork, Ireland, April 1854

James Anderson, 41 York Place, Edinburgh

John Maclean, near Lochgoilhead (*sic*), Near Greenock. 100 papers of seed, 1855

Lord John Manners, Belvoir Castle, Belvoir, Leics, May 27th 1859

The Hon Lady Adeliza Norman, Bottesford Rectory, Grantham, Aug 4th 1859

Viscount Valentia, Beltchington Park, Kirlington, Aug 31 1859

---

species at Killerton, *R. ciliatum, R. falconeri, R. glaucophyllum, R. hodgsonii* and *R. thomsonii*. In a survey undertaken by Michael Lear in 1993 only *R. hodgsonii* could be located.

Carclew in Cornwall was one of the earliest gardens to obtain plants from Kew. Sir Charles Lemon received the following in 1851, *R. falconeri, R. hodgsonii, R. griffithianum, R. maddenii, R. ciliatum, R. dalhousiae, R. cinnabarinum* var. *roylei, R. glaucophyllum, R. niveum, R. thomsonii* and some numbered rather than named plants. In 1917 Millais[7] described the following: 20 to 40 years old, *R. grande, R. falconeri, R. barbatum, R. arboreum, R. griffithianum, R. grande, R. lanatum. Rhododendron arboreum* 'Sir Charles Lemon' (probably *arboreum* subsp. *cinnamoneum* x *campanulatum* subsp. *campanulatum*) and a young *R. falconeri* propagated from a Hooker *R. falconeri* are still growing in the garden.

John Luscombe of Combe Royal, Devon, a subscriber to *Rhododendrons of Sikkim-Himalaya*, wrote to Sir William Hooker in December 1851 requesting plants of *R. griffithianum, R. hodgsonii, R. maddenii, R. grande* and *R. wightii*[8]. He already had *R. arboreum* in cultivation, probably, the Indian introduction. In January 1852, he requested any Sikkim rhododendrons that were available and on 6 April wrote to William Hooker thanking him for a 'magnificent present of Rhododendron [which] arrived in safety last Thursday'. The plants he received from Kew on 3 April were as follows, *R. dalhousiae, R. glaucophyllum, R. cinnabarinum, R. ciliatum, R. thomsonii, R. campylocarpum, R. niveum, R. fulgens, R. barbatum, R. griffithianum, R. maddenii, R. edgeworthii, R. hodgsonii, R. campbelliae, R. arboreum* vars. and *R. barbatum*. Correspondence continued between Combe Royal and Kew. The plants were growing satisfactorily, with the exception of *R. dalhousiae* and *R. edgeworthii*. and one can sense the excitement created by the new species 'showing their paces' in the garden. Luscombe also planted rhododendrons supplied by Messrs Henderson and Low who had both also received plants from Kew. Luscombe received seed again from William Hooker in 1858. Then *R. dalhousiae* flowered in

1858, *R. cinnabarinum blandfordiiflorum* in 1859 (described by Luscombe as 'very distinct and pretty') and *R. thomsonii* in 1864. Luscombe was an enthusiastic gardener and planted a range of other exotic trees and shrubs in his American garden. Several dozen *R. arboreum* forms, some 15m (49 ft) tall and *R. niveum*, considered to be a Hooker form, still grow at Combe Royal.

In 1859 *R. campylocarpum, R. campanulatum, R. barbatum, R. ciliatum, R. falconeri, R. dalhousiae, R. edgeworthii, R. griffithianum, R. hodgsonii, R. fulgens, R. thomsonii, R. grande, R. cinnabarinum* and *R. arboreum* were sent to Belvoir Castle. The Duchess of Rutland reports that there are several old rhododendrons still growing at Belvoir and it is possible that they may be the original plants. According to J G Millais, by 1917 *R. falconeri* had attained a height of 5m (16ft).[7]

Rhododendrons were among the

---

**Table 5. Distribution of Hooker rhododendrons to nurseries**

Mr Jackson, Kingston upon Thames, Sept 15th 1851 long list of species

Mess Veitch, Exeter Nurserymen long list of species, Nov 9 1851, Oct 6th 1855

Mess Fisher, Holmes and Co. Handsworth Sheffield. Nurseryman, 1852

Mess Urquhart & Son. Dundee, Jan 24 1852, May 22 1852

Mess Standish and Noble, Bagshot, 15th Mar 1852

Mr Masters, Cantebury (*sic*), April 16 1852

Mr Rollison, Upper Tooting, London

Mr Pince and Co. (Robert Taylor 1804-1871), July 29 1852

Mr Low, Upper Clapton, 1852, Sept 8th 1855

Mr Henderson, Pine Apple Place, Edgeware Rd, London, 1852 Oct 19th & 30 1855

Mr Epps, Maidstone, Kent, May 1st 1853, June 26th 1853

plants that the Viscountess Doneraile received from Sir William Hooker in 1854, but the estate at Doneraile, County Cork is now a public park and there are no rhododendrons growing there. Mr Counihan was head gardener at the Vice-Regal Lodge, Phoenix Park, Dublin. However none of the species received by him exist at what is now the residence of the President of Ireland.

Of these nurserymen in Table 5, Rollisson, Henderson, Jackson, Standish and Noble, and Veitch all subscribed to the *Rhododendron of Sikkim-Himalaya.*

Messrs Standish & Noble of Bagshot received plants of six species of rhododendron from Kew in 1852 and they may also have received seed. They offered 'a collection of twenty-four distinct sorts from 5-10 guineas'. Later the two partners separated and in 1898 Noble's nursery became known as the Sunningdale Nursery. In 1939 there were seven large *R. thomsonii,* large plants of *R. cinnabarinium, R. falconeri, R. lanatum* and a fine plant of *R. campanulatum* var. *aeruginosum* in the nursery. Mr James Russell took layers of these plants to Castle Howard, Yorkshire, in 1968, where they are now established in Ray Wood.

Rhododendrons were sent to many parts of the world in glazed cases and it is interesting to see in the record books a tiny illustration of the various types that were used.

In the 1850s four consignments of plants were sent to the Belgian nurseryman L Jacob-Makoy of Liège. The travel arrangements for the consignment to Dr Asa Gray of Cambridge, Massachusetts USA were recorded by Kew as 'a close box by Mail Steamer from Liverpool forwarded to Liverpool by Passenger train, October 20th'. The consignment sent from Kew to the Arnold Arboretum included *R. barbatum, R. ciliatum, R. arboreum, R. wightii* var.*, R. edgeworthii, R. niveum, R. fulgens* and *R.* sp. *Assam* and *R.* sp. *Bootan Hills* (*sic*) and *R. formosum* (not a Hooker introduction).

Glazed cases that included *Rhododendron arboreum* were sent to Canterbury, New Zealand and to Mr Walter Hill, New South Wales, Australia. In 1856 two glazed cases which included two specimens of *R. ciliatum* and one specimen of *R. dalhousiae* were sent to W S Grahame, Auckland, New Zealand. Marby[9] writing in 1977 records that a selection of species was listed in a catalogue issued about 1880 by William Martin, a Scottish settler, who had a nursery at Fairfield, Dunedin. These were *R. falconeri, R. griffithianum, R. arboreum* red, *R. campanulatum, R. ciliatum, R. dalhousiae, R. edgeworthii, R. glaucophyllum* and *R. thomsonii,* and one might surmise that the plants had been grown from seed.

As the Hooker rhododendrons were propagated and became more freely available, many articles in *The Gardeners' Chronicle* recorded how the plants were used in gardens. Gill, writing in 1898,[10] mentioned collections at Tremough,

---

**Table 6. Distribution of Hooker rhododendrons worldwide**

Mr Held, Carlsruhe, Baden, Sept 6th 1850

Mr Makoy, Liège, Sept 10th 1850, Mackoy 1852, Oct 17th 1853, July 29 1856

(L. Jacob Makoy et Cie. Horticulteurs, près de la station de Guillemins et du Viaduc de Ste
  Veronique, Liège, Belgium)

Mr Linden, Bruxelles, Nov 13th 1850, all numbered plants, Feb 28 1852

Mon. de Duc de Mondmovency (*sic*), 18th Sept 1851

Mr Smith, Jamaica, 30th Sept 1851

Canterbury New Zealand, 2 glazed cases including rhododendrons, 1851

Mr Walter Hill, New South Wales. Glazed case *R. roseum,* 1851

Woodland, Hannover

Baroness J. Nahuys, Arnheim, Holland, 1853

Mr Chatin, Paris, July 24th 1853

St Helena glazed box

Fred A Haage, Erfurt, 1853

Sir H Barkley, Jamaica, Sept 14th 1853.

Grand Duchy of Mecklenburg Strelitz, Oct 21 1853, Oct 4th 1855

Prof. Parlatore, Florence, April 26th 1855

RH the Duke of Montpensier, Spain, 1855

Mr Hanneman Leipzic (*sic*), 1855

PWD Brackenbridge, Govanstown, near Baltimore, USA, 1855

WS Grahame, Auckland, 1856

Dr Asa Gray, Cambridge University (*sic*) [Harvard University] USA,

Mons C Boissier, Geneva, May 10th 1859

---

Tregothnan, Scorrier, Carclew and Killiow, all in Cornwall. At another Cornish garden, Menabilly,[11] established in the 18th century, Mr Jonathan Rashleigh started a rhododendron collection about a century later in an area known as the Hooker Grove, a compliment to Sir Joseph Hooker. Menabilly was a coastal garden of 8.5ha (21 acres) with 11.25km (7 miles) of paths and a 3.25km (2-mile) avenue lined with rhododendrons, hydrangeas and fuchsias.[12] In 1886, 29 Himalayan species were in cultivation.

From Carclew, situated between Truro and Falmouth, plants were sent to another garden, Heligan, where John Tremayne had begun planting in 1851. W Roberts, writing about this garden in 1896, noted the following Sikkim rhododendrons: *R. griffithianum, R. thomsonii* (7.5m/25ft) *R. falconeri* (15 years old) which produced 258 flowering heads, *R. hodgsonii, R. arboreum* (*R. campbelliae*), *R. glaucophyllum*. In the Upper Drive *R. grande, R. falconeri, R. arboreum* pink forms, *R. griffithianum* and *R. niveum*

*The garden at Carclew in Cornwall. Hooker sent plants to Sir John Lemon on 5 December. 1851, including* R. arboreum *and* R. falconeri

were recorded.[13] In 1983 Major Magor[14] noted that this old garden had become totally neglected, but was worthy of conservation: restoration began in 1990 and by 1994 *R. arboreum, R. grande, R. griffithianum, R. campylocarpum, R. niveum* and *R. thomsonii* were all found to be growing in the garden (see figure 3).

More recently, in 1925 Charles Tremayne of Carclew, gave a plant of *R. cinnabarinum* var. *roylei* to Treve Holman at Chyverton, near Truro, as a 'garden warming present'. The layer and some of its children are still in the garden.

As well as distributing plants, the Hookers also sent seed to various garden owners. At Tremough[15] near Penryn, Cornwall, Mr Shilson received seed from Sir William Hooker. The 8ha (20 acre) garden was richly planted with rhododendrons. Both sides of the drive were lined with 170 plants of *R. barbatum, R. arboreum* var. *cinnamomeum, R. falconeri* and *R. cinnabarinum*. Some 800 rhododendrons were planted in borders: they were *R. griffithianum, R. thomsonii, R. falconeri, R. cinnabarinum, R. campanulatum* var. *aeruginosum* and *R. dalhousiae*. Mr Richard Gill, head gardener who wrote the later article 'Himalayan Rhododendrons' noted the success of rhododendrons in the garden. *R. dalhousiae* had been in cultivation for 20 years. Also present were *R. arboreum* in all its varieties and by 1898 had attained a height of 8.3m (27¼ft) while *R. barbatum* achieved 6.6m (21½ft).

The grounds at Castle Kennedy and Lochinch were developed from 1844 onwards by the Earl of Stair. In the 1850s Sir Joseph Hooker visited the Earl and advised the planting of rhododendrons in the policies. He later sent him seed of *R. arboreum, R. thomsonii, R. barbatum* and *R. campanulatum*. Mr Fowler, the gardener, stocked the 'American' ground with rhododendrons, kalmias and azaleas. In 1864 the *R. thomsonii* was reported to have 40 to 50 heads of bloom.[16] In June 1993, three *R. arboreum* var. *cinnamomeum* were measured by the author, one tree had a single trunk 2m (6½ft) diameter at base with a height of 17m (55¾ft). A second multistemmed tree close by was 17m (55¾ft) tall also. A third tree 2.1m (7ft) in diameter, 15.5m (51ft) tall was in flower 1 June 1993 and there was a group of the same sized trees nearby. By the pond a multistemmed specimen of *R. barbatum* was approximately 6m (19½ft) tall.

*Rhododendron edgeworthii* first flowered in the open air in Britain on the Isle of Rothesay, in the west of Scotland in 1863. Mr Clarke, the curator of the Botanic Garden, Glasgow, had received seed from Sir William Hooker and in 1856 gave 12 species to 'R. B.' in Rothesay.[17]

In 'Rhododendrons in the Western Highlands', Balfour[18] describes the rhododendrons at Poltalloch, Argyll; Kilmoy, Lough Fyne; Glenarn and Stonefield. At Glenarn a large specimen of *R. falconeri* reputed to be from Hooker seed is still growing in the garden. The gardens at

*Joseph Hooker's herbarium sheet showing* R. cinnabarinum, *preserved at RBG Kew (see figures 5 and 7 for Hooker's drawing made in the field and W Fitch's lithograph of the same plant in* Rhododendrons of Sikkim-Himalaya)

Stonefield Castle also contain a wide selection of rhododendrons, many considered to be grown from Hooker seed.

Tregothnan,[19] Cornwall received plants from the sale of Canon Arthur Boscawen's garden at Lamorran Rectory in 1862; 110 lots were purchased for the garden. Old specimens still growing in the garden include *R. falconeri, R. griffithianum* and *R. thomsonii.* In front of the summer house, an expanse of formal grass is flanked by a crescent of red *R. arboreum.* The rhododendrons some 13 to 16m (40-50ft) tall bloom in late April.

In Ireland, the gardens of Thomas Acton at Kilmacurragh, Co. Wicklow, contain some very fine rhododendrons, dating from the late 1800s. The following were measured in 1994: *R. arboreum,* believed to be the first planted into Ireland, 9m (30ft); *R. arboreum roseum; R. barbatum* regarded as the Menabilly form 8m (25ft): *R. falconeri* 6m (20ft); *R. griffithianum* 8m (25ft).

At Fernhill, Sandyford, Co. Dublin, a woodland garden laid out in the mid 19th century by the Darley family still retains the original Broad Walk of conifers and a number of *R. arboreum* var. *roseum.* These rhododendrons were probably given to the Darleys by the Keeper of the Botanic Gardens Glasnevin, David Moore. One plant has been given the cultivar name, 'Fernhill Silver'. This multistemmed tree, with a cinnamon flaking bark, has a diameter of 3.1m (10ft) and a height of 15m (49ft). The flowers are in tight flowerheads.

Another *R. arboreum* var. *roseum* is also multistemmed with a diameter of 2.5m (8¼ft) and a height of 12m (39ft). On one side of the Broad Walk a group of eight specimens of *R. arboreum* var. *roseum* are about 15m (49ft) tall.

Another woodland garden at Ardnamona, Co. Donegal, Ireland, was planted with rhododendrons by Sir Arthur Wallace in the 1890s. The following numbers of specimens were counted by the author in the garden in 1993: 31 *R. falconeri;* 17 *R. arboreum;* 14 *R. arboreum* var. *roseum;* 9 *R. arboreum* var *cinnamomeum;* 5 *R. arboreum* var. *arboreum;* 11 *R. niveum;* 1 *R. hodgsonii;* 4 *R. griffithianum;* 4 *R. grande;* and 4 *R. barbatum.* So many fine old specimens of plants occur in the garden today that one must assume that they were grown from seed. Tree heights varied from 5.5m (18ft) for a *R. niveum* to 13 to 14m (42½-46ft) for *R. arboreum, R. falconeri,* and *R. grande.* Tree trunks measured in 1993 had 90 rings.

At Castlewellan National Arboretum, Co. Down, Northern Ireland, Hooker rhododendrons were planted in the 1880s and 1890s. Tall specimens of *R. falconeri, R. grande, R. barbatum* are alive, but the *R. niveum* mentioned in the Year Book 1983/84 has died.[20]

At the former Balfour garden near Colinsburgh, Leven, Fife, now a hotel, *R. cinnabarinum,* considered to be from Hooker seed, is in cultivation. It also was mentioned by Millais in 1924.[21]

At Hethersett, Littleworth Cross,

Surrey, part of the old Mangles' garden, *R. wightii,* and a neat form of *R. campylocarpum* known as a Hooker seedling was noted by Millais.[21]

At South Lodge[22], Horsham, *R. campylocarpum,* a dwarf rounded bush with sulphur yellow flowers, was distinct from other forms. It came to this garden, established by F D Godman in 1883, from Reuthe's nursery. They had raised it from seed received from Sir Joseph Hooker.

At Royal Lodge in Windsor Great Park, *R. barbatum* 5.5m (18ft)[23] was considered to be one of the old Hooker introductions. *Rhododendron falconeri, R. cinnabarinum, R. thomsonii, R. campylocarpum* and *R. arboreum,* pink and white shades 8m (24ft) high were also in cultivation.

While many of the gardens already mentioned had a mild equable climate, Biddulph Grange in Staffordshire, was a cold location for the cultivation of rhododendrons. In the 1850s, based on a description of a Himalayan ravine, James Bateman[24] constructed a dark rocky glen with a stream of water. In it he planted a selection of species including the following Sikkim Himalayan species, *R. fulgens, R. thomsonii, R. lanatum R. hodgsonii* (all hardy) *R. falconeri* and *R. wightii* (nearly hardy). *Rhododendron lepidotum, R. setosum, R. glaucophyllum* and *R. ciliatum* flowered but were damaged by frost. The temperatures were too low for the other species and they did not flower. He also constructed a Rhododendron House for

the cultivation of the more tender species, *R. dalhousiae, R. edgeworthii, R. fulvum, R. aucklandii, R. campanulatum* var *aeruginosum, R. thomsonii, R. campylocarpum, R. niveum, R. wightii, R. argenteum, R. hodgsonii, R. lanatum* and *R. virgatum.* By 1862 *R. maddenii* was in flower and many species in the Ravine were transferred to the Rhododendron House. Bateman also noted the attractive young foliage of some of these species.

In the 1890s at Minterne[25], Dorset, *R. falconeri, R. thomsonii, R. campylocarpum, R. arboreum* and *R. barbatum* were planted by Lord Digby in a setting of shrubberies and beneath the shade of beech trees. Other old plants are recorded at Benmore, Dunoon.[26] *R. campanulatum* a fine old specimen 10.6m (35ft) high, *R. cinnabarinum, R. griffithianum, R. arboreum;* at Borde Hill[27] where *R. barbatum* and *R. falconeri* were planted in 1893 from seed collected by Hooker; and at Westonbirt[28] where *R. falconeri, R. lacteum* and *R. arboreum* some 100 years old are considered to have been grown from Hooker's seed.

Many of the species introduced by Sir Joseph Hooker became progenitors of well known rhododendron hybrids (see Chapter 10).

While few rhododendrons can be authenticated as plants of known wild origin, the legacy of the Hooker introductions is evident in so many Victorian gardens. It is a memorable experience to visit these places, where in the midst of native trees, tall arboreal specimens of *R. falconeri, R. griffithianum* and *R. arboreum* have withstood the vagaries of weather and garden management for well over 100 years to become the 'lilies of the sky'. Nor is his contribution confined to tree rhododendrons, the medium-sized shrubs, *R. campylocarpum, R. cinnabarinum, R. thomsonii* and their hybrids, are available everywhere and widely planted in present day gardens.

## Acknowledgements

Lady Cynthia Postan; Mrs Cheryl Piggott, Archivist, RBG Kew; Mr Donal Synnott, Director, National Botanic Gardens, Glasnevin; The Librarian, Lindley Library, RHS, London; The Librarian, University College, Dublin; John Main, RBG Edinburgh; Mrs Chope, Carclew, Cornwall; H Sharp, Combe Royal, Devon; The Duchess of Rutland, Belvoir Castle; James Russell, Castle Howard, Yorkshire; Nigel Holman, Chyverton, Cornwall; Sue Pring, Heligan, Cornwall; Michael Lear, Killerton, Devon; John Anderson, Kilmacurragh, Wicklow; Sean O'Gaoithin, Ardnamona, Donegal; Lady Adam Gordon, Hethersett, Surrey.

## Notes

[1] HOOKER, J (1849, 1851). *Rhododendrons of Sikkim-Himalaya.*

[2] ANON, (1863). 'Drumsheugh', *The Gardeners' Chronicle and Agricultural Gazette.* 1251.

[3] BAINES, T (1875). 'Botanic Garden Belfast', *The Gardeners' Chronicle.* **III**: 818.

[4] MACQUEEN COWAN, J (1953). 'Rhododendrons in the Royal Botanic Garden', *The Rhododendron and Camellia Yearbook.* 1953. 7: 33-57.

[5] ANON, (1876), 'Himalayan Rhododendrons at Kew', *The Gardeners' Chronicle.* **V**: 370.

[6] ANON, (1881). 'Sikkim Rhododendrons at Kew', *The Garden.* **XIX**: 322.

[7] MILLAIS, J G (1917). *Rhododendrons.*

[8] Correspondence between Luscombe and Sir William Hooker for the years 1851 to 1865 was consulted at RBG, Kew.

[9] MARBY, R (1977). 'Rhododendrons in Dunedin', *Rhododendrons 1977 with Magnolia and Camellias.* 14-21.

[10] GILL, R (1898). 'Himalayan Rhododendrons', *The Gardeners' Chronicle.* **XXIII**: 65, 80.

[11] ANON, (1886) 'Plants Growing Out of Doors at Menabilly', *The Gardeners' Chronicle.* **XXV**: 817.

[12] SWF (1903) 'Menabilly Cornwall', *The Gardeners' Chronicle.* **XXXIII**: 234-235.

[13] ROBERTS, W (1896). 'Heligan, Cornwall', *The Gardeners' Chronicle.* **XX**: 747-748.

[14] MAGOR, W (1983). 'The Garden at Heligan in Cornwall', *Rhododendrons 1982/3 with Magnolias and Camellias.* 1-3.

[15] MILLS, H (1876). 'Tremough, Cornwall', *The Gardeners' Chronicle.* **VI**: 719.

[16] JL (1864). 'Garden Memoranda', *The Gardeners' Chronicle and Agricultural Gazette.* 679.

[17] RB (1863). 'Home Correspondence', *The Gardeners' Chronicle and Agricultural Gazette.* 534.

[18] BALFOUR, FRS (1946). 'Rhododendrons in the Western Highlands', *Rhododendron and Camellia Yearbook.* **I**: 32-4.

[19] FALMOUTH, Viscount and Viscountess, (1968). 'Tregothnan – a Camellia and Rhododendron Garden in Cornwall', *Rhododendron and Camellia Yearbook.* **22**: 2-9

[20] DAVID, J (1984). 'The Rhododendron and Camellia Group 1983 Tour of Ireland'. *Rhododendrons 1983/4 with Magnolias and Camellias.* 53.

[21] MILLAIS, J G (1924). *Rhododendrons and the Various Hybrids.*

[22]MILLAIS, J G (1921). South Lodge. *Rhododendron Society Notes II.* **No. 2**: 73.

[23]FINDLAY, T Hope and Hardy, A (1973). 'The Garden at Royal Lodge'. *Rhododendrons 1973 with Magnolia and Camellias.* **27**: 5-11.

[24]JB (1862). 'Sikkim and Bhotan Rhododendra out of Doors'. *The Gardeners' Chronicle and Agricultural Gazette.* 356, 381, 404.

[25]DIGBY, Lord (1956). 'The History of Minterne Rhododendron Garden'. *Rhododendron and Camellia Yearbook.* **10**: 9-15.

[26]HALL, A (1967). 'Rhododendrons at Benmore'. *Rhododendron and Camellia Yearbook.* **22**: 34-47.

[27]CLARKE, RNS (n.d.). 'The Rhododendron Species at Borde Hill'.

[28]ANON, (1965). 'Rhododendrons at Westonbirt Arboretum', *Rhododendron and Camellia Yearbook.* **19**: 47.

DR MARY FORREST *is a lecturer in horticulture at the University College, Dublin, specialising in Plant materials and Garden History. Her inventory of woody plants in Irish gardens was published as* Trees and Shrubs Cultivated in Ireland

# CHAPTER 6

## THE IRRESISTIBLE SPREAD OF THE RHODODENDRON IN BRITISH GARDENS

### KEN HULME

As recently as 150 years ago very few species of *Rhododendron* were known in the western world. Linnaeus (1707-78) had been aware of only a handful of species. In the 19th century a small number (of mostly deciduous species) trickled across the Atlantic from North America. More notably by the dawn of the 19th century army personnel and surveyors were discovering rhododendron forests in the Himalayas. Dr Buchanan Hamilton is credited with the earliest introduction of *Rhododendron arboreum* from that region, closely followed by Nathaniel Wallich, who collected on a wider scale and provided a catalogue of his acquisitions. In 1825 we have the first report of the crimson form of *R. arboreum* flowering in Alexander Baring's garden at the Grange, Alresford, Hampshire. Then Robert Baxter of Dee Hills, Chester, received an award for the white form of *R. arboreum* in 1839.

Baxter's plant had been raised from seed received in 1821 from N Wallich, by H Shepherd, Curator, City of Liverpool Botanic Garden, an establishment founded in the centre of the city and declared open in 1802. (This was two years prior to the meeting in Hatchard's bookshop which led to the formation of the London Horticultural Society, later to become the Royal Horticultural Society.)

Accounts in the *Botanical Magazine* reveal that many early introductions from the Far East were grown under glass. Uncertainty about the degree of hardiness of particular species was complicated by the variation in response to climate – within a species – due to provenance. It is widely recognized that the flower colour in *R. arboreum* varies with altitude; the deeper colour forms are generally from lower levels and the paler ones from higher up. The rich colour forms are less hardy than the paler ones and thrive only in gardens with notably mild climates. The accounts of *R. edgeworthii* mention that it first flowered in cultivation in 'a cool greenhouse'. This species is found growing wild over a wide area and plants of different provenance are likely to show variable response to climatic conditions. The point is borne out by reference to specimens in gardens. I have been familiar with *R. edgeworthii* in the open in the Royal Botanic Garden, Edinburgh (RBGE), for almost 50 years. The Award of Merit (AM) form of this species with delightfully pink-flushed petals is trained against a sheltered wall at Bodnant and, one assumes, is less hardy than the Edinburgh plants. Similarly, *R. cinnabarinum* was originally given protection, but it became widely grown in the open in many gardens.

Huge rhododendrons are to be found on a number of estates, some nearly 20m (65½ft) high and over 140 years old. These venerable specimens are found in areas of high rainfall, high humidity and relatively mild winters. This represents the maritime climate of West-Coast Britain, but the varying requirements of species makes it possible to grow rhododendrons in almost any part of the British Isles.

The main limiting factor is an alkaline soil: in areas where chalk or limestone is present there are difficulties in growing most members of the Ericaceae. From observation in Yunnan, George Forrest concluded that some species of *Rhododendron* could be accommodated on soils derived from limestone rock. Attempts to grow these species on base-rich soils in Britain have, however, ended in failure. Several explanations for these results spring to mind. First, there are very different types of limestone, and, secondly, climatic conditions could account for the difference between success and failure. In areas of high rainfall and humidity plants can thrive on a thin layer of organic material above the influence of the underlying rock. (A number of species are epiphytes in their natural habitat.) There are well-known examples in Britain where a classic calcifuge plant can form thriving populations on layers of organic soil above limestone, for example the heather moors of North Wales.

The Westonbirt Arboretum is in the Cotswold limestone area but in certain parts there has been an accumulation of organic matter which makes it possible to grow rhododendrons quite successfully. In such cases the high levels of lime, which raise the soil pH and make it difficult to take up the minor elements so essential to rhododendrons, have been leached away. Trials at RBGE demonstrate, however, that the optimum pH for rhododendrons is in the range 5.0-6.0. Readings above this figure give rise to the sickly state known as 'lime induced chlorosis'. On the other hand, significantly lower figures result in unsatisfactory growth. That mistakes were made in attempting to cultivate some of the earlier importation of plants on unsuitable soils is beyond doubt.

F & J Dickson of Upton Nurseries, Chester, recorded the first flowering of *Rhododendron campanulatum* in Britain in 1839. Proximity to the port of Liverpool and the presence of H Shepherd, of the City Botanic Garden, must have helped. The Dicksons acquired seed of *R. lacteum* in 1841 and flowered it in 1848. Though no longer in existence, the firm continued well into the 20th century. Another nursery firm, Standish & Noble, were early handlers of rhododendron seed, including some of Joseph Hooker's importation of *R. campylocarpum* which they had in flower in a frame in 1856 (see Chapter 5). Rollisons of Tooting received an award for one of the forms of *R. arboreum* in 1836 and Victoria Nursery, Highgate, were awarded the First Class Certificate (FCC) for *R. nuttallii* in 1846. Before long the firm of Veitch was assuming an important role. As well as growing a number of species hybridization began. The fact that the best forms of *R. arboreum* and the magnificent *R. griffithianum* were not hardy in many parts of Britain may have provided the incentive. To combine the qualities of these species with the hardiness of others seemed a worthy target. Plant breeders must have a reason for their activities. Many early hybrids had genuine garden value, however most have vanished from current nursery catalogues (see chapter 10).

That cultivars of the 19th century have been superseded is a general rule verging on a truism. Few are still on offer and those that are, owe their position to some feature beyond intrinsic appeal. For example, *R.* 'Cunningham's White' raised by the man whose name it bears in his Comely Bank Nursery, Edinburgh, about 1830, grows in more extreme conditions than almost any other rhododendron. It also roots so readily from cuttings that it is often used as an understock for grafting. Then, *R.* 'Nobleanum', an Anthony Waterer hybrid of the same period, will flower throughout mild spells in winter. Another, *R.* x 'Praecox' raised by Isaac Davies in his Ormskirk nursery, also survives as a fairly tough winter-flowering shrub – the pale purple flowers of this plant are in evidence in half the gardens in the street where I live. A K Bulley refused to have this early flowering cultivar in his garden at Ness, and the colour of *R. mucronulatum* is infinitely more pleasing. Yet another, *R.* x 'Fragrantissimum' was awarded the FCC when exhibited by Rollisons in 1868 and was presumably raised by them.

The mixed blessings of hybridization became evident with the arrival of the vast array of new species between 1880 and 1930. Information on the flora of West China was beginning to reach Europe; the firm of Veitch had received seed of *R. racemosum* and presented it in 1892 to receive the FCC. They were keen to add to their success. They commissioned E H Wilson to collect for them in China in 1899 and among his considerable haul of new species were *R. orbiculare*, *R. sutchuenense* and *R. calophytum*. A few years later he introduced the superb *R. williamsianum*. The horticultural world was enthralled with the new rhododendrons and a period of intense collecting activity soon followed.

In 1904 A K Bulley launched George Forrest on his career as a plant collector. The success of his first expedition led him to concentrate his six further explorations on the floristically rich area of Yunnan and the adjoining territories. The earlier claims on the number of new species Forrest introduced are now seen to be an overstatement, but the significance of his work cannot be exaggerated. Among his discoveries are *R. impeditum*, *R. russatum*, *R. clementinae*, *R. rex* subsp. *fictolacteum*, *R. sinogrande* and *R. griersonianum*. The list could be extended to resemble an index of the genus: to quote P D Williams, 'Wilson's plants came in manageable proportions, those of Forrest came in a tremendous and sustained flood.' The contribution to the garden scene was only one aspect of George Forrest's contributions; his earlier training in herbarium work resulted in his compilation of a wealth of dried specimens. Most are lodged in the Herbarium of the RBGE and did much to establish that institution as the international centre for research on the genus *Rhododendron*. (The purchase of specimens from a French Herbarium by A K Bulley for his old friend Professor Sir Isaac Bayley Balfour also helped.)

In 1911 Frank Kingdon-Ward began

*A K Bulley, who first sent George Forrest to China to collect garden-worthy plants. He bequeathed his garden at Ness in Cheshire to Liverpool University*

to collect for A K Bulley and his finds included *R. pemakoense*, *R. leucaspis* and *R. wardii*. He is also credited with reintroducing the magnificent *R. macabeanum*.

R R Cooper travelled for A K Bulley in Bhutan and Sikkim from 1914 to 1916, from where he introduced *R. dalhousiae* var. *rhabdotum*. It was Cooper's misfortune to arrive home with his material in the midst of World War I, but Ludlow and Sherriff found his notes a valuable aid. Only the last named pair and Kingdon-Ward continued with extended plant exploration activity after World War II. Ludlow and Sherriff discovered the appealing *R. ludlowii*. It has proved to be an outstanding parent in breeding programmes.

The plants which arrived at the peak of the exploration activity were rapidly distributed to gardens on the large estates from Caerhays in Cornwall to Blackhills in Morayshire and all favourable locations in between. Nurseries were by no means excluded from the distribution and some became keen exhibitors, as evidenced by Messrs Gill of Falmouth gaining the AM for *R. falconeri* in 1922 and Harry White of Sunningdale receiving the AM for *R. rigidum* (in 1933). Both firms became involved with hybridization, Gill producing *R.* 'Shilsonii' which has stood the test of time and is considered by some to be one of the all-time greats.

It is on the large estates, nonetheless, where so many of the fine specimens are to be found. Who can ever forget the first encounter with genuine trees of *R. arboreum* at Benmore near Dunoon, where conditions are so favourable that Dick Shaw could compile a long list of species which naturally regenerate. So many of the gardens of Argyll contain mature specimens of great age: Stonefield Castle, for example, has specimens raised from seed collected by Joseph Hooker on his celebrated Himalayan journeys. One is tempted to ask: did our Victorian forebears know something about the mild winter climate in West-Coast Scotland – a fact beyond belief by many in England. The truth is more prosaic, the Campbells of Stonefield were friends of William J Hooker, then in Glasgow, and knew of his son's travels in the Himalayas. Several Scottish gardens began growing rhododendrons a generation before most of the Cornish ones.

Members of the subsections Falconeria and Grandia reach tree proportions in the milder districts of Britain. One of the finest collections of species in these groups is at Brodick on the Isle of Arran. On my first visit in 1954 Jim Russell spent some time contrasting the growth habits of specimens of *R. macabeanum*, raised from seed collected by Kingdon-Ward on one hand and by J F Rock on the other. Today there is much discussion on the comparative quality of flower colour in various plants of this species. One enthusiast from the North of England, who paid regular visits to the Cornish gardens, was fond of reciting 'that the *R. macabeanum* at Trewithen is the finest yellow-flowered rhododendron in the Western World'. I have read that the plant at Trewithen was a gift to George Johnstone from Colonel Bolitho of Trengwainton. It would be poetic justice if this proved to be the case, because Colonel Bolitho's plant was awarded the FCC in 1938. I do not wish to imply that there are no other specimens of comparable quality; to do so would remind me of H H Davidian singing the praises of the Edinburgh plant, followed by a chorus of claims for some of the plants in other parts of the country. The group of *R. macabeanum* at Muncaster shows quite a degree of variation and the size and number of plants lead one to believe they are of a batch raised from Kingdon-Ward's seed, a view sustained by the knowledge that Sir John Ramsden was a member of his sponsoring syndicate. It was Sir John who led Brodick into the rhododendron world by a gift of plants some 70 years ago. Today Brodick can boast of one of the finest collections to be seen anywhere. This claim applies particularly to the large-leafed species. My most impressive photographs of *R. sidereum* and *R. falconeri* were taken at Brodick. One of the large-leafed species – *R. montroseanum* – is named in honour of the former owner, the Duchess of Montrose. The collection since then has been carefully managed for the National Trust for Scotland, mostly by one head gardener, John Basford, and only inevitable retirement could have drawn him away from this garden.

Other gardens in 'the West', as the Scots say, add interesting facets to the 'Rhododendron story'. J A Campbell started planting rhododendrons at Arduaine around the turn of the century and his enthusiasm was passed on to his son and daughter-in-law who devoted much attention to the garden. I paid my first visit in 1949 with Dr J M Cowan and H H Davidian. Sir Bruce and Lady Campbell, the head gardener and the former nanny were then tending the garden. It was here, in 1936, that *R. protistum* first flowered in cultivation. One writer described it as having grown into a 'monumental tree'. It is claimed that J A Campbell brought seed of *R. arboreum* subsp. *zeylanicum* from Sri Lanka and the plants he raised are still growing at Arduaine. Outstanding in the garden are amazingly large and floriferous specimens of *R. griffithianum,* quite unusual outdoors in Britain. My second visit to Arduaine took place in 1959 when I saw the former nanny collecting flowers for the funeral wreath of the head gardener. We realized that this elderly lady was the sole survivor of the gardening quartet of 10 years previously. The garden went into utter decline but was restored by the brothers Wright, who after 20 years, handed over this remarkable garden with its superb collection of plants to the National Trust for Scotland.

Another Campbell family has developed and maintained the garden at Crarae (see figure 8) and a number of the large-leafed species can be found thriving here. This garden has good forms of *R. wardii*; the same species is also well represented at Strone Palace.

The favourable climate for large-leaf rhododendrons extends further north than Argyll. Osgood McKenzie and his daughter, Marie Sawyer, established a selection in their celebrated garden Inverewe, Wester Ross. In the same county J Holms propelled himself with vigour into a planting programme at Larachmhor, Arisaig, but as the plants were reaching maturity the owner died and the property became vacant. Some of the staff of the RBGE began a rehabilitation programme some years ago and significant plants, threatened by competition, are being given scope to thrive. It was here that *R. sinogrande* first flowered in Britain in the early 1930s. The most impressive specimen of this species I have encountered is at Trewithen and it seems entirely appropriate that George Johnstone should have received the FCC for it in 1926.

It is not only on the large estates that members of the genus have found congenial conditions. A C and J F A Gibson built up an exciting range of species at Glenarn, Rhu, a large suburban garden; when the Gibsons arrived they inherited established specimens of *R. falconeri* and *R. thomsonii* and little else. The brothers greatly extended the rhododendron collection. They were also keen exhibitors, winning many awards, including the AM for *R. glischrum* subsp. *rude* in 1964 and the AM for *R. hirtipes* in 1965.

The extreme South-west of Scotland provides an ideal environment for rhododendrons and it is not surprising to find a group of estates with a long association with the genus. Logan on the Mull of Galloway is almost akin to an island site with the sea on three sides. The estate is now divided with wall garden and immediate surrounds now in the care of the RBGE. In this area are rhododendrons of the Maddenia subsection and *R. edgeworthii.* In the other part around Logan House there are a number of huge specimens, including the largest example *R. grande* I have ever seen. There is a veritable forest of different rhododendrons belonging to the subsections Falconera and Grandia. One specimen brought down in a gale more than 30 years ago was then accurately aged at within a whisker of 100 years. That some of these plants could have been raised from the earliest importations from the Far East is entirely feasible. Interestingly, Kenneth McDouall and his brother who owned Logan before the 20th century and for many years on made a significant contribution to the cultivation of dwarf rhododendrons. It was they who first cut blocks of peat and built them into low terrace walls, a system which has been imitated around Britain and has proved so successful. The Hambro family took over Logan and George Steadwood served as a loyal head gardener. Martin College succeeded him and laboured with great commitment through a very lean spell, to be rewarded with the Assistant Curatorship when the RBGE took over.

Slightly inland from Logan is Lochinch, an estate in the grand style, long associated with rhododendrons. Thomas Calla and a Mr Fowler spent many years working in the garden and were certainly involved in propagating

*The Earl of Stair's garden at Lochinch in South-west Scotland. Many of Hooker's seeds and plants came to this garden, long associated with rhododendrons and tended by a succession of dedicated and skilful gardeners*

rhododendrons from seed. The Earl of Stair was a member of the Rhododendron Society, a group of estate owners, many of whom supported the collectors in their search for their favoured genus. During the First World War R Findlay was encouraged to move from Logan to Lochinch; his sons followed him into horticulture and one, T Hope Findlay, held a senior position in the Savill Gardens, Windsor. R W Rye had the longest association with Lochinch in the 20th century, working there for 38 years. A cultivar derived from members of the Maddenia and Boothia subsection is named after him.

The Cornish gardens began early to recognize the potential of the new Sino-Himalayan rhododendrons and by 1885 J C Williams had started a planting pro-gramme at Caerhays Castle. This activity was to grow in volume and significance to the point when he became the principal member of the syndicates supporting the later expeditions of George Forrest. Much of the seed raising was undertaken by the then head gardener, James Martin. The mature plants of *R. williamsianum*, I esti-mated, could have been raised from Wilson's seed by him and no doubt he, too, raised the large trees of *R. sinogrande* and *R. rex* subsp. *fictolacteum* from For-rest's seed. His successor, Charles Michael, spent much time with J C Williams decid-ing where in the garden certain plants should be placed. He and George Bland-ford carried out the actual planting, later to be maintained by Reggie Uglow. The present head gardener, Philip Tregunna, has spent many years at Caerhays ensuring the preservation of fine old specimen plants, some of which are extremely rare in Britain.

In the sheltered parts of the garden many plants grow exceedingly vigorously and the blossom on rhododendrons becomes remote in the sky above. To obvi-ate this problem many species of rhodo-dendron are cut back hard from time to time and most will again develop into shapely bushes bearing flowers at eye-level. There are, however, words of caution on the universal application of this treatment; the smooth-barked species fail to sprout new shoots from severely pruned trunks. The seemingly ideal climate at Caerhays is not suitable for all species and some were transferred from the mild coastal garden to the inland Werrington Park (also belong-ing to J C Williams). *R. lacteum*, it was reported, grew far better at Werrington Park than at Caerhays and this is conso-nant with the claim that this species requires a cooler climate for it to thrive. Certainly the best plants are in cooler areas; at Corsock House in South-west Scotland, for instance, rather than Logan and Lochinch in the balmy influence of the Gulf stream. The other notable plant of *R. lacteum* of which I am aware is at Blackhills in Morayshire, the garden owned and maintained by the Christie family. My visits have never coincided with the flowering of *R. lacteum* but the description indicates that the quality of clear yellow flowers is similar to the Cor-sock plants.

To focus attention a little longer on species requiring milder conditions, such as many in the Maddenia subsection: the most representative selections of these pre-dominantly sweetly scented rhododen-drons are at Brodick and Trengwainton, but there are also massive plants of *R. johnstoneanum* at Muncaster and Clyne Castle Swansea. The former owner of

Clyne, Admiral Walker-Heneage-Vivian, grew several slightly tender species in the sheltered tree-clad valley and in the inter-war years was awarded the FCC for *R. dalhousiae* and for *R. lindleyi*. The huge funnel-shaped flowers of *R. lindleyi* vary in colour from pure white to white with a strong tinge of pink and those who have observed this plant over a number of seasons at Arduaine say that the colour varies in individual plants from one season to the next. Differing temperature regimes obviously influence chemical reactions in the pigmentation. Careful siting of the less hardy species can often lead to success in districts not recognized as being particularly favourable. For example, *R. lindleyi* flourishes on a sheltered patio in Dr Florence Auckland's garden near Bolton in Lancashire, as does Peter Cox's plant against a sheltered wall in Perthshire. A marked degree of variation in several species in this subsection have often been recognized with awards to particular clones. Major A E Hardy received the AM for his plant of *R. maddenii* 'Ascreavie' grown at Sandling Park, in Kent, a part of England most prone to icy blasts generated by high pressure systems over the continent in winter. *R. spinuliferum* is reputedly grown in gardens in various parts of Britain but one recalls seeing it in only sheltered gardens. A clone called 'Jack Hext' received the AM when shown by Nigel Holman, Chyverton, Truro. The AM was also awarded to another clone, 'Blackwater', when exhibited by Brodick

Castle. A connoisseur of the deciduous species assured me that the flower quality of *R. schlippenbachii* at Chyverton was equal to any he had seen of this plant.

Many selections of *R. cinnabarinum* were made in former times in gardens of the South-West, and several from Caerhays were given clonal names. Some were crossed with other species to give rise to well-known cultivars, for example *R.* 'Alison Johnstone'. The garden at Minterne in Dorset began growing rhododendrons just before World War I when Lord Digby brought a plant from Inverewe and from then on the collection developed steadily. Arthur Smith managed the collection most economically for several decades around the middle of the 20th century.

Many species can be cultivated widely throughout Britain, granted a degree of protection from wind. Members of the Fortunea subsection such as *R. sutchuenense* and *R. oreodoxa* provide early blossom in many gardens. At Bodnant in North Wales the magnificent *R. orbiculare* regularly provides a stunning display and it seems appropriate that Bodnant received the AM for this species in 1922. Lord Aberconway, for many years President of the RHS, was a supporter of the collecting work of Forrest, Farrer and Kingdon-Ward; his staff raised their seed and cultivated the progeny with great skill. F C Puddle was the first in a dynasty of head gardeners; he was succeeded by his son C E Puddle, who in turn handed over to his son Martin Puddle. The combined period of their stewardship is now approaching 90 years – how near to the century will they reach? There are notable specimens of species at Bodnant, *R. augustinii* in superb blue form, for instance, and the circle of *R. williamsianum* around 'the Bath'. FC Puddle was an experienced breeder of orchids and turned his skill to raising hybrid rhododendrons, one of which bears his name.

*Rhododendron williamsianum* and *R. griersonianum* were among the species most frequently used at Bodnant in their breeding programme. The arrival of the last named species from Forrest's 1917 expedition with its distinctive geranium-red flowers caused a considerable stir in the rhododendron world. Within seven years of arrival it was awarded the FCC when exhibited by E de Rothschild of Exbury and T H Lowinsky of Tittenhurst, Sunninghill. (The latter property is the latest to be restored to its former glory.) Unfortunately *R. griersonianum* is not hardy and this has given added impetus to try to transfer its features into hardy progeny.

Exbury became one of the noted centres for successful hybridization activity as well as for the cultivation of the species of *Rhododendron*. The first plants of *R. yakushimanum* to reach these shores went to Exbury and the original plants set out in 1934 can still be seen there. This species has achieved an unparalleled level of attention. World War II delayed recognition

until 1947 when the specimen exhibited by Wisley received the FCC. It is compact, free flowering, hardy and an excellent foliage plant with potential for breeding, although none of the progeny quite equal *R. yakushimanum* in all its qualities. Francis Hanger, who was head gardener at Exbury before going to Wisley, believed the *R. yakushimanum* would provide the modern gardener with a range of cultivars appropriate to this more confined space. Arthur Osborne, his successor, no doubt was involved in breeding work at the instigation of his employer. Fred Wynniatt, who was in charge of the garden at Exbury for many years, certainly raised a number of cultivars, one of which is named after him. The present head gardener, Doug Betteridge, continues in the Exbury tradition of combining the desirable features of existing plants through breeding and one cultivar, *R.* 'Pearl Betteridge' is named after his wife. Not far from Exbury the Whitaker family planted Pylewell Park with rhododendrons and their head gardener, W F Hamilton, raised a very fine cultivar which is simply known by his initials – *R.* 'W. F. H.' – a replacement for the immensely popular *R.* 'Elizabeth' when the effects of 'powdery mildew' were at their worst. Years ago we heard a lot about Lord Swaythling's estate Townhill, near Southampton, when F J Rose was head gardener. Mr Rose represented the typical old-time horticulturist with experience in every aspect of the profession. There is no longer the same scope for such men, and as I can find no reference to the current status of Townhill I fear it may have been submerged in some modern development.

After World War I, Mr and Mrs J B Stevenson began to create a garden at Tower Court, Ascot, with an emphasis on rhododendrons which came to be recognized as among the finest in Britain. Every effort was made to acquire every species and plant of merit. They grew, for instance, the unnamed McLaren T41 and exhibited it before Dr Cowan described it and named it *R. aberconwayi*, after the sponsor of the collector. J B Stevenson was Editor of *The Species of Rhododendron*, for many years the accepted text book on the genus.

On the death of J B Stevenson his widow took up the challenge of preserving the large number of important rhododendrons. This was achieved – against all odds – by reaching an agreement with the Crown Estate Commissioners to transferring most to Windsor Great Park. The work was completed with the stirling support of Robert Keir, for many years head gardener at Tower Court, and Stevenson's plants now form the nucleus of the collection at Windsor. In the three decades since that notable operation the collection in the Valley Gardens has been regularly augmented. A glance down the list of *Rhododendron* species to which awards have been made, shows a goodly number presented from Windsor: *R. rex* and *R. diaprepes* the FCC in 1955 and 1974 respectively, and also to *R. soulei*. The list of AM awards to

Windsor includes *R. thomsonii, R. lanigerum, R. argyrophyllum* and *R. hodgsonii*. A number of good cultivars have been produced at Windsor, such as the cross between *R. roxieanum* and *R. maculiferum* subsp. *anhweiense*, called *R. 'Blewbury'*, a very attractive plant.

J J Crosfield, Embley Park, near Romsey, made a significant contribution in the cultivation of rhododendrons for a number of years before World War II and for some time after. His plant of *R. oreotrephes* received the AM. There appears to have been something akin to a 'blue hybrid race' between Bodnant with their entry *R. 'Bluebird'*, J J Crosfield with *R. 'Blue Diamond'* and the Cornish entry – almost certainly started by E J P Magor at Lamellen and further selected by Major General Harrison – to give us *R. 'St. Tudy'* and *R. 'St. Breward'*. Some of the collection of plants assembled by E J P Magor remained for his son Major E W M Magor, in his restoration, including the original plant of *R. 'Damaris'*, which continues to thrive near the main drive.

Several estates in Sussex each in turn played a part in the progress of the genus in cultivation. G W E Loder, later Lord Wakehurst, established many fine plants at Wakehurst Place. This is now an annexe of the RBG Kew, thus giving them scope to cultivate plants which find conditions on the banks of the Thames unsuitable. Further inland is the Loder estate of Leonardslee with a paramount claim to fame. It was here at the dawn of the 20th century that

Sir Edmund Loder crossed *R. fortunei* with *R. griffithianum*, to give rise to *R.* 'Loderi' one of the most celebrated of cultivars of all time. Those who admire the magnificent scented blossom of *R. griffithianum* but find it impossibly frost sensitive, can enjoy quite similar qualities in its progeny.

In the 1920s Colonel L C R Messel received batches of rhododendron seed collected by Kingdon-Ward and Rock and these were raised and planted at Nymans by his head gardener, J C Comber. Although originally catalogued under collectors' numbers, many of the labels were lost and efforts to re-identify the plants were made in the late 1960s. The great gale of October 1987 struck Nymans with full force and one fears that many of the rhododendrons were flattened. Mr C G Nice must have spent the whole of his working life in the garden at Nymans, for many years as head gardener. The High Beeches is another Sussex estate associated with the Loder family. Colonel G H Loder resided there for 60 years, planting throughout the period. Edward and Anne Boscawen, who carried on his work, report that excellent forms of *R. griersonianum, R. campylocarpum* subsp. *caloxanthum* and many more species thrive there. They devised a modern maintenance programme with Eric Stockton, who cared for the woodland garden from 1927 until his retirement, and with Len Burren who moved to The High Beeches with the Boscawens (the garden is now a charitable trust). Mr H A Mangles' garden at Little-

worth Cross, established towards the end of the 19th century, was well known, but declined between 1939-45. The present owner, Lady Adam Gordon, has restored it, with periodic interruptions from gales. There are good mature plants of *R. barbatum* and *R. wightii*, as well as most of the hybrids raised by Mangles, which have now been successfully propagated. There is a striking selection of rhododendrons at Hergest Croft, Kington, Herefordshire, within a stones throw of Offa's Dyke . The estate has been in the Banks family for a very long time, but the major work of laying out the garden was undertaken at the beginning of the 20th century. The area known as Parkwood is formed like an amphitheatre. Paths run along the contour lines and one walks along them between the vast array of species. There is an outstanding form of *R. mallotum* and the plant *R. rex* subsp. *arizelum* has the most impressive indumentum I have ever seen on this species.

A group of inland gardens has a place in the history of the cultivation of the genus. Raymond Baldwin's impressive collection is at Penn, Alderley Edge, Cheshire. The Hon. Michael Flower is planting an enthusiast's selection in the Grove at Arley Hall in the same county: popular species such as *R. yakushimanum* and *R. pseudochrysanthum* are supplemented by a range of cultivars. The University of Liverpool Botanic Garden at Ness has been associated with rhododendrons since its founder, A K Bulley, launched George Forrest on his career as a plant collector. The plants were cared for by Mr J Hope, for many years head gardener, who often pointed to plants which were raised from Forrest's seed. The records and the labels were however lost through wartime neglect and without continuous documentation it is no longer possible to claim provenance for these plants. The winter of 1981-2 inflicted severe damage on many rhododendrons in gardens fringing the Irish Sea. It was therefore a pleasant surprise to see the thriving plantation in Ray Wood, Castle Howard (North Yorkshire) in 1982. Plants brought from the old Sunningdale Nursery by Jim Russell in 1975 had connections with Joseph Hooker (see Chapter 5).

The most representative selection of all today is in the Royal Botanic Garden, Edinburgh. It is also the most carefully and accurately labelled collection and all serious students of the genus should give it the attention it deserves. There are complete demonstrations of particular subsections, for example Lapponica and Saluenensia, and many others are widely represented. The whole range of species has been replanted in recent years so that all the species in one subsection are grouped together, thus making it easy to compare the characteristics of related plants.

A number of species in the Grandia and Falconera subsection are found in Edinburgh and, although flowering quite freely, they produce much more compact growth and less luxuriant foliage than their west-coast counterparts. The climate in this part of Scotland is distinctly on the dry side for rhododendrons and frosts are frequent, but the plants do adapt. The generally cool conditions in summer relieves one potential source of additional stress to the plants. For many years the plants brought back by the collectors were managed by Charles Lamont and he was succeeded by James Duncan who worked in collaboration with Dr J M Cowan and H H Davidian on the labelling of the collections. The more scientific classification, which has been openly explained, is the work of Drs James Cullen and David Chamberlain.

Many of the dwarfer growing species grow well in cooler conditions and the late R B Cooke demonstrated this in his garden, Kilbride, Corbridge. This garden was on the north slopes of the Tyne Valley in Northumberland, where he used to glance-around at his amazing range of rarities and say, in essence: 'beware of those mild areas where plants are induced into early growth, only to suffer damage in subsequent frosts'. After his death a number of his valuable plants were transferred to other gardens for safe keeping; are there for instance plants in cultivation of *R. pronum* other than those traceable to R B Cooke?

A successful rhododendron garden is to be found at Howick in Northumberland. Howick is near the coast of the North Sea and is regarded by many to be in a veritable 'banana belt'. Microclimate is very important in the cultivation of rhododendrons. The recent sequence of mild winters begins to raise the prospect of climate changes beginning to take place, and the scene is set to encourage all rhododendron growers to be more adventurous with the less hardy species.

KENNETH HULME *trained at RBG Edinburgh and was taken round the gardens of Argyll by H H Davidian and Dr Mac-Queen Cowan in 1949, since when he has had a special interest in rhododendrons. This interest continued during his subsequent 32 years as Director of the Liverpool University Botanic Garden at Ness*

# CHAPTER 7

# THE VIREYA STORY

## GEORGE ARGENT

Rhododendrons of section Vireya are often simply referred to as Vireyas sometimes loosely as 'Malesian Rhododendrons' or even more vaguely as 'Tropical Rhododendrons'. Vireya is best for a popular name, it was coined by Carl Blume for his new genus of *Rhododendron* 'allies' from South-East Asia and was used to honour a French pharmacist friend of that name, but it was never widely accepted as a good genus. Malesia, the geographical area of the South-East Asian archipelago from the Malay Peninsula and Sumatra in the West, New Guinea in the East and the Philippine Islands in the North, is the region from which most of the Vireyas come but it is not all encompassing. A few of the species 'escape' the confines of this zone and a few rhododendrons from other sections have inconveniently penetrated this area so 'Malesian' is not without exceptions if used to describe this group. 'Tropical rhododendrons' in the strictest sense is also inappropriate as again, although the majority technically occur within the tropics, a few do occur north of the Tropic of Cancer. Worse, the term is badly misleading to growers, as the majority are montane plants from high altitudes which like cool conditions far removed from those obtained in the traditional stove house.

The first Vireya described was *Rhododendron malayanum* by William Jack, a Scotsman from Aberdeen. He was a surgeon in the employ of the East India Company and served as botanist to Sir Stamford Raffles on the west coast of Sumatra. Jack climbed Mt Bunko (Bengkoh) popularly known as the Sugar Loaf, just inland from Bencoolan. He commented that despite its low elevation 'the character of its vegetation is decidedly alpine'. Here he collected this first Vireya which he correctly attributed to the genus *Rhododendron* despite (for the time) the surprising location. His plant descriptions were a model for their day: 'corolla crimson, tubular, expanding into a five-lobed limb, sprinkled with callous dots, tube gibbous at the base and marked with five furrows'; describes well the flower of *R.*

*malayanum* so, despite the loss of the herbarium material upon which this description is based, there is no doubt about its identity. It is tragic that in the same year that Jack published this first Vireya he also died of pulmonary tuberculosis probably complicated with malaria, and even more so that most of his specimens, drawings and manuscripts were lost two years later when the *Fame* burned and sank at sea off Sumatra. Merrill gave the warmest tribute and said of Jack that he 'was indeed the pioneer post-Linnaean Malaysian botanist' and had he lived he might have added so much more.

Carl Blume was second in the field, a medical doctor who became director of the now Bogor Botanic Garden in 1822. He travelled widely in Java and published five species under his genus *Vireya* in 1826, three of which he must have seen at first hand. These plants were first brought to the attention of the public in an article in the *Journal of The Royal Horticultural Society* for 1848, where John Lindley firmly rejected the concept of the genus *Vireya* and reported on Sir Hugh Low's findings in Borneo where the Vireyas were described as 'perhaps the most gorgeous of the native plants'. He also hypothesized about the problems of their cultivation as epiphytes and must have aroused considerable interest. He may well have been partly responsible for the nurserymen Messrs Veitch of Exeter sending Thomas Lobb on an expedition to South-East Asia from where he brought back the first live Vireyas for cultivation in Britain in 1845. This was a very considerable feat. Anyone who collects today with the advantages of air transport knows to his cost how easy it is to lose Vireyas with even a small delay. What care and attention must have been given to these plants over a journey of many weeks by sea in closed glass Wardian cases.

*Rhododendron javanicum* (Bl.) Benn. caused a sensation on its introduction as its bright orange colour was at that time new for the genus. Veitch sent the plants for figuring in the *Botanical Magazine* (tab. 4336, 1847) with the remark that 'it is certainly one of the finest things ever introduced to our gardens'. This was quickly followed by *R. jasminiflorum* Hook. (see figure 9) which was exhibited at the Chiswick Gardens exhibition in 1850 where it was reported that 'few plants excited greater attention among the visitors most distinguished for taste and judgement', and the strangeness of the flowers caused *The Gardeners' Chronicle* to imply it was 'probably no Rhododendron at all'. From seven listed species (six in the modern concept) hundreds of forms were obtained by cross pollination of what were passingly known as the javanico-jasminiflorum hybrids. They included double 'balsamaeflorum' types which have never been equalled and formed the basis of a remarkable genetic study (this was before Mendel's classic genetic work on peas was known) by Professor G Henslow which was published by the RHS in 1891.

Several of these hybrids such as 'Princess Alexandra', 'Ne Plus Ultra' and 'Triumphans' are still found in cultivation.

From 1865 the great Italian explorer Odoardo Beccari was making his massive collections of plants in South-East Asia, among which he collected several notable rhododendrons. In *Malesia* (I, 1878) he described nine new species and put together a synopsis of the known species of this group up to this time. He listed 27 species in total from four islands, 23 of the species still stand today. Five were from Java, seven from Sumatra, 14 from Borneo and the first records from New Guinea, which included the superb *R. konori* Becc. now so well known and admired in cultivation for its enormous and beautifully scented, pale pink to white flowers.

In 1886 Vidal, a Spanish botanist, listed six species of *Rhododendron* in his revision *De Plantas Vasculares Filipinas.* Two species, *R. apoanum* Stein and *R. kochii* Stein had been recorded in 1883 with comment about their great potential for cultivation – a potential still hardly realized for the Philippine species. The first collection of a Vireya in the Philippines was made as early as 1839 by Hugh Cuming, a British naturalist on Mt Banahao. Cuming was noted for collecting living orchids for Loddige's nursery but there is no evidence of his having collected any Vireyas as living material, but perhaps they failed to survive the difficult journey.

However, as the Victorian period came to a close the Vireyas were in decline.

The limited genetic base of rather lowland species and rather unrealistic ideas about growing even these in very hot stove conditions meant fewer people troubled with them, particularly as there now came an enormous influx of new exciting hardy species from China and the Eastern Himalayas. Partly the Vireyas went out of fashion and partly they were squeezed out of the hothouses by tougher and even more gaudy orchids. They certainly could not compete in Britain with the new hardy Chinese rhododendrons, both species and hybrids, which were being grown more and more widely. World War I almost gave the *coup de grace* when ornamental horticulture went into decline with the shortage of manpower and conservatories everywhere being left abandoned and unheated. What, however, was rather surprising was that although the cultivation of these plants was in decline the number of species being described increased. In the 1890s, eight species were newly described; in the 1900s, 15 more species were described; but from 1910-19, 50 more species were described despite the ravages of World War I.

The next four decades saw only 45 more species names appear in the literature. Herbert Copeland, an American, produced a landmark account of the Philippine Vireyas in the *Philippine Journal of Science* (40: 1929, 133-79). He described five new species in a paper which enumerated 21 species of *Rhododendron* (20 of them Vireyas) and provided a very workable account of the group. Another significant piece of work was that of Professor Holttum who was experimenting in the Singapore Botanic Gardens to produce good, free-flowering Vireyas that would be successful in the tropical lowlands. These were described in the Malayan *Agricultural/Horticultural Magazine* in 1939 (pts 9 & 11). Using the local species, especially *R. longiflorum* Lindl., *R. jasminiflorum* and *R. brookeanum* Low ex Lindl. (all of which can occur at sea level in the tropics), he was raising plants of great promise when the work was curtailed by the invasion of the Japanese in World War II. This work has never really been developed since within the tropics, and it is very sad that the most commonly encountered cultivated rhododendrons in tropical gardens are poorly growing azaleas. An effort has been made by John Swisher to grow low altitude Vireyas in Florida, but I know of no formal breeding programme to produce Vireyas which would flourish in the lowlands as Professor Holttum envisaged.

When Australia took possession of German New Guinea at the beginning of World War I the interior of the island was a great blank on maps. Very little penetration of this area occurred until a prospector found gold in 1929. Gold fever took over and exploration quickly followed. After that came missionaries and administrators, and plant collecting began as the mountainous area was opened up. An article by C R Stonor (*The Rhododendron Year Book,* 1951-2, 6; 48-51) gave a glimpse of what rhododendrons were to be found. He managed to bring back seed which germinated in the late 1940s at Edinburgh. A few of his plants still survive today.

A significant publication in 1949 was that of Professor Hermann Sleumer who, (*Bot. Jahr. Syst.* 74(4) 511-33) in a 'Systema Generis *Rhododendron* L.' gave the first properly organized classification of the genus into subgenera and sections, including the Vireyas. It was a portent of his future contribution to the group. Leonard Brass, who was responsible for the plant collections on the three large-scale and highly successful Archbold Expeditions to New Guinea culminating in that of 1938-39 to Mt Wilhelmina (G Trikora) and the Lake Habbema area, provided Professor Sleumer with abundant material of exciting new species. Professor Sleumer started work in the 1950s on a revision of *Rhododendron* for *Flora Malesiana* with the wealth of material that had accumulated and was rapidly being added to by the New Guinea Department of Forests. John Womersley, for many years Chief of the Division of Botany in New Guinea, took a particular interest in the genus, as did the Rev. Norman Cruttwell, an Anglican missionary with a first class honours degree in botany. He spent a lifetime in New Guinea and was very active in the pioneer days (and up to the late 1980s). In the early 1960s Professor Sleumer published 122 new species of Vireya, the last great explosion in the size of the genus *Rhododendron*. His account of the genus for *Flora Malesiana* appeared in 1966, the classic reference work, even today nearly 30 years on. It stimulated a great revival in Vireya growing, particularly in Australia, New Zealand and America, all countries where the species could, in selected places, be grown outdoors.

John Womersley, Norman Cruttwell and Hermann Sleumer all sent living material, mainly the small light seed, to botanical establishments and enthusiasts in America, Europe and Australasia and the number of species in cultivation burgeoned. RBGE sent Paddy Woods and Bill Burtt to bring back new species into cultivation from the Malay Peninsula, Borneo and New Guinea, but much of the activity and interest in the group was moving out of Britain. There were Australians like Lou Searle, an agricultural extension officer for the Australian Administration working in the highlands, who took a fancy to the group and spent much of his leisure searching for Vireyas. He will be remembered for the exquisite *R. searleanum* Sleum. named in his honour but Searle also deserves mention as someone who strove to beautify the New Guinea highland roads and towns with plantings of the native species; both then and since his efforts were often unappreciated. More than once he had to rescue his plantings from the bulldozers as they were being swallowed up by unannounced road widening schemes, but he doggedly continued to grow, propagate and distribute plants from his highland base.

A collection of plants was being accumulated at the Strybing Arboretum in the United States and experiments in growing and hybridizing were being undertaken at Boskoop in The Netherlands from the new materials which were being sent out. But the greatest interest was growing in Australia and New Zealand, where people who had often seen the plants at first hand were returning from tours of duty in New Guinea. John Womersley in retirement from his post in Papua New Guinea led 'Rhododendron tours' which bred a band of enthusiasts in Australia and New Zealand. Graham Smith, the remarkable and energetic director of the Pukeiti Rhododendron Garden, collected many species and developed the group as a feature which stimulated much of the interest which is current in New Zealand today. Graham and Wendy Snell abandoned a solid livelihood growing camellias to invest everything in a Vireya nursery and became outstanding breeders of modern Vireya hybrids developing especially small-leafed plants with large flowers. Michael Cullinane similarly invested his heart as well as his money into a Vireya nursery in New Zealand; Clyde Smith wrote the beautiful introductory book *Vireya Rhododendrons'* for the Australian Rhododendron Society (1989) and Os Blumhart, another nurseryman, went on to collect on his own account and has bred some amazing new hybrids compacting the growth with the use of the tufted cushion-like and aptly named *R. saxifragoides* J.J. Smith. This difficult plant from the alpine bogs high in New Guinea has the ability to compact many of the flamboyant but straggly forms. Once in hybrid combination, they grow with true hybrid vigour showing none of the temperamental nature of the *R. saxifragoides* parentage.

Another major input was that of Paul Kores, an American funded by the Stanley Smith Foundation to collect and study Vireyas in Papua New Guinea over a four-year period with a special remit to introduce plants into cultivation. Many plants were distributed via the American Rhododendron Species Foundation and an account of high altitude Vireyas was published in P van Royen's *The Alpine Flora of New Guinea* (vol. 3 1982 Cramer). It was a consolidation of Sleumer's mainly herbarium-based taxonomy with more species being reduced to synonymy than were newly described, but it added considerably to our understanding of the wild populations of these plants. Others contributed in very different ways and it is impossible to mention everyone who has played a part in the development of the modern Vireya cult. Peter Valder collected on isolated forays into South-East Asia; his lively broadcasting and sharp mind have both entertained and stimulated many people. He gave a remarkable account of the collection of *R. aequabile* J.J. Smith from Mt Singgalang in 1974 following the travel instructions from a Dutch East Indies railway guide for 1910. This must rank as one of the most offbeat ways to use a railway guide: 'the only significant difference to the journey as described,' he remarked, was 'that there were buses instead of horse-drawn carriages.'

John Rouse deserves special mention for a major contribution to the Vireya scene. A professional physicist he applied a sharp scientific mind, an eye for beauty and a very generous spirit to the group. He built up what was probably the finest collection of species and hybrids in cultivation in his garden in Melbourne where he can grow most of the plants outside. He developed the best seed-raising apparatus yet devised for these plants and made numerous hybrids, but he used this work to develop our understanding of the breeding systems often leaving others to register his best forms. He had grafted specimens both within and without Section Vireya and used this information to provide remarkable insights into the relationships of *Rhododendron*. He has published a great many papers, taken superb photographs, shown plants and helped scientists and laymen all over the world.

There are at least three 'Vireya Buffs' newsletters: *Vireya Venture, Vireya News* and *Vireya Vine*. The last is a tribute to the Education Committee of the Rhododendron Species Foundation and especially to the efforts and vigour of E White Smith, its editor. He persistently asks, persuades and cajoles people to write all manner of news, thoughts, recipes, observations and anecdotes, and his energy in getting these mailed all over the world has made this a truly international medium of communication. It has brought together very diverse people in very different places – growers, nurserymen and scientists – and is a must for all who take a serious interest in the group. Another of the Americans who should not be forgotten is Bill Moyles who, working on behalf of the American Rhododendron Society, has patiently cleaned, packeted and tested seed, sending out many thousands of packets and has certainly been important in spreading these plants to diverse collections all over the world. The vulnerability of all plant collections if they are maintained only in one place cannot be overstressed and it is a tribute to the fraternity of Vireya growers that so many species are quickly spread around. It takes dedicated work to do this on a large scale.

The present situation is that Vireyas are having another vogue period, albeit largely outside the United Kingdom. The RBGE achieved a gold medal at the March show of the RHS in 1992 followed by the Rothschild Challenge Cup for an exhibit of Vireya species. Currently it has probably the largest list of species in cultivation in any one collection. The cool summers give Edinburgh an advantage over many more southern areas for growing these plants under glass, but the real interest is in areas where they can be grown outside. There is virtually no hybridizing going on in Britain at present and very few of the plants are commercially available here. In contrast Australia, New Zealand and America are producing exciting new forms which are more vigorous, more compact and free-flowering with a range of habit, colour and perfume to suit most plant-lovers' tastes. They also have several specialist nurseries to cater for enthusiasts. There is potential for these plants to be grown in Britain: they require relatively little heat and flower throughout the year, but they do not take kindly to living-room conditions. The big challenge for the future is to develop a Vireya garden within the South-East Asian area from which they come. This must be done with care as where species are moved they could so easily hybridize with wild populations and play havoc with indigenous species. However, if an accessible, well-maintained garden can be found in an isolated mountain area without its own endemic species, this could prove a great attraction for rhododendron lovers and a site for further study. There is still enormous potential for the development of these plants. Many areas that do not already do so could grow them in the future, and there is unbounded potential for hybrids, given the species we already have in cultivation.

DR GEORGE ARGENT, *a tropical botanist at the RBG Edinburgh, has spent several years working in New Guinea on the local flora. He has made many field trips collecting Vireyas and is now working on the Ericaceae of the Malesian region*

# CHAPTER 8

# COLLECTORS' TECHNIQUES: THEN AND NOW

❦

## PETER COX

All professional plant hunters have had to discover within themselves a standard of dedication to their work far beyond that required for most other vocations. All the great plant hunters of the past proved to be people capable of getting themselves out of the most desperate situations by sheer fortitude and being able to keep calm when to panic might have meant near certain death.

These explorers were usually selected by the then leaders in the botanical or horticultural world from among their own staff and they often had great foresight in their choices. Who could have picked more successful collectors than Robert Fortune, George Forrest and Ernest Wilson? Others, like Joseph Rock, achieved what they did by sheer determination, arrogance and daring. A few like Reginald Farrer and George Sherriff were sufficiently well off to pay their own way and hunted plants purely for their own amusement. Perhaps the most dedicated of all was Frank Kingdon-Ward who spent his whole life exploring, and then gave us the pleasure of being able to read of his travels in his books and articles. The chief reason he had to carry on into old age was because he was paid so little for his efforts and could not afford to retire.

Often two or more years were spent on one trip out East, usually with a break or two in some town in the foothills or on the coast. With only ships to travel out to the East (or elsewhere), river boats to take them part of the way into the interior and rough tracks onwards, travelling was slow, often very uncomfortable and sometimes dangerous.

Nowadays there are no full-time professional plant hunters, though a few still pay their way by selling what they collect (often in the form of shares of seed). Visits to good plant areas are short, the plant hunters are usually in and out within a month; very often little serious trekking is done and only hotels and guest houses used for accommodation.

The methods of collecting have, of course, also changed and the results have not necessarily changed for the better. Some of the great collectors of the past will be described here and their methods compared with plant hunting today. As we rarely have to suffer the same degrees of hardship, solitude or danger, it is not easy to select those of today who would have equalled the great achievers of the past. The great majority of rhododendrons (other than Vireyas) are found wild on the mainland of South-East Asia: therefore I will only cover this area.

## Robert Fortune

Robert Fortune was a gardener by trade and had a thorough apprenticeship. He joined the staff at the Royal Botanic Garden, Edinburgh (RBGE) under the famous William McNab and after only two and a half years was recommended for the post of superintendent of the hothouse department at the Royal Horticultural Society's garden at Chiswick. He was soon appointed as the Society's collector in China where he collected over the period from 1843 to 1862. He proved to be a first-rate choice for the job. Not only was he skilled at transporting plants but he was able to recognize a good plant and introduced few poor ones. He was a great correspondent and made copious notes and diaries but sadly, most of these were destroyed by his family on his death.

Very little was known about the plants of China in 1843. Fortune was asked to look out for one particular rhododendron in what is now Guangdong province in south China, but he was also told to search for yellow-flowered camellias, which in the event were not to be introduced into cultivation until over 100 years later. Packets of seed were to be large enough for general distribution wherever possible.

Peace had only just been made with China, so Fortune was unable to travel far away from the treaty ports, especially on his first expedition. Many plants were acquired from local nurserymen who at first locked their gates as they were frightened that he would take their plants without paying. In the end he gained their confidence and was offered every plant in Shanghai! He introduced some evergreen azalea cultivars including *R.* 'Amoenum' (which he named himself) and, subsequently of course, *R. fortunei* which he found in the mountains where he was able to collect a quantity of seed. He remarked on the wide-spread azaleas in the wild, mostly *R. simsii* (see figures 15 and 16).

Fortune took live plants with him from Britain to Asia, partly as presents, but partly to gain experience in looking after plants collected in China. Similarly, he took vegetable seeds, for presents and to see how they would travel. He remarked that there were great difficulties in preserving the seeds of trees and shrubs in south

*Wardian Case. A miniature greenhouse of wood and glass sealed with pitch. Plants were established for 10 days in soil. Fortune sent his plants home from China in these cases strapped to the deck. After a voyage of four months 215 out of 250 plants survived*

China because of the attacks of maggots and we still have this problem in the present day. All his live plants were sent home in Wardian cases, designed by Mr N B Ward of London. These cases were constructed of wood and glass and made as airtight as was possible by sealing with strips of canvas dipped in boiling tar and pitch. Before the journey, the plants would be established in the cases for 10 to 14 days in 23-26cm (9-10in) of soil and this was often covered with moss. During this time the plants would be watered frequently. A promise had to be obtained from the ship's captain that the cases would remain on the poop deck for the whole voyage where they would be least frequently washed by sea water in rough weather. It was also important for the cases to be raised 15cm (6in) to allow water used for washing the decks to pass underneath. Water condensed on the glass when the sun shone and then dropped back on the plants in the evening like dew. If the cases were not accompanied by Fortune himself or anyone else expert enough to inspect them regularly, they were kept closed for the entire four months' voyage to England. If expertise was at hand, they would be opened during the day (not at night), using sliding doors in calm weather to allow a good clean-up. On one voyage, Fortune left China with 250 plants in 18 cases and 215 arrived in good condition. He sometimes took the precaution of splitting a consignment between two ships to spread the risk. On one occasion he took with him two little hand cases containing very special plants, on a partially overland route.

Fortune was obviously very levelheaded and could keep calm in the face of danger. On one trip he was twice attacked by pirates. He told the crew to shelter as best they could from the shots from the pirates' guns and waited until their ship was near enough for his shotgun to be effective. He then let them have it and on both occasions they were beaten off. But for all his virtues, apparently Fortune lacked a sense of humour.

## Sir Joseph Hooker

Sir Joseph Hooker started with the great advantage of having an illustrious father who was also director of Kew. Hooker junior had had the best available training as a taxonomist and geographer and few people to this day have been so well prepared for the job as he was for Sikkim. He fully understood the possible variations to be found within a species, and also the importance of distribution, which some later taxonomists seem to have forgotten. He was also quite a competent artist.

Hooker's first expedition had been to Antarctica so he had some experience of roughing it before setting off in 1848 for his famous travels in Sikkim and district. His friend and helper, B H Hodgson, had studied ethnology and zoology in Nepal for 25 years and had completed a natural history of birds and animals in the region. As a consequence he had a considerable influence on Hooker's travels and studies. Hooker's first collections amounted to 80 porter-loads taken to the foot of the mountains, then for five days by cart and then to Calcutta by river. On his second expedition in 1850, food had to be sent to the party at intervals, because the country's resources were not capable of feeding 40 or 50 men. Compared to nowadays extra porters were needed due to the bulk and weight of the equipment, instruments and clothing. Hooker subsequently spent two months in Calcutta arranging the shipment of his collections and completing manuscripts, maps and surveys.

## Missionaries

The first westerners to travel into the richest rhododendron areas of Sichuan and Yunnan were either not interested in plants or else collected very little. The first to collect plants were not professional collectors but were there for other purposes, notably to convert the natives to Christianity.

The most famous of these missionaries were the Frenchmen, Pères Armand David, Jean-Marie Delavay, Paul Farges and Jean Soulié. All collected herbarium specimens, most of which were sent to the Musée d'Histoire Naturelle in Paris, to Adrien Franchet the only taxonomist to do any serious work on them (see Chapter 3). Many of the specimens disappeared or were left unexamined. Most species were subsequently rediscovered and successfully introduced as seed by such collectors as Wilson, Forrest and Rock. However, these missionaries had one positive advantage over later collectors in that they worked from an established base in China. Whether one approves of missionary work or not, undoubtedly these dedicated men must have suffered loneliness, depression, discomfort and some were tortured and murdered by Tibetan lamas.

Armand David (1826-72) was a trained naturalist and it is for his work on the fauna of China that he is best known. Jean-Marie Delavay was a model collector making excellent herbarium specimens and field notes, most of which he accomplished single-handed. He was reputed to have collected 200,000 specimens. W G Bean saw a large number of rhododendron seedlings from Delavay's collecting in the Jardin des Plantes in Paris in October 1889 and he brought back a few tiny plants to Kew. According to him, nearly all had perished at an early age from being kept too hot. Paul Farges discovered some fine rhododendrons and other plants in an area not renowned for its richness in rhododendrons. Jean Soulié was especially popular because he was a skilled physician. He had little opportunity to send back seeds and was finally murdered along with one of his assistants.

## Augustine Henry

Augustine Henry went to China as a maritime customs official and was stationed at Yichang. He then became a medical officer. He took to collecting plants only out of boredom and trained two natives to help him. Many species he discovered were collected later by Wilson.

## Ernest Wilson

My father, E H M Cox, considered Ernest Wilson to be the best of the collectors, but he is not my favourite. He studied botany for which he won a Queen's Prize Award and then went on to teach the subject. In 1899 at the age of 23 he was picked by the Director of Kew to collect for the famous nursery firm of James Veitch and Sons. He was told by his employer to concentrate on finding *Davidia involucrata* as almost every other worthwhile plant in China had probably already been introduced!

Wilson proved to be an excellent collector. He liked the Chinese, was very diplomatic and always got on well with people. His memory was excellent and he was very knowledgeable on trees and shrubs. Although his books are interesting and informative, it is difficult to follow his actual itineraries. He disliked heroics and was very modest, so little is known about his adventures.

His early days in China were spent in the company of Augustine Henry, from whom he learnt much. He travelled lightly compared with other explorers of his day, but he always used a full-plate camera. His first expedition was so successful that Veitch sent him out again in 1903 to collect *Meconopsis integrifolia*. Alas, not long after he returned from another very successful expedition, Veitch's Coombe Wood nursery was sold up and a huge clearance sale took place. Thus the plants Wilson collected were not as well distributed as those of Forrest and Kingdon-Ward a few years later.

Wilson was then appointed by Professor Sargent of the Arnold Arboretum, Boston, to carry on collecting until 1919. He eventually settled in the USA to work on his collections with Alfred Rehder, a skilled taxonomist. Sadly, Wilson and his wife suffered untimely deaths in a road accident. Splendid old specimens of Wilson's original introductions are still growing in the Arnold Arboretum.

Wilson covered an amazing amount of ground in north-west and north Sichuan in areas I have myself driven through, so I can vouch for the distances involved. Although some new rhododendron species have been discovered in areas covered by Wilson, he did not miss much.

A team of eight helpers assisted Wilson to press and dry his herbarium specimens, prepare and pack his seeds, roots and bulbs for shipment to England and the USA. More than 13,000 seedlings of *Davidia involucrata* germinated which, with one assistant, he potted himself. At the end of his first expedition for the Arnold Arboretum he had collected (by native collectors ) 18,237 lily bulbs, something that fills us with horror these days. If only 837 arrived in America in good condition, it was because he tried to save money by not packing every bulb individually in clay as he had done for Veitch. The following year he repeated the exercise, sending 25,000 bulbs. This time each bulb was coated in moist clay which was allowed to dry before being packed in a crate and surrounded by pulverized charcoal. Vulnerable seeds and cuttings were packed in moist sphagnum and wrapped in oiled paper. Wilson also wrapped beech seedlings in sphagnum and packed them in a ventilated trunk. This shipment accompanied him home and arrived in excellent condition.

### George Forrest

George Forrest was a man who knew what he wanted to do, determination being stamped all over his somewhat grim features and sturdy frame. He was always very much a countryman, fond of shooting and fishing. Several years in Australia, partly looking for gold, toughened him up. Returning to Scotland, he worked for two years handling herbarium specimens which he always did standing up. This taught him the importance of good quality herbarium specimens.

When A K Bulley of the firm of Bees was looking for someone well-qualified to undertake botanical exploration, Forrest was recommended by Sir Isaac Bayley Balfour of the RBGE. One reason for his success was his personality. He always had friendly relations with the Chinese and minority tribesmen. He was genuinely interested in their well-being and made use of the brief time he had spent as an apprentice pharmacist to doctor them and help them in other ways. He took out lymph for inoculating the locals against smallpox at his own expense. Forrest's great organizing ability was another reason for his success. His excellently trained native collectors helped him to cover more ground and collect quantities of good specimens and seeds. This produced many mule-loads of seed weighing many pounds. Such quantities were unnecessary and resulted in much unsown seed and many unwanted seedlings. I well know how far even a small packet of rhododendron seed can be divided up and still give ample for everyone, even a nurseryman. But conservation was hardly considered in those days. Collecting enormous quantities of rhododendron seed has little or no

*Forrest in China with his dog and gun.*
*He never shot for sport, only for the pot*

*George Forrest's HQ at Tengyueh (now Tengchong). Seed bags hang from the rafters. The campbed, collapsible*
*chair and bare boards reveal the austere and comfortless conditions in which collectors lived for months on end*

*A group of Forrest's trained collectors in the field. Note the dog, guns and plant presses, essential tools of their trade*

*Forrest's porters about to start on their last journey with loads of plant presses full of herbarium specimens*

impact on long-lived rhododendrons, but stripping hillsides of all available seed of, say, a monocarpic meconopsis with its localized distribution could have dire consequences for the future of that species.

Over 30,000 herbarium specimens were collected by Forrest, the most important contribution to the flora of Yunnan ever likely to be made. He also made fine collections of mammals, birds and insects and studied geological formations and soil character. Nor did he leave his loyal staff to do all the collecting: he himself saw nearly every plant he collected and he took all his own photographs. He was a keen observer with an eye for beauty, also self-

disciplined and a man of his word; he always did his best for his sponsors.

In a letter written while resting in Bhamo, Burma, Forrest gave the only clear account of how he organized his collecting. If he wished to collect seed of any plant seen in flower, he would select a good herbarium specimen, noting in his field notes that it was desirable. When returning to collect seed, he would show the flowering specimen to his collectors, giving its location. From the combined flowering and fruiting specimen he would then draw up a full botanical description. His chief collector was evidently so good that he was able to remind Forrest of the details he had forgotten (see Chapter 3).

## Reginald Farrer

Reginald Farrer's early interest in plants started in the Ingleborough hills of Yorkshire behind his home. His was a curious, complex, strange and fascinating personality; he was a tireless traveller, great walker and fearless climber. His eye for a good plant was usually sufficient to spot its potential garden value. Though he introduced enough good plants to be classed among the great collectors, he tended to be over-optimistic about his finds succeeding in gardens at home. Farrer was well-read and had a great memory. He had a peculiar power of living within himself and a fertile imagination that stood him in good stead. He adored the work of plant collecting and liked to take all the credit for himself. The names of Purdom and my father who accompanied him on his Gansu and Burma trips respectively were never included in his field notes or seed numbers.

Farrer and my father found it difficult in the monsoon period to stop herbarium specimens from becoming mouldy and had constantly to search for maggots and wood lice. The seeds were dried on racks, but they also sent home some plants. During the autumn they were hard at work from first to last light sorting and labelling seeds and specimens.

## Frank Kingdon-Ward

Frank Kingdon-Ward has always been my idol as a collector. He accomplished almost everything alone, only occasionally having another European or, latterly, his second wife as a companion. He travelled through more difficult and wetter country than any other collector. He had the temperament to endure solitude and was obsessed with the wilderness. His ambition was to be an explorer and he accepted the career of a plant hunter only because there appeared to be more money in it. He started with little interest or knowledge of plants and this is borne out in his earliest book, *The Land of the Blue Poppy* (1913). Although he received medals for exploration, he did not reach the top rank of geographer-explorers, finding surveying and map-making irksome and being happy in his latter years to hand the job over to others.

Like most collectors, Kingdon-Ward had an excellent eye for a good plant and would go to extraordinary lengths to collect seed of outstanding plants that he had seen in flower. Like Farrer too, he had an unerring memory for the exact position of a plant, even if buried under snow. Examples of his tenacity were in his collecting of *R. cinnabarinum* subsp. *xanthocodon* Concatenans Group growing in impenetrable thickets and finding *R. cephalanthum* Crebreflorum Group after endless searching on cliffs in snow.

Kingdon-Ward had two methods of collecting. The first was to stay in one valley, covering the ground thoroughly and the second was to be constantly on the move. He used both techniques with great success, but on the whole the former seems to have been more satisfactory. He found many new species in the autumn in the Tsangpo Gorge when he collected 'blind', that is, without seeing them in flower.

He did not get on as well with the local people as Wilson and Forrest did, and he had many difficult moments especially with the notorious Mishmis in what is now eastern Arunachal Pradesh.

I had the good fortune to meet Kingdon-Ward briefly at an RHS show in London when my father introduced me to him. I shall always remember this tiny wizened old man who looked so frail that a puff of wind could blow him away.

## Joseph Rock

Joseph Rock was perhaps the most extraordinary of all plant collectors. From a humble background in Vienna, he escaped from his father to turn up penniless in Hawaii in 1907. He had by then learned several languages and proceeded to investigate the wildlife of Hawaii, becoming the acknowledged expert on the flora. He could be very moody and had peculiar reasoning but nevertheless usually got his way. He was always restless, never making any attachments that could tie him down.

He was sent to China as an agricultural explorer and soon learned to travel in style with two cooks and a butler, using a clean table cloth, silver and napkins and maintaining an Austrian diet. On his return to civilization he would indulge in operas, fancy hotels and *haute cuisine*. Staying with an elderly friend of mine Rock insisted on being fed on lily bulbs every day, much to his host's annoyance. It is surprising that he could afford such a life, but apparently his exploring paid handsomely. His scholarship did not and in his old age he had to live off his savings.

Rock organized his collecting largely by using trained native collectors, although not to the extent that Forrest did. He tended to collect many consecutive numbers of one species, with what purpose I am not sure, but presumably to show the variation within certain populations. These collections aggravated gardeners who could not be bothered to grow say, 14 almost consecutive numbers of *R. crinigerum* and the sheer bulk of his collections put growers off. Rock collected in China from 1923 until the Communist takeover in 1949 forced him to leave his beloved Lijiang for ever.

He once made the dreadful blunder of claiming Minya Konka in Sichuan to be the highest mountain in the world, when it proved to be only 7,590 metres (24,900ft). My own observations indicate that he invariably overestimated the altitudes on his herbarium specimens. His photographs must be among the finest monochrome photographs ever taken and a unique study of China as it was before the Communist revolution.

I once met Rock when he came to see our garden. At that stage, little had been done to it since the neglect of World War II, and it had also suffered from a particularly damaging spell of weather. I well remember his remark that our garden was not as good as that of Windsor Great Park. I did not take to the man.

**Ludlow and Sherriff**

Frank Ludlow read botany under Professor Marshal Ward, Kingdon-Ward's father, and on leaving university, became a teacher in Asia including Tibet. After some years in various posts he went to Kashgar where he met George Sherriff. Ludlow the biologist and Sherriff the soldier soon found they had much in common and went on shooting trips together. They became great friends and planned to explore Bhutan and Tibet in the years ahead. Oddly, they always called each other by their surnames.

Their expeditions were precisely planned and Sir George Taylor, later Director of Kew, acted as their home agent, apart from the 1938 expedition when he accompanied them. Like Rock, Sherriff was an accomplished photographer and took unique films of Tibet before it was changed for ever by the Communist Chinese. Sherriff was a great organizer, due to his temperament and military training. He even had vegetable seeds sown at intervals along their proposed route and arranged for the produce to be collected and brought to their camps. They had an excellent Turki cook and all, including their staff, lived in style. They even carried a small library with them.

Ludlow and Sherriff systematically explored Bhutan from west to east and then, similarly, south and south-east Tibet, collecting hundreds of bird skins and herbarium specimens. In 1936 they sent four crates of living plants in the cold room on a P&O liner. In 1938 they made what was possibly the first ever air transportation of live plants from South-East Asia to Britain. Alas, World War II led to the loss of many of these introductions. Their 1949 trip to Bhutan produced enough seed for 20,000 packets. It was amazing that they collected so much since they were often frustrated, as when most of the seed was devoured by grubs or when browsing yaks had eaten all the flowering shoots on the meadows or, to crown it all, early snow had obliterated everything.

I knew Geordie and Betty Sherriff very well and loved visiting their beautiful garden at Ascreavie, Angus, where they grew primulas and meconopsis so successfully. It was the Sherriffs and Frank Ludlow who inspired me to take up plant hunting. Once my wife and I visited Ludlow in his cubby hole in the Natural History Museum's herbarium where he gave us advice before our 1965 trip to north-east India. He told us that Sherriff always wore gym shoes but that he always wore boots and that we could take our choice! We chose the latter.

**The End of an era**

The final expeditions of Kingdon-Ward,

Rock, and Ludlow and Sherriff, in 1956, 1949 and 1949 respectively, could be called the end of an era, as both China and Burma closed their borders and Bhutan and Arunachal Pradesh became harder to get into. There was a time when the only great plant hunting area open was Nepal. China did not reopen its doors until 1980, but Arunachal Pradesh and Burma remain almost out of bounds to the present day, as do most of the frontier areas between India and Tibet. It is these parts that are still the least botanically explored of all South-East Asia. In this interval of around 30 years many changes have taken place in the world, not the least being the vast increase in air transport and in the number of people who can afford to travel long distances. Although many people have at last become aware of the need for conservation, natural resources are alas being plundered without a thought for tomorrow. All these events have completely revolutionized the way we now set about plant hunting, often with a self-imposed ban on collecting any plants. Many countries make some attempt at conservation, such as banning all collecting of plant material. Unfortunately, despite these rules, the illegal collecting of whole populations of plants like orchids, bulbs and corms continues apace.

### 1956 to the present day

My first trip to South-East Asia in 1965 took place at a time of transition between the year-long plus expeditions of old and the whistle-stop tours of today. By pulling strings with Indian authorities, my wife and I managed to get briefly to the Subansiri division of Arunachal Pradesh, in an area not previously explored by westerners. We flew out, while our luggage, including food for the mountains, went by sea. Although we spent two and a half months in India, most of this time was wasted arguing with officials about our permit for entering Arunachal Pradesh (known then as the North-East Frontier Agency). But we were able to collect plants, and this can make all the difference to the success of a spring-only trip when seed can be very scarce.

On our way we stayed with a retired tea planter in Shillong and, while waiting to go on to Darjeeling after leaving the Subansiri, we wrapped some hundreds of our rhododendron seedlings in little balls of moss tied on with cotton and bedded them down in a shady place in our friend's garden. For the journey, our plants were put into baskets. Luckily our agents in Calcutta had an air-conditioned office where we were able to leave the plants until near our departure. Before finally leaving, the baskets were thoroughly searched and then surrounded with sacking, so we were not able to check their well-being until our arrival in London. The arrangement was that the plants would be cleared at Kew and they would keep a selection and pass the rest back to us. I had to stay on in London to collect them, and so far so good, but rounding a corner in a taxi in Hyde Park, the basket slid off the shelf next to the driver on to the street and the plants were scattered all over the place. Luckily there was little traffic and I was able to collect every one, little the worse for their experience. The plants had travelled very well and losses were small. To our disgust, our collection of *R. grande,* the bulk of our seedlings, proved to be early into growth and hopelessly tender.

In 1966 James Keenan of RBGE went to Burma, the last person to get in on a collecting trip from the West. After months of wrangling with the Burmese government, he was finally given his permit in December to go to Bumpa Bum, a mountain that had not been previously explored. The forest proved to be almost impenetrable so Keenan had to scramble up river beds. He made some interesting collections, both herbarium and seed, and flew home, leaving his collections to travel by sea. This proved to be a disaster for only one seed lot germinated and that was a berberis. Undoubtedly the seeds had either been cooked or rotted off. It was a lesson I have never forgotten.

After years of effort at attempting to get into China we succeeded in 1981. The Kunming Botanic Institute put a tremendous effort into making this expedition a success. Five of us plus our hosts spent a month on the Cangshan, central-west Yunnan, from late April to late May camping at four different sites. It would be fair to say that this was the first ever successful spring seed collection as most, if not all, earlier collections had been made in the autumn when most seed ripens naturally. We were undoubtedly lucky that the previous season had been a bumper one for flower and also that the spring weather had been kind and had not knocked all the remaining seed out of the capsules. Fairly plentiful seed was had off nearly every rhododendron species we found, giving an adequate amount for a good distribution. There was no question of the pounds of seed as collected by Forrest; just one small fairly full packet of many seed numbers.

In those days, there were no restrictions on collecting plants. Two of us were put in charge of the plant collections while the rest of the party looked after the herbarium specimens. After each camp we returned to a base where all the plants were stored in a small outhouse with some light but no direct sunlight. We had to be exceptionally careful not to over water as rot could have set in and rapidly spread. Losses were small and mainly restricted to primulas, notoriously difficult to transport when in growth. The plants were packed into baskets with part of a basket for a lid. It took the two of us until 2am to finish the job. On our first leg of the journey to Guangzhou we had the baskets in the compartment with us but in Hong Kong, where we knew the governor and his wife, it was better still. Talk about VIP treatment! Into the first-class lounge; escorted onto the plane where our plants were handed to us and placed with us in first class on the upper deck. Eventually all, including ourselves, arrived in excellent condition at RBGE where the plants started their six-month quarantine.

Seeds were easier to handle. On fine days they were laid out by our tents or hung up in cotton bags to dry and were given a rough cleaning before packeting for the journey. Spring-collected seed is never as clean as that collected in autumn due to all the rubbish associated with old seed capsules. Germination was excellent and seed of the larger species kept its viability for up to five years in a refrigerator.

After four years of trying to get back into China with no success, three of us went on a private trek to Nepal in May 1985. This time I was allowed to make my own quarantine arrangements, provided I collected certain plants only and kept them for six months in an insect-proof frame away from any other plants. The plants were tied to round woven bamboo mats in a layer of moss and these mats were wired into a basket. One day I was horrified to see polythene tied over the top of the basket: the heat that might have built up under the polythene if the sun had been out could have killed the lot. The polythene was promptly replaced with an umbrella (see figure 6). Despite the roasting trek back to the roadhead by way of the Arun valley, all went well until Delhi Airport. An Airline official, no doubt hoping for a backhander, refused to allow the plants on to our plane, the excuse being that the plane was full. We telexed from London to Delhi and they actually arrived the next day, looking rather the worse for wear. On arrival at my home they were nicely bedded into the frame and most made a good recovery. Alas, this was not the end of their troubles. There was one of the rare plagues of field voles that year and when I came to open the frame again after two weeks of snow almost every plant had been mown off just above ground level; luckily some did recover.

Our seed collections in Nepal were the poorest I can remember on any spring trip. On our trek we were constantly soaked by either heavy rain or violent hail storms, once bad enough to knock (locally) all the leaves off *R. thomsonii* and tear the tough leaves of *R. hodgsonii* to shreds. This sort of weather can also knock off any remaining seed capsules. Autumn seed collecting is invariably more certain, particularly after a poor flowering season. On several occasions, I have collected very green capsules in early to mid-September, and with just two or three exceptions, the germination has been fine. Also, in the autumn, just one or two large, or a handful of small, capsules are ample, while in the spring, to obtain a few seeds, every available capsule has to be grabbed.

In recent years seed from South-East Asia has been coming in from various sources. With a few exceptions, seed collected by other people does not germinate as well as my own. Often the seed looks good and yet proves to be dead after sowing. Some seed may have been stored in a drawer for some years but most has undoubtedly been killed by over-heating. I prefer paper seed packets to polythene for collecting in the wild, although in wet weather paper packets can disintegrate. Some people use little polythene packets but I reckon they could end by losing their seed from sweating in heat. Viability can also be lost by being crushed in non-padded envelopes in the post.

Herbarium specimens also need to be treated very carefully. The best specimens are those where the drying paper has been laboriously changed day after day until the specimens are dry. These days many people are in a hurry and cannot be bothered with this paper changing. So they rig up a sort of oven where the specimens are cooked, supposedly very slowly, over very gentle heat. Invariably the specimens end up partly shrivelled and on occasion, I have even seen the drying paper singed.

However expert plant hunters may be, many seed batches reach their recipients either as *Rhododendron* sp. (short for species) or wrongly named. Naming plants in the field can be tricky, even for the most knowledgeable, and I have certainly made mistakes myself, though I will not put 'sp.' on a rhododendron packet.

Present-day plant hunting trips to South-East Asia can be roughly divided into three categories: 1 Parties of up to 20, or even more, organized by travel companies. These rarely camp, making use of any local accommodation available, and are not necessarily entirely botanically orientated; 2 Smaller groups from two to eight in association with local botanical institutions; 3 One or more persons travelling on their own, making use of public transport, and often roughing it in the worst accommodation. This third group may have difficulties in reaching the most remote areas, but has the advantage of flexibility on time spent in each area. There are, of course, variations on these categories, according to country. Some spring trips are now being followed up by autumn trips for seed.

Post-1949 plant hunters are numerous and many have been on only one or two trips. The question arises, who among the present-day plant hunters could have accomplished what the likes of Fortune, Forrest and Kingdon-Ward did? I like to think that people such as Roy Lancaster, Ron McBeath, Tony Schilling and Chris Grey-Wilson would have achieved just as much.

PETER COX VMH *is a director of Glendoick Gardens Ltd, Perth, Scotland which specialises in rhododendrons. He has written several books on rhododendrons and has made 11 plant hunting trips to South-East Asia including eight to China*

# CHAPTER 9

# HYBRIDS FOR A COLD CLIMATE: THE SEIDELS

## WALTER SCHMALSCHEIDT

The leading German specialist in the breeding and selection of rhododendrons during the 19th century and the early 20th centuries was without doubt the firm of T J Rudolf Seidel, whose nursery garden at Grüngräbchen near Dresden is still in existence. Their records contain something like 600 entries of new cultivars. Their achievement can perhaps be compared to that of the British family of Waterer: certainly no other German nursery of the past can compete with it.

The first member of this important family of gardeners was Johann Heinrich Seidel (1744-1815). He began his career as a garden apprentice in Dresden in 1764, but he spent seven years training and studying abroad in Vienna, the Netherlands, England and, finally, Paris before returning to his native Saxony in 1771 when he was appointed assistant curator (Adjunkt) of the Elector of Saxony's orangery. In 1778 he was promoted to be the Elector's head gardener (Kurfürstlicher Hofgärtner) and later the King's gardener (Königlicher Hofgärtner). Early in the year 1807 he began selling his own *Rhododendron ponticum,* and it is said that he had six different species of rhododendron in cultivation.

Four of his sons became gardeners and in 1813 two of them, Jacob Friedrich Seidel (1789-1860) and Traugott Jacob Seidel (1775-1858) established the nursery known as Gebrüder Traugott Jacob Seidel (T J Seidel Brothers). At first their main business was growing camellias and the story of how this came about is an intriguing one. Jacob Friedrich, the younger brother, had been working from 1810 to 1812 as a garden inspector at the Jardin des Plantes in Paris where he quickly recognized the horticultural potential of camellias as winter-flowering shrubs. When he was forced to join the French army in 1812 and set out on Napoleon's

*109*

*Johann Heinrich Seidel (1744-1815), the founder of
the dynasty. Gardener to the King of Saxony and the
first to sell* R. ponticum *at his nursery in Dresden*

march to Russia, he took the camellia plants he had acquired in his knapsack. However, he got no further than Erfurt before deserting and making his way back to Dresden where he soon started growing camellias in the family nursery which he set up with his brother in 1813.

Later another speciality – rhododendrons and azaleas – was added, and in 1820 T J Seidel Brothers put *Rhododendron* 'Azaleoides', *R. catawbiense, R. dauricum, R. dauricum* var. *atrovirens, R. ferrugineum* and *R. hirsutum* on the market as hardy plants. By 1822 Jacob Friedrich was already hybridizing rhododendrons.

Towards the end of the 1850s Jacob Friedrich Seidel's son, Traugott Jacob Herrmann Seidel (born 1833) joined the family business after learning his trade as a gardener both at home and in France and England. When Jacob Friedrich Seidel died in 1860 Traugott Jacob Herrmann took over the management and changed the name of the firm to T J Seidel. At the same time he gave up growing other plants in order to specialize in rhododendrons, camellias and azaleas. He had already visited John Standish at his Bagshot nursery in Surrey and worked at the nursery for a time in 1859, and this undoubtedly influenced his decision to concentrate on

*T J Rudolf Seidel (1861-1918) of the Dresden firm of
Gebrüder T J Seidel, the leading German hybridizer of
hardy rhododendrons. He owed his success to grafting
his hybrids on R. 'Cunningham's White', thus
producing them rapidly in quantity*

breeding rhododendron hybrids.

About 1860 he made his first hybrid, 'Jacob Friedrich Seidel', for which he was to be awarded the first prize of one ducat at an exhibition at Berlin. His next novelty, 'Eduard Bäseler' ('crimson, one of the biggest flowers'), appeared in his catalogue for 1867. In 1869 he offered 'Marie von Woedtke' and in 1873 'Justizrath Stein'. From then on further novelties followed regularly. In 1877 he started the first trials with hardy rhododendrons. His eldest son, Rudolf (T J Rudolf Seidel) joined the business in 1883 and his second son, Heinrich, followed six years later. T J Herrmann Seidel died on 28 April, 1896.

A property at Grüngräbchen near Dresden (Niederlausitz or Lower Lusatia) was acquired in 1897. There T J Rudolf Seidel (1861-1918), the foremost breeder of rhododendrons of the dynasty, produced hardy Seidel hybrids on a large scale; his aim was to produce even hardier rhododendrons. Some 150ha (360 acres) of the estate at Grüngräbchen with extensive areas of moorland, as well as a stand of 100-year-old Scots pine (*Pinus sylvestris*), provided the ideal habitat. Grüngräbchen lies 40km (25 miles) north of Dresden, with a harsh climate – the average temperature around 4°C (39°F) lower than at Dresden. This offered optimal conditions for the selection of absolutely hardy plants.

.Of the 106 taxa of rhododendrons selected from the experimental garden at Dresden and moved to Grüngräbchen, 48 were killed by frost in the winter of 1899-1900 (temperatures of -33°C/-27°F with no snow cover); 41 suffered frost damage each year; and only 17 proved thoroughly hardy. Building on the experience of his forebears as well as his own knowledge, T J Rudolf Seidel used only well-tested hardy parents, such as the cultivars *R.* 'Alexander Adie' (syn. *R.* 'Jay Gould'), *R.* 'Boule de Neige', *R.* 'Mrs. Milner', as well as a *R. campanulatum* hybrid 'Viola' of which he knew the inherited qualities and potential. These were crossed, following a special breeding programme, with *R. catawbiense, R. metternichii* (which was in fact *R. brachycarpum*, although this was not known at that time) and *R. smirnowii*.

T J Rudolf Seidel reported to the *Mitteilungen der Deutschen-Dendrologischen Gesellschaft*, Jahrbuch, 1902 (Report of the German Dendrology Society, Year Book, 1902): '. . . based on my trials, and I make them systematically, there are 12 crosses likely to lead to success. They are (the first mentioned being the mother plant):

1. *Rh. catawbiense* x 'Mrs Milner'
2. *Rh. catawbiense* x 'Jay Gould'
3. *Rh. smirnowii* x 'Mrs Milner'
4. *Rh. smirnowii* x 'Jay Gould'
5. *Rh.* 'Boule de Neige' x 'Mrs Milner'
6. *Rh.* 'Boule de Neige' x 'Jay Gould'
7. *Rh.* 'Viola' x 'Mrs Milner'
8. *Rh.* 'Viola' x 'Jay Gould'
9. *Rh. japonicum metternichii* x 'Mrs Milner'
10. *Rh. japonicum metternichii* x 'Jay Gould'
11. *Rh.* 'Boule de Neige' x 'Viola'
12. *Rh.* 'Viola' x 'Boule de Neige' '

His breeding principles were:
1. Readiness to flower when young;
2. Clear-cut colour differences;
3. Good growth and strong roots;
4. Dark, medium-sized foliage, not liable to wind damage;
5. Hardiness;
6. Needing no special care;
7. Late flowering;
8. Buds on the earliest shoots;
9. Coming true from seed (if possible).

New cultivars had therefore to meet stringent requirements. The aims laid down by TJ Rudolf Seidel are still valid and reflect his experience and foresight, based on his life-long experience with hardy rhododendrons.

The hardiness of the Seidel cultivars was clearly superior to nearly all other similar cultivars. This was strikingly proved during the hard winters of 1962-63, 1965-66, 1978-79 and 1984-85, when many of the nearly 2,000 different rhododendrons at the Lehr-ünd Versuchsanstalt fur Gartenbau (Horticultural College and Research Institute) at Bad Zwischenahn were badly damaged by frost.

The earliest crosses were made by T J Rudolf Seidel at Dresden in 1891, frequently using the hybrid 'Everestianum'. The cultivars 'Allah', 'Anton', 'August',

*Figure 1: rhododendrons growing in a valley in Bhutan, typical of the Sino-Himalayan habitat of the genus (see Chapter 1)*

*Figure 2 (above left):* R. maddenii, *one of the lepidotes recognized by the presence of scales by Clarke in 1882. Illustration from* Rhododendrons of Sikkim-Himalaya *(see Chapter 2). Figure 3 (above right):* R. arboreum *at Heligan in Cornwall. Sir John Lemon of Carclew gave this garden rhododendrons from those he received from Kew in 1851 (see Chapter 5). Figure 4 (below): Joseph Hooker on his second Himalayan journey surrounded by his Lepcha collectors and Ghorka guards. Sketched in Sikkim in 1949 by the artist Frederick Taylor*

*Figure 5 (top left): W Fitch's engraving of* R. roylei *(*cinnabarinum*) in* Rhododendrons of Sikkim-Himalaya *(see below). Figure 6 (top right): plants collected by Peter Cox in Nepal in 1985 were tied to woven bamboo mats for transportation back to Britain. Here they are protected from the sun by an umbrella (see Chapter 8). Figure 7 (above): Joseph Hooker's drawing of* R. roylei *(*cinnabarinum*) made in the field from the same plant as his herbarium specimen preserved at Kew (see Chapter 5)*

*Figure 8: the ravine at Crarae in Argyll is very similar to the Sino-Himalayan landscape and many large-leaved rhododendrons are at home there (see Chapter 6)*

*Figure 9 (top left): the Vireya* R. jasminiflorum *was first exhibited in 1850. The strangeness of the flowers led to a comment that it was 'probably no Rhododendron at all' (see Chapter 7). Figure 10 (top right):* R. 'Humboldt', *one of TJ Rudolph Seidel's cold-hardy hybrids (see Chapter 9). Figure 11 (above): Borde Hill, the Sussex garden of Colonel Stephenson Clarke, a prominent member of the original Rhododendron Society (see Chapter 15)*

*Figure 12 (top):* R. *'Beauty of Littleworth' in the Home Wood at Exbury, one of James Mangles' best hybrids.*
*Figure 13 (above left):* R. *'Loder's White', a beautiful hybrid whose authorship is uncertain. Figure 14 (above right):* R. *'Luscombei' bred by and named after John Luscombe of Combe Royal in Devon (see Chapter 10)*

*Figures 15 and 16:* R. simsii, *found in a Shanghai nursery by Robert Fortune, was sent to Standish & Noble at Bagshot in 1851 – (top left) an engraving of the plant from* Curtis's Botanical Magazine *and (top right) a living plant (see Chapter 13). Figure 17 (above left):* R. 'Lem's Cameo', *Halfdan Lem's superb American hybrid. (see Chapter 11). Figure 18 (above right): John Charles Williams of Caerhays, one of the first Englishman to grow Chinese rhododendrons and Chairman of the Rhododendron Society 1916-27 (see Chapter 15)*

Figure 19: Azalea rustica *Flore Pleno hybrids: 'Murillo', 'Virgile' and 'Phébé (all still available) illustrated in a Belgian Horticultural journal of 1893 (see Chapter 12)*

'Carola', among others, originated from these crosses. These novelties were named in 1899 but were not introduced until after 1905. The names were generally chosen from male and female first names, and followed an alphabetical sequence; thus, those named in 1899 included 'Alfred', 'Allah', 'Anton', etc., 'Bertha' and 'Botha' in 1900, 'Emil', 'Erich', and 'Eva' in 1903, and so on.

Every year between 40,000 and 50,000 seedlings were produced, and from 1913 onwards 12,000 to 15,000 four- and five-year old specimens were prepared for sale each year. A decisive factor in this success, or rather in the rapid propagation and distribution of these cultivars, was that about 1870 the Seidel nursery succeeded in propagating 'Cunningham's White' from cuttings. In the early 1880s some 20,000 specimens were produced each year for grafting stock. Cultivation and propagation of novelties on a large scale were thus ensured.

A particular tradition of the Seidel family was to repeat the same names for the male children. The first specialist of the family bore the names Traugott Jacob, and all his male descendants have since been given the same two first names, plus a third, which was their real personal name, for example, Traugott Jacob *Herrmann* Seidel. Part of the tradition was the spelling of the German first name 'Herrmann' with two r's, the usual spelling, never accepted by the Seidel family, being 'Hermann'.

The Horticultural College and Research Institute (at Aurich, East Frisia till 1975) is now at Bad Zwischenahn (Oldenburg). Here, I have been collecting Seidel cultivars for years in order to preserve them and there are now nearly 120 growing at the Institute. It forms the largest collection of Seidel hybrids in the world. In 1971 the Institute received 'Bella', 'Echse', 'Eva' and 'Fee' from the Arnold Arboretum at Boston, USA. These four cultivars, extinct for a long time in Germany, had been sent to the United States by the Seidels along with a number of others in 1908. They had survived many of the harsh North American winters. This fact alone proves that the Seidel hybrids are very hardy. I have managed to acquire other cultivars lost to the Seidel nurseries from Hermann A Hesse, the well-known nursery at Weener/Ems. In 1974 the late Mr Michael Haworth-Booth (Farall Nurseries, Haslemere, England) sent propagation material of 'Bernhard Lauterbach' dating back before 1890. This cultivar had been erroneously listed in the *Rhododendron & Camellia Year Book* (1956), No 10, as 'Baron Leuterbach'.

In 1973 I found the beautiful bi-coloured 'Leo XIII' in an old garden in Oldenburg town, and in an old park at Lütetsburg, E.Friesland, I found 'Edwin II'. Last, but not least, the Seidel nurseries provided scions of 'Else Seidel', 'Markgraf', 'Peter Seidel', 'Rebe', 'Rudolf Seidel', 'Textor', 'Ute' and other rarities no longer in cultivation in the West. The search for long-forgotten Seidel cultivars is a never-ending adventure, as is their correct naming.

Ludwig Leopold Liebig (1801-72) was another important rhododendron breeder in the 19th century. In 1837 he acquired Elisenruhe, a private nursery, and made it a commercial undertaking. By 1887 his nursery was, after the Seidel's, the third largest at Dresden. Of his cultivars, so far as is known, the following are still in existence: 'Jewess', a very hardy *R. caucasicum* hybrid which originated before 1857; 'Ludwig Leopold Liebig' (bright scarlet) from before 1880; and 'Gabriele Liebig' (white, petals slightly tinged towards the edge with soft rose-violet, and with strong dark red marking) from before 1863. An *R. edgeworthii* hybrid called 'Suave' produced by Liebig is known to exist in England, introduced before 1863.

The other German rhododendron breeders of the past, such as Otto Schulz, head gardener of the Royal Porcelain Manufactory at Berlin, Johann Baptist Müller, breeder of 'Wilhelma', a race of heavily speckled rhododendrons, Sebastian Rinz of Frankfurt-on-Main, Louis Roth of Stuttgart, the Mardner brothers of Mainz, and some others, produced comparatively few cultivars which have all disappeared almost without trace.

It is worth mentioning here that a Scotsman, James Booth (at his nursery at Klein-Flottbek, now a suburb of Hamburg) was (in 1837) the first to hybridize rhododendrons in northern Germany. They have all vanished, presumably because they possessed too many of the tender *R. arboreum* genes.

**Acknowledgements**

With thanks to Leon Declerq and Albert De Raedt. Translated by David McClintock and Heino Heine.

*From 1961 to* 1995 WALTER SCHMALSCHEIDT *was officially in charge of fruit and woody plants at Oldenburg for the Weser-Ems Chamber of Agriculture. He is now responsible for a large collection of old and rare rhododendrons in Bad Zwischenahn*

# CHAPTER 10

# HYBRIDS IN THE BRITISH ISLES: THE 19TH CENTURY

## LIONEL DE ROTHSCHILD

Rhododendrons are promiscuous. Such an anthropomorphic statement cannot be judgemental but we can be grateful that they are so; quite what rhododendrons would make of us with our families of hybridists is another question. It is certainly true that the history of hybridization is written in blood lines, with the same families of rhododendrons and the same families of people occurring generation after generation. The obvious reasons – that gardens and nursery businesses tend to be handed down from father to son and that the crosses of one generation may not appear until the next – are not, I think, the only ones to explain the peculiar fascination exerted by the possibility of breeding something new: a case of *exegi monumentum*, perhaps, or as James Mangles wrote over a hundred years ago, 'It may almost seem, for instance, a profanation to think of refining the ineffable delicacy of *R. veitchii*, or gilding the golden glory of *R. javanicum*, and yet I do not envy the cultivator who has no ambition to leave his own mark among his flowers, for the sake of science as well as for his own.' (*The Gardeners' Chronicle* 9.4.1881). It sometimes seemed to me, as I researched this article, that there were few cultivators indeed who lacked such an ambition: the problem has been, quite literally, to see the wood for the trees. If, therefore, I omit someone's favourite hybridizer or hybrid or insert others deemed less worthy, I would ask the reader to forgive it as the lottery of the author's memory and the threat of the editor's red ink.

### The 19th Century

By common consensus the first hybrid was an azaleodendron, *R. ponticum* x *R. periclymenoides* at Mr Thompson's Mile End Road nursery at the turn of the 19th century: the result, now known as 'Odoratum', was recorded in the Royal Botanic Garden, Edinburgh by 1814 and won an Award of Merit (AM) in 1994, surely the longest delayed recognition to date! While this hybrid has always been spoken of as an accident, I prefer to believe it was deliberate (cf. R Gorer *RYB* 1980-81).

Azaleodendrons, popular at the time, represent something of a genetic dead-end (not least because they are usually sterile, 'mules'), though one to which we shall return. Purposeful breeding of rhododendrons began in the second quarter of the 19th century with a handful of major species. The dates of their introductions vary from source to source, so I shall pick one while well aware that another article in this issue may well give another. For our purposes the most important species were *R. maximum* (1736), *R. ponticum* (1763), *R. caucasicum* (1803), and *R. catawbiense* (1809) and to a lesser extent, *R. dauricum* (1780), *R. campanulatum* (1825) and *R. barbatum* (1829). These rhododendrons all introduced certain characteristics: for example, *R. catawbiense* had great hardiness and a good habit; *R. maximum* was late flowering and hardy, as well as giving the distinctive blotch on the upper lobe so beloved by Victorian hybridizers; *R. ponticum*, as we all know, adapted to its new surroundings all too well; *R. caucasicum* flowered earlier and for longer; *R. campanulatum* introduced a different shape to the flowers; *R. dauricum* flowered even earlier but had to wait until 1853 for its lepidote groom *R. ciliatum* for its moment of glory in 'Praecox' (I Davies; cf. Bean for parentage error in Register).

However, while some crosses were made between these species, such as 'Everestianum', 'Album Elegans' and 'Roseum Elegans', or occurred naturally, the single most important species was *R. arboreum* : to some extent the early history of hybridization can be seen as combining the colour of *R. arboreum* with the hardiness of the rest. The blood-red *R. arboreum* was first seen by Captain Hardwicke in 1796 in Kumaon (of Corbett's man-eating tigers appropriately enough) and this magnificent rhododendron was not introduced until about 1809-10 (Davidian) and did not flower until 1825 at The Grange, Alresford. The pollen was used the following year by J R Gowen (later Secretary and Treasurer of the RHS) for the second Earl of Carnavon of Highclere to produce 'Altaclerense' (the latinization of Highclere, now orthographically corrected, in line with *Ilex* 'Altaclerense') from a *catawbiense* x *ponticum* hybrid. Two other crosses were figured in the same year (1831) as 'Altaclerense', namely 'Smithii' (*arboreum* x *ponticum* , made both ways, possibly containing *R. maximum* , possibly syn. 'Cornish Early Red'), made by William Smith, gardener to the Earl of Liverpool and later nurseryman at Norbiton, and 'Russellianum' (*catawbiense* x *arboreum*), of which an enormous clump, under its synonym 'Southamptonia', graces the lawn at Exbury House. From this point hybridization took off, with much back-crossing to reinforce the hardiness.

Carnavon may well have been inspired by his younger brother, Rev. William Herbert of Spofforth (later Dean of Manchester), a man of considerable learning who urged, among other things, the use of *R. maximum* to promote later flowering. Herbert himself made several crosses, notably the azaleodendron 'Hybridum' (*viscosum* x *maximum*, 1817), 'Jacksonii' (*caucasicum* x 'Nobleanum' or *arboreum*, 1835; W Jackson & Co probably also raised a similarly named hybrid and there is some confusion) and 'Aprilis', said to be *ponticum* x *dauricum*, 1843, but Gorer (*op. cit.*) thinks *R. caucasicum* more likely in these cases rather than breaching the elepidote-lepidote divide.

One of the more adventurous hybridizers was William Smith, mentioned above: he (presumably) made 'Smithii Album' (probably again *arboreum* x *ponticum*, there being white forms of both; the later similar cross 'Boddaertianum' [Van Houtte, intro. 1863, probably *arboreum* x *ponticum* or *ponticum* hybrid, not *campanulatum* x *arboreum* as registered, cf. Bean] is particularly wonderful in the garden as I write these words); he certainly made 'Venustum' ('Nobleanum Venustum', *caucasicum* x *arboreum*, 1829), which my grandfather thought 'easily the best of that hybrid . . . a much clearer pink than the dull form which is sometimes exhibited' (RYB 1953). Smith was also responsible for some highly popular yellow azaleodendrons, notably 'Norbitonense Aureum' and 'Norbitonense Broughtonianum' (both [*maximum* x *ponticum*] x *molle*, syns. 'Smithii Aureum' and 'Broughtonii Aureum') in the 1830s.

Many other firms were active (for example Lee & Kennedy, and Loddiges, notably associated with *ponticum*) but pride of place must go to the extraordinary dynasty of Waterers. I shall not attempt a detailed exposition of the Waterer family tree: suffice it to say that there were eventually two branches, running nurseries at Knap Hill and Bagshot, and that I shall differentiate between generations with regal numerals, as in the excellent Note on the family in Bean by G Donald Waterer, a paradigm of clarity.

Thus after Michael I (1745-1827) and II (*c.* 1770-1842), ownership split with Bagshot going to Michael II's younger brother John I (1784-1868), thence to his son John II (1826-93) and then to his sons John III (1865-1948) and Gomer (1867-1945) (who ended up back at Knap Hill); Knap Hill went to Michael II's youngest brother Hosea I (1793-1853), thence to his nephews Anthony I (1822-96) and Robert Godfrey and then to Anthony I's sons Anthony II (*c.* 1850-1924) and briefly Hosea II (USA)(1852-1926). Easy really.

The Waterers had what has been termed a 'collective anonymity' (F Street ) and while there may have been some differences of approach – PD Williams, for example, noted that 'the elder Anthony relied principally on hybridization, while the younger usually preferred to breed by selection' (*R. Soc. Notes* Vol. II No. V, 1924), they shared the basic aim of the hardy hybridist, 'to raise plants that were hardy, sturdy and shapely in growth, so that when not in flower they were good-looking shrubs, whilst the flower-heads, to satisfy the requirements of the time, were to be large and full, the flowers holding themselves up, of good substance, the colours pleasing, and, most important of all, they were not to expand before June' (Watson). Hardiness was the pre-eminent desideratum for the Waterers, a belief reinforced, I think I read somewhere, when an entire crop of *araucarias* was lost to frost in the 1850s.

The first flower of note I shall mention is not in fact late-flowering: 'Nobleanum' (*caucasicum* x *arboreum*) was raised by Michael Waterer II by about 1832; it is almost certainly *not* named after Charles Noble of Standish & Noble as Standish was born only 15 years earlier and Standish & Noble commenced trading only 15 years later (cf. Bean and Willson). This and another *R. caucasicum* hybrid, 'Christmas Cheer', are still widely planted for early colour, as is 'Lee's Scarlet'. His brother John I of Bagshot produced 'Lady Eleanor Cathcart' (*maximum* x *arboreum* [or x 'Altaclerense' type hybrid, cf. Bean]) in the late 1830s; like his youngest brother Hosea I of Knap Hill, who made some 'judicious' crosses with *R. catawbiense*, he believed in using *R. arboreum* as the pollen parent to achieve later, frost-free flowering. Smith of Norbiton also found that $F_1$ hybrids with *R. arboreum* as seed parent were less beautiful and more sensitive to cold than the reverse

crosses (Focke, referred to in Bowers). Of course, as F Street has pointed out with regard to *R. arboreum*, *R. griffithianum* and *R. yakushimanum*, when these plants were initially introduced and were still rare, pollen was available but not plants so they predominated as male parents. These and other nurserymen made hundreds of hybrids, crossing, re-crossing and back-crossing. They made excellent use of what we would regard as limited resources; it should be added that then as now far too many cultivars were named and introduced as fashionable 'new' plants each year – but business is business.

Rhododendrons were highly fashionable. I have in front of me some documents from the Rothschild archives. First, there are letters to my great-great-great grandfather, N M Rothschild (NM) from Conrad Loddiges & Sons of Hackney and Lee & Kennedy of Hammersmith from as early as 1814 onwards: most of them concern NM sending plants to his brother Amschel in Frankfurt; though rhododendrons are not mentioned specifically, both firms were active in that field (RAL). It is also amusing to note similarities in any business: NM's father Mayer Amschel wrote to his son, 'They say the lack of order would make a beggar out of a millionaire' (RAL 1805); J C Loudon wrote in reproof of Michael Waterer II, 'We never knew a nursery or market garden, where any money was made that was not kept *orderly* ' (*The Gardener's Magazine* 1829, quoted in Willson). Then there are two lists; because the names in both are quoted directly from documents from a period when there was considerable confusion and variability, I have not attempted to regularize the spelling and typography to modern standards of nomenclature – all names are *sic*. The first is of Camellias, Rhododendrons and Azaleas at Ferrières in 1850 (whether they are being imported or exported is not absolutely clear), owned by NM's brother Baron James de Rothschild; he was credited as having 'encouraged the introduction of these hybrids into France, and large consignments of these splendid standard Rhododendrons were exported there, and this example was imitated by many others' (Henry Knight, *The Gardeners' Chronicle* 25.8.1881). This pre-dates his use of Paxton to remodel the château, so 'the taste English' was already evident. The list includes some 31 rhododendrons, among which are 'Aureum de Smith', 'Altaclarense' 'Campanulata', 'Cinamomeum' and 'Nobleanum'. The second is an invoice to NM's son Baron Lionel de Rothschild (that is Lionel of Exbury's grandfather) from Waterer and Godfrey, Knap Hill Nursery, dated 11.12.1856, for Kalmias, Azaleas and Rhododendrons totalling £37 7s 6d, including 19 different rhododendrons, among which are 'Cunningham's White', 'Pictum', 'Multi Maculatum' (still admired by Gertrude Jekyll many years later), 'odoratum', 'Catawbiense', 'Jackmanii' (pre-dates Methven entry in Register), 'Rusellianum', 'Lucidum' and 'Isabel'. The most expensive are 'Standards', 6 for £9 9s 0d. There is also 'Victoria Van Houttii', so trade went both ways. The bill from Waterer for the five years 1856-61 totalled £89 7s 0d. (RAL)

I have gone into some detail in order to show how thriving the businesses were in a relatively short time. In 1849, however, another transformation took place: seed started arriving from Joseph Hooker's expedition to the Sikkim-Himalaya and publication commenced of his beautiful drawings. In all he introduced some 45 new species (Macqueen Cowan, RYB '49), including *R. campylocarpum, R. ciliatum, cinnabarinum, R. dalhousiae, R. edgeworthii, R. falconeri, R. grande, R. griffithianum, R. maddenii* and *R. thomsonii.* Much of the seed was distributed by Kew to private gardens, which now become of increasing importance (see chapter 5).

Six years later the first Chinese rhododendron arrived, *R. fortunei*, discovered by Robert Fortune on an expedition to find new varieties of tea. This coincided with debate about the virtues of *R. arboreum* and it is interesting to note the reaction of the nurserymen of the day. The firm of Standish & Noble was one of the great rivals to Waterers. Standish had already done some hybridization at Bagshot Park under Andrew Toward before the partnership commenced in 1847; it was dissolved in 1856 – 'two suns could not stand in the same horizon', said Standish. Standish retained an older site at Bagshot Bridge and then created a new nursery at Ascot; Noble remained but started work that winter on a new site (the present Sunning-dale Nurseries) near the railway station (cf. *The Gardeners' Chronicle* 4.11.1882).

In 1850 they contributed a chapter on hybrids to *The Journal of the Horticultural Society* (reproduced in Watson) in which they detail their back-crossing, 'By crossing the American species again with the first hybrids, such as Altaclarense (*sic*), &c., we have still retained the rich tints of the Indian kinds, with all the hardiness of the American;' they also claimed these new hybrids bloomed young and late in the season. The terms 'American' and 'Himalayan', incidentally, came to be used quite loosely as well as polemically; even quite late in the period, owners talked of creating an 'American garden' when referring to an area set aside for rhododendrons (cf. *Journal of Horticulture and Cottage Gardener* 31.8.1871 and *The Gardeners' Chronicle* 2.2.1904 with regard to the 'American garden' at Combe Royal – of which more later and see chapter 4 – which contained both 'American' and 'Sikkim' rhododendrons). They then comment that 'the wider the cross the more healthy the progeny, and that breeding "in and in" produces weak . . . constitutions'. Here they cite an $F_2$ cross of *caucasicum album* (*ponticum album* x *caucasicum*) called 'Bride' (wrongly described in Register but correctly described under 'The Bride', with which it appears to be in synonymy); further selfing of it was a failure. They then list their second generation crosses (i.e. the third generation), showing

they were aiming at distinct 'sections' of hybrids, though few I think now survive with the exception of 'Bride'; 'Standishii' ([*ponticum* x *maximum*] x 'Altaclerense', according to this document, *pace* Register) was used for some hybridizing, chiefly by Sir Edmund Loder ('Dame Nellie Melba', 'Leonardslee Giles'). This is not the same as the white *griffithianum* hybrid 'Standishi' (Register with one 'i'; erroneously in Bean Note with two 'i's); it is registered under Veitch but whether it is theirs named in his honour or one of his later crosses introduced by them, I cannot tell. In 1855 there was again discussion on *arboreum* crosses in *The Gardeners' Chronicle*; they reproduced their remarks in their catalogue (extracts in Russell, RYB 1947 and in *R. Soc. Notes* Vol. III No. II, 1926), 'Now it is well known that seedlings from, or even once removed from *arboreum* are not suited for general culture', again on grounds of blooming too early in the season and only after 20 years, and they go on to say, 'In the Sikkim Rhododendrons we have the material for giving new features to succeeding crosses.' The merit of back-crossing with the other parent or of having *R. arboreum* only as grandparent is almost exactly reproduced 120 years later in the criticism of the first *R. yakushimanum* crosses.

One new cross was 'Ascot Brilliant', put out by Standish in 1861 after his move to Ascot; it is probably the first *R. thomsonii* hybrid (S&G have 'Blandyanum' as the seed parent) and it is reported that this species first flowered in (the old) Standish & Noble's greenhouse in 1857, probably grafted onto old standards to 'speed things up'. While their expertise with species was considerable, handling Fortune's 'sendings' and offering 24 different Sikkim rhododendrons in *The Gardener's Chronicle* in 1853 only three years after their introduction, it is less likely that their other most famous cross was similarly speeded up: 'Cynthia' was put out under that name by Standish and under 'Lord Palmerston' by Noble, both in 1860, and was therefore probably made a few years prior, say before 1856 (dissolution), before the first flowering of *R. griffithianum* in 1858 in Wandsworth (*griffithianum* was first offered for sale by Noble in 1858 too and won an FCC for Standish in 1866). It is generally regarded, therefore, as a *R. catawbiense* hybrid and the *R. griffithianum* parentage can be discounted; it was once second only to 'Pink Pearl' in general popularity.

It is at this point that something of a divergence occurs between the nurserymen and the amateurs. Tenderness continued to be the chief concern of the nurserymen: they made some use of *R. griffithianum* but were only really satisfied at several generations removed, when they had built on and developed their existing lines of hardy hybrids; they also made use of the Maddenia subsection for avowedly tender plants (as well as Vireyas, which are dealt with separately in this volume, see chapter 7).

To both these we shall return. Frank Kingdon-Ward (*On the Roof of the World.* From the late 1940s he hyphenated his name; for simplicity I have done so throughout.) later wrote of *griffithianum*, 'There is an ethereal quality about the enormous bell flowers – their vital milk-whiteness, their careless rapture of form, their exquisite effortless grace as they hang clustered from the leafy shoots, their subtle fragrance – which defies description.' (He had a good go!) James Mangles of Valewood (1832- 84) was quick to grasp the importance of *griffithianum*. He was as much influential for his writings as for his breeding: Millais called him 'the High Priest of the Rhododendron cult', as well he might when one remembers Mangles' explanation of an exasperating failure, '[there are] certain atmospheric moments for the union of vegetable species . . . Never try such things when an east wind is blowing.' This is not to say he only enjoyed the *rôle* of *vates* , for he was keenly scientific too: 'It is indeed a problem for Rhododendron growers to solve to throw colour into the white Sikkim, and especially the scented species. Mr. Darwin alludes to '"the singular fact that white varieties generally transmit their colour much more truly than other varieties".' (*The Gardeners' Chronicle* 7.6.1879). And again, 'As we advance, Nature is always presenting fresh problems for solution. So much the better, provided we arm ourselves with intelligent and industrious research, and German concentration, to meet the emergency.' (ibid 19.7.1879).

His influence carried on a generation later: J C Williams, for example, wrote that 'a constant reading of all I could get together of what Mr. Mangles had said and written pressed me into crossing species rather than hybrids . . . seeing . . . that apparently the more he crossed species and the less he admitted mixed blood, the more even was the quality of the flower, drew me more to the policy which he followed'. (*R. Soc. Notes* Vol. III No. II, 1926). In the period of what J C Williams called 'almost limitless species', pedigree was to become all-important.

In practical terms, too, Mangles' contribution, especially with *R. griffithianum* crosses, was important. There is considerable confusion in the literature on some of the parentage – as this writer has found all too often – so I have not shown all the guesses. It also seems likely that a couple of the crosses attributed in the past to James were made by James' brother Henry Mangles (d. 1908), another rhododendron enthusiast; it was to Littleworth Cross, owned by Henry and his sister Clara (d. 1931) that some of James' collection moved after his untimely death. James won the first award for a *R. griffithianum* cross with 'Alice Mangles' (x *ponticum*, FCC 1882); his 'Isabella Mangles' (x unknown) was much admired by Millais and his 'Beauty of Littleworth' (x *campanulatum*?), raised by Clara to win an FCC in 1904, looks especially splendid on the main path of the Home Wood at Exbury (see figure 12). There is also an enormous

group of 'Loder's White' (see figure 13) in the Winter Garden at Exbury: this famous plant came to Sir Edmund Loder via F D Godman of South Lodge, though J Mangles' original consignment also included some of Luscombe's hybrid seedlings, so authorship is uncertain. Parentage is even less certain: the Register entry (*arboreum* subsp. *cinnamomeum* var. *album* x *griffithianum*) has been widely discounted but the latest suggestion of ('Album Elegans' x *griffithianum*) x 'White Pearl' (Cox, Hillier Manual and S&G) seems unlikely given that 'White Pearl' (syn. 'Halopeanum', *griffithianum* x [*arboreum* x *maximum*?] was only introduced into commerce in 1897 (cf. Bean). Better of itself than as a parent, its best offspring is probably 'C.I.S.' (x 'Fabia'). Finally there is 'Mrs Randall Davidson' (x *campylocarpum*), which though superseded by 'Penjerrick' is still a lovely plant (cf. Lady Adam Gordon RYB 1976); a sister seedling, 'Mrs Kingsmill', won an AM when exhibited by Clara in 1911, when described as creamy white, now in commerce as pale yellow.

Henry Mangles was almost certainly responsible for that fore-runner of 'Royal Flush', 'Rose Mangles' (*cinnabarinum* x *maddenii*; several others were named, including the hardy yellow 'Primrose Queen', renamed 'Hethersett' in 1962 by Lady Adam Gordon, who has restored some of his garden) and for one of the most enduringly beautiful and striking though reputedly demanding azaleodendrons, 'Glory of Littleworth'; indeed it is probably still one of the best known azale-odendrons, though I hope the lovely 'Martha Isaacson' (Ostbo, pre-1956) gains in popularity.

Moving further west, John Luscombe of Combe Royal was another gentleman hybridist: he was particularly famous for his citrus collection, winning the Banksian medal for an exhibition of them in 1827 and presenting a 'magnificent basket' of fruit to the Queen in 1850. He was a friend of James Mangles, who wrote of him 'there has been no more enthusiastic Rhododendron grower' (*The Gardeners' Chronicle* 19.3.1881) and he was one of the first to use *R. fortunei*, which first flowered in his garden (1866), to produce 'Luscombei' (x *thomsonii*, exh. 1880), 'the fame of which' wrote Mangles approvingly, 'has reached German science' (ibid). It is still a lovely flower (see figure 14) and a cross repeated and 'improved by Sir Edmund Loder in 'Pride of Leonardslee' (using the same *fortunei* as for 'Loderi') and by my grandfather in 'General Sir John du Cane' (using subsp. *discolor*). He was probably also responsible for the *griffithianum* hybrid 'Coombe Royal' (for some unknown reason spelt with two 'o's in all reference books) which in turn was the seed parent for the ever popular 'Mrs G. W. Leak' as well as 'Mrs Charles E. Pearson'.

Moving yet further west, we come to what was soon to be the epicentre of the rhododendron world, Cornwall. No other county can grow such tender plants with impunity nor can boast of so many fine rhododendron gardens. Captain Tremayne of Heligan crossed blood-red *R. arboreum* with *R. griffithianum* to produce 'John Tremayne' and 'Mrs Babington'; my grandfather made reference to both parents being good forms and used both on occasions at Exbury. He wrote of the *R. griffithianum* that it was 'a very fine form indeed which has been sent out by Smith, of Guernsey, and which I believe was Mangles's original variety and was used by Sir Edmund Loder in his famous 'Loderi' strain' (RYB 1953). He also commented that 'the form known as "roseum superbum" largely used by Lowinsky, a form which he obtained from Gill, produces very tender offspring and . . . the form used by Mr. George Johnstone is also much too tender for northern gardens.' (ibid). The cross was made several times elsewhere (Tregrehan: 'Carlyon's Hybrid' or 'Carlyon's Cross'; Scorrier: 'Scorrier Pink') but most notably by Richard Gill (1849-1927), who was gardener at Tremough and then set up his own nursery business on land leased from the Shilson family. This much decorated grex – one FCC and five AMs at a recent count (W Magor RYB 1982-83) – includes 'Beauty of Tremough' (FCC 1902), 'Gill's Triumph' (AM 1906), 'Gill's Goliath' (AM 1914), 'Glory of Penjerrick' (AM 1904) and 'Glory of Leonardslee'. He used the good form of *R. griffithianum*, which he called *R. aucklandii roseum superbum* (mentioned by Lionel, above), which Mrs

Shilson had been sent by a friend from a plant in the Italian Lakes, and did so extensively, especially as a seed parent. He also made 'Shilsonii' (*thomsonii* x *barbatum*; Loder made the reverse cross in 'Nestor') and raised many *R. arboreum* and *R. barbatum* seedlings and crosses between the two. Finally, he crossed 'Kewense' with *R. thomsonii*: because of its similarity to 'Pride of Leonardslee', Lord Aberconway (as H D McLaren, *R. Soc. Notes* Vol. III No. III, 1927) suggested Gill might have used *R. fortunei* as seed parent ('Richard Gill' is registered as such), but also noted the latter hybrid's slightly smaller flowers and deeper edges to the petal. Be that as it may, a fine plant was named 'Aurora' by Lionel in 1922, won an AM and was seed parent to two of the more famous of his early crosses, 'Naomi' (LR108, x *fortunei*, named after his younger daughter) and 'Yvonne' (LR112, x *griffithianum*, named after his sister-in-law).

At Penjerrick, under the supervision of Robert Fox and his son Barclay Fox (1873-1930), Samuel Smith as head gardener from 1889-1935 made only 11 crosses but with an extremely high success rate – an object lesson perhaps to indiscriminate hybridizers. Lord Aberconway wrote that this record is all the more remarkable when one considers that he had 'no knowledge of the science of heredity and . . . but rare opportunities of visiting other gardens, of discussing his work with other hybridisers or of obtaining pollen from far afield. Close observation of the qualities of a flower, and fine judgement in selecting the parents, have evidently been the mainspring of this success.' (As H D McLaren, *R. Soc. Notes* Vol. III No. IV, 1928.) He was one of the first to make second generation Himalayan crosses, putting the pollen of Gill's 'Shilsonii' onto blood-red *R. arboreum* to make 'Cornubia' (so named by Gill; Smith subsequently named the best of this cross 'Liliani' cf. W Magor RYB 1981-82), and that of 'Glory of Penjerrick' onto *R. thomsonii* to make 'Barclayi'. 'Cornish Cross' (*thomsonii* x *griffithianum*) has always been popular and was remade by my grandfather using a different form of *R. griffithianum* ('Exbury Cornish Cross'); 'Werei', after Robert Were Fox (*arboreum album* x *barbatum* cf. W Magor) was much admired by Millais. However, his most famous cross was 'Penjerrick' (*griffithianum* x *campylocarpum* var. *elatum*): both Smith himself, emphatically (quoted in W Magor's article) and Lord Aberconway (*op. cit.*) were in no doubt that *R. griffithianum* was the seed parent, so I am puzzled why the Register and later reference books show the reverse. I am less sure that because var. *elatum* is not specified, it was therefore Hooker's dwarf form, as Magor infers (the same as 'Mrs Randall Davidson' *et. al.*); my grandfather (RYB 1933) was in no doubt that it was var. *elatum*, and its different colour forms would fit with his observation (RYB 1953) that var. *elatum* throws yellows, pinks and whites whereas Hooker's gives 'constant pale yellow.' Of course, this is an horticultural rather than a scientific distinction; P Cox *(Larger Species)* notes there are many grades between the two.

What is in no doubt is that it was an influential and beautiful hybrid: Aberconway considered it 'that most lovely of all rhododendrons' (RYB 1947) and planted a whole grove at Bodnant. He thought one reason for 'the effectiveness of the planting' at Penjerrick was that two-thirds of the rhododendrons were of but five kinds (*arboreum*, 'Barclayi', 'Penjerrick', 'Cornish Cross' and 'Liliani'/'Cornubia'): this clearly points the way to the mass plantings of the same rhododendron so beloved by many of the next generation of gardeners, including my grandfather and taken to its most spectacular conclusion by the serried ranks at Mount Congreve. Aberconway also compared the 'well-filled conical truss' of the Bagshot catalogue, which 'has it' on the show bench, to 'the shower of drooping bells' of 'Cornish Cross', 'Barclayi' or 'Penjerrick', 'where one truss seems to melt into the other [and] has a beauty . . . unobtainable with the other type of flower.' (*R. Soc. Notes op. cit.*). This again is a clear pointer to trends in taste and to some disparity of approach between the great gardeners and the great nurserymen. The importance of the best form as parent, with so much greater choice now becoming available, was to become paramount; but before leaving Cornwall – to which we shall return – for the blue blood lines of 'Loderi', it is as well to remember

that Nature can produce the occasional fine hybrid too and that Carclew boasts one of the finest in 'Sir Charles Lemon', which my grandfather (RYB 1934) thought was probably a hybrid between *campanulatum* and *arboreum* subsp. *cinnamomeum*. It delights me every year.

Human as opposed to natural selection was taken a step further by Sir Edmund Loder. I have already mentioned 'Pride of Leonardslee' and 'Nestor'; the former cross was also repeated in 'Betty' and 'Hullabaloo'. Millais wrote that his 'greatest successes were those obtained by mating species or hybrids that were near one another in specific character and habit . . . success was more or less certain in the case where a "dominant" species, such as *R. griffithianum*, *R. thomsonii*, *R. fortunei*, *R. barbatum* or *R. caucasicum*, was used in conjunction with another species closely allied . . . or with a vigorous hybrid that did not contain a strain of an undesirable species'. (*R. Soc. Notes* Vol. III No. II, 1926).

He also noted that certain 'apparently good' hybrids 'often had a tendency in the second or third generation to throw up some bad strain which in the plant itself was hidden, and which only appeared as the result of hybridisation' (ibid): an example of this hybrid-induced variability might be his 'Sussex Bonfire' (*haematodes* x 'Cornish Cross'). Certainly Sir Edmund used the best possible forms of species available for his most famous cross, 'Loderi': the seed parent was a good form of *R. fortunei* in his own collection; the pollen came from the good *R. griffithianum*, already mentioned above, in his neighbour F D Godman's greenhouse at South Lodge. The cross had been made before, at Kew ('Kewense') in 1874 but the parent plants were poorer and the results less spectacular; now in 1901 (both dates from *R. Soc. Notes* Hybrid Register of 1926; Bean differs) Loder made systematic use of his material in three batches, twice with *R. griffithianum* as male parent giving 60-70 per cent success rate and once in reverse with only 12 per cent success. They first flowered in 1907 and continued after his death in 1920: many have been named, of which some of the finest are 'King George', the later flowering 'Venus' (the original plant came to Exbury) and 'Pink Diamond'. At a recent count 'Loderi' had won two FCCs, three AGMs and five AMs and to my mind, while I concede there may be too many named clones (I realise I am using the word 'clone' with historical accuracy but botanical inaccuracy: perhaps the word 'sibling' should be used more widely), it richly deserves the accolade of most decorated hybrid (W Magor RYB 1982-83) and represents something of an apogee in 19th century hybridization and indeed hybridization to date – and it has fragrance!

'Loderi' has been much used for further hybridization. Within the grex there is 'Princess Marina' ('King George' x 'Sir Edmund'), and 'Olga' ('Pink Diamond' x 'King George'; not to be confused with Slocock's 'Olga'), and the $F_2$ cross made at Townhill, 'Julie', the nearest to a yellow Loderi. 'Pink Diamond' produced 'Sunkist' ( x *griffithianum*), 'White Lady' ('Halopeanum' x), 'Ruthelma' and 'H. Whitner' (x 'Cornish Cross'), the latter named after the gardener. In other crosses the exact clone is unspecified: one of the finest whites is 'Snow Queen' ('Halopeanum' x 'Loderi'), a plant of which I am particularly fond; 'Halopeanum' was also used (x *thomsonii*) for 'Gem' and 'Leonardslee Brilliant'. Other members of the family have also raised or registered some Loderi crosses, notably 'Seagull' (x *sutchuenense*, Lady Loder), 'Mrs C. Whitner' ('Snow Queen' x 'Sir Edmund', Sir Giles), 'Cretonne' ('Barclayi' x 'Loderi', Sir Giles) and 'Sarita Loder' (*griersonianum* x 'Loderi', Col G H Loder). Finally, it is certainly no accident that one of the finest yak crosses, 'Seven Stars', is with 'Loderi' ('Sir Joseph Hooker' x *yakushimanum*, Crown Estate).

Now we must return to the nurserymen but first not to the hardy hybrids but rather the opposite extreme, the tender rhododendrons. This was the era of the glasshouse, or stovehouse as it was sometimes called, when plentiful labour tended vast quantities of bedding plants to be planted out each year in complicated patterns. They also tended a dazzling array of hothouse and indoor plants and the Vireyas and tender rhododendrons were extremely popular. The better known of these include 'Princess Alice' (*edgeworthii* x *ciliatum*, Veitch FCC 1862), 'Countess of Haddington' (*ciliatum* x *dalhousiae*, Parker FCC 1862), 'Countess of Sefton' (*edgeworthii* x 'Multiflorum', I Davies 1877), 'Lady Alice Fitzwilliam' (possibly *edgeworthii* x *ciliatum* or, less likely, *formosum*, Fisher FCC 1881) and 'Fragrantissimum' (*edgeworthii* x *formosum*, Rollisson FCC 1868). We shall return to tender hybrids in the 20th century and, of course, one man's tender is another man's hardy but by and large these are conservatory plants or at best plants for sheltered positions. What is notable about this list, I think, is the high proportion of FCCs, in part reflecting the premium put on scent in a largely unscented genus; it is also notable that every one has a different raiser or exhibitor – in this field, unlike Vireyas (Veitch) or hardy hybrids (Waterer) no one name dominated.

This is not to say that others did not try. Standish and Noble have already been discussed in detail and I think it fair to say that neither flourished in the same way after separating, and Noble's 'Prometheus', one of the better reds of the period ('Michael Waterer' x 'Monitor', the latter named after the 'ironclad' Union battleship), was propagated only in Harry White's day and was used as a parent (x 'Doncaster') of 'Madame de Bruin'. G Paul raised a whole series of *R. fortunei* hybrids, highly regarded by William Watson, but he is better known for the parent he used, 'Sir Charles Butler' (syn.

'Mrs Butler', widely thought to be a form of *fortunei* though J Street imputes hardy hybrid blood). This has often been used as a parent: for example, x 'Halopeanum' by Van Nes to produce the delightful 'Mrs A.T. de la Mare', the even better 'Admiral Piet Hein' and finally 'Van Nes Sensation', which in turn produced the spectacular Australian hybrid, 'Colehurst' (registered *fortunei* subsp. *discolor* Houlstonii Group x; though pollen parent might be 'Admiral Piet Hein' or unknown [cf. Cox ]). Paul is also remembered for 'Essex Scarlet', which having good colour and being late flowering has also been a useful parent, notably for the 'Elisabeth Hobbie' grex (x *forrestii* Repens Group).

Isaac Davies has already been mentioned in connection with 'Praecox'; he is probably also responsible for 'Stanley Davies' (1890), best known as the pollen parent of 'Britannia' (Van Nes). Ivery is remembered for 'Ivery's Scarlet' (incl. *arboreum* and *ponticum*, 1850), which we have at the top of the Home Wood. At the same date Cunningham of Edinburgh introduced another old stand-by, 'Cunningham's White' (*caucasicum* x *ponticum* var. *album*), a rhododendron of such versatility and hardiness, it tolerates cold, pollution and even some alkalinity; it is much used as rootstock for grafting in Germany, in preference to *R. ponticum*. Methven is another Scottish name that should not go unmentioned (for example the aptly named 'Leopardi', one of the earlier introductions to the USA). Another old rhododendron which is still popular for its unusual colour is 'Lord Roberts' (*catawbiense* x, Fromow 1900 [Bean] or Mason [Register]; the former took over part of the latter's nursery in 1894).

European hybridizers were also influential. Work on the continent spanned the same range from tender ('Suave', 'Sesterianum', 'Victorianum') to hardy and some of the latter are still common: I have already mentioned the lovely 'Boddaertianum' and 'Halopeanum' (a good parent); 'Fastuosum Flore Pleno' (*catawbiense* x *ponticum*, Francoisi pre-1846) is a versatile semi-double bluish mauve and 'Helene Schiffner' (*arboreum* x, Seidel FCC 1893) is one of my favourites, strikingly pure white. Two which are often linked are 'Prince Camille de Rohan' (*caucasicum* x, possibly incl. *maximum* and/or *arboreum*, raised Van Houtte [F Street] or Waelbrouck [Bean] int. Verschaffelt 1855 [Bean] or 1865 [Register]) and the darker 'Chevalier Felix de Sauvage' (*caucasicum* x, Sauvage *c*.1870); the latter was the pollen parent of 'Mrs G.W. Leak' (Koster, 1916 [Register] or later [Cox]) which, while definitely not my favourite, is much admired by visitors. We shall see more of these heavily blotched pinks in the next century. Finally, a few of Otto Schulz's crosses were named and put into commerce by Van Nes of Boskoop, notably 'Mrs A.M. Williams' and 'Queen Wilhelmina' (both *griffithianum* x, int. 1896); the latter was the seed parent (x 'Stanley Davies') of a number of Van Nes' stable, of which the finest is 'Britannia', in turn parent of 'Kluis Sensation' and 'Leo'. I do not think there are obvious generalizations to be made on the continental hybridizers though it is said they used *R. maximum* more for hardiness – the British liking the quicker turnover of generations available with *R. ponticum* and *R. catawbiense* – and they made much less use of *R. ponticum* as rootstock.

The number of generations, which were sometimes accelerated into as little as four years by grafting the seedling tops onto *R. ponticum*, as Standish & Noble did, meant the nurserymen could make maximum use of the proliferating characteristics of multiple crosses from a limited number of parents. Bean argues that they did not really achieve 'their aim of putting the glowing red of the best *R. arboreum* onto a late-flowering, hardy plant' because the 'blue basis to the flower' was never entirely absent. Purity of colour became more important: Gertrude Jekyll, for example, prized 'Bianchi' (named after an Italian motor car) for its *pure* pink; my grandfather and others of his generation eschewed magenta, that bluish tinge in red from *R. ponticum* and *R. catawbiense*.

I think finer reds came later with *R. griersonianum*: the greater 19th century achievement, and particularly that of the Waterers, lies in the deep red to purple range or those that have exploited the other characteristics, the flares, the blotches, the speckles; *R. arboreum* played little or no part in many of these. Where specific attribution has been made it is noted; otherwise the 'composite personality' to which G Donald Waterer refers (Bean Note) must suffice; the dates give some indication. At the lilac end of the spectrum is 'Lady Grey Egerton' (*catawbiense* x [or perhaps *maximum* x, Cox] A Waterer pre-1888), a colour apparently shown to good effect under canvas; it was used by Slocock as pollen parent for the beautiful 'Lavender Girl' (*fortunei* x). At the other extreme are 'Old Port' (*catawbiense* x, A Waterer before 1865; S&G indicates another in commerce in the USA, possibly *R. ponticum* x, deeper purple without blotch) and 'Cetewayo' (perhaps *ponticum* x, A Waterer before 1883); of the latter, J Russell wrote that 'a large bush has all the melancholy dignity of a superb prune mousse.' The most popular and striking purple is 'Purple Splendour' (*ponticum* x, incl. *catawbiense* and *maximum*, A Waterer II before 1900): with its sumptuous colouring, it really is the standard for these dark purples, as well as being the parent of that fine and unusual Reuthe hybrid, 'Sonata' (x *dicroanthum*). Another favourite of mine is 'Frank Galsworthy' (*ponticum* x, A Waterer), with its bold yellow flare, named after the flower painter brother of the novelist. One of the so-called 'ironclads' is 'Caractacus' (*catawbiense* x, A Waterer FCC 1865); Hosea II emigrated to Philadelphia and his father shipped 1,500 hybrids to exhibit in the 1876 Centennial Exhibition, doing much to popularize rhododendrons in general

and 'ironclads' in particular in the USA The Waterer links with the USA had started in about 1850 when Knap Hill sent plants for the Capitol House grounds (cf. Willson). One of their few obviously red *arboreum* crosses is 'Doncaster', a good compact red, popular in itself and as a parent, including four of the (*yakushimanum* x) Seven Dwarfs.

Moving away from the darker colours, 'Lady Clementine Mitford' (*maximum* x, A Waterer 1870) is a pale peach-pink, darker at the edges, and in 'Picotee' (probably *ponticum* x, A Waterer; not to be confused with Veitch's 'Picotee Roseum' FCC 1863), as the name suggests, the pink edging is more pronounced. Anthony I admired the blotched or spotted upper petal (mainly from *maximum*), which he thought gave form and substance: this type of orchidaceous-looking hybrid continued in the next century but the finest in this century and perhaps of them all, and certainly the most famous 19th century Knap Hill hybrid, is 'Sappho' (possibly *maximum* x [S&G] or 'Smithii Album' x [Cox], before 1867 though the name was used earlier for a rosy crimson hybrid).

Moving to the Bagshot branch, again there was a fine range of hardy hybrids along much the same lines. 'Chionoides' (*ponticum* x, possibly incl. *maximum*, J Waterer pre-1886 [Register] or 1865 [Bean]) is a reliable late white – F Street's favourite white in fact – and 'Mum' (*maximum* x, 1897, very near to 'Maximum Album') is another, though less common

*The original plant of* R. *'Pink Pearl' photographed at Bagshot around 1890 with Charlie Rose, the gardener entrusted with its care*

now. 'Joseph Whitworth' (*ponticum* x, J Waterer pre-1864 [Bean]) has been described as 'purple lake' or 'deep maroon', a colour more fashionable then than later though the trend now, with so many new hybrids, must be towards greater catholicity: plummy colours and plummy accents may finally converge! Two of the first really late-flowering *R. arboreum* hybrids, 'John Waterer' and 'Mrs John Waterer' (probably incl. *R. ponticum* and *R. catawbiense*) were introduced by them in 1855 (Bean, who gives this early date and possible parentage, calls the Register entry

'certainly erroneous' but he is mis-reading for 'John Walter' on the line above!); they may be siblings. One of the few occasions when floral fiction did follow genealogical fact was with 'Donald Waterer', which is 'Alice' x 'Gomer Waterer' – all three good rhododendrons. The latter, made by John II before 1900, is a *catawbiense* x, according to J Street including 'Madame Carvalho' (*catawbiense* x, like a white form of *catawbiense*, J Waterer 1866) and *griffithianum*; the former, a *griffithianum* x, might be a seedling of 'Pink Pearl'.

This brings us to the most famous

hardy hybrid of them all, 'Pink Pearl' itself, raised by John II and first exhibited by Gomer at the Temple Show in 1896, winning an AM on its introduction the next year and an FCC in 1900. Its parentage is generally now described as 'George Hardy' x 'Broughtonii', following the note in Gomer's papers, but 'Cynthia' has also been posited as the putative seed parent, the two having some similarities. The compact habit would support the former as father but against that, 'Broughtonii' does flower rather early compared to 'Pink Pearl': we may never know (but see below). In any event, it has been extremely popular, as well as commercially named and represents something of a summit in hardy hybrids in general and *R. griffithianum* crosses in particular. The one notable characteristic of *R. griffithianum* which eludes it, scent, is present in its sport 'Mother of Pearl' (int. 1925): this plant – named for its colour rather than its relationship! – has not proved quite as popular as its famous parent, though it apparently looks good under electric light and my grandfather, for one, while noting that 'comparisons are odious', preferred the latter and thought it would replace the former (JRHS LXV, 1940).

To this writer it has sometimes seemed that the Waterers did dominate the hardy hybrids of the latter part of the 19th century; certainly Millais, in Volume I of *Rhododendrons* (1917), listed 484 hardy hybrids raised in Europe and at that time obtainable of which 292 came from the two Waterer firms. It is arbitrary to make a divide at the end of the century, for hybridization continued, but I think it true to say that there was a change. Nurserymen, particularly in Holland, built on 'Pink Pearl' or looked to other lines – the Hooker introduction *campylocarpum* for yellow, for example. The great garden owners used mainly the old Himalayan rhododendrons and continued to do so but, while there was some new collecting in the latter part of the century, particularly by French missionaries or officials (*augustinii*, for example, introduced in 1900 and providing a whole new range of blue), it was in the early part of this century that they were to be faced by an unprecedented flood of new species. 'Loderi' and 'Pink Pearl' do represent ends and new beginnings.

The problem for the writer also changes. This has been an exercise in gathering facts: who crossed what with what to produce what and when. On any given plant I have found at least one of the secondary source books, or compendia (Bean, Cox, S&G, Register) differs on at least one of the variables! I have generally taken a majority vote or, in the case of dates, I have tended to go for the earliest. I am well aware that the reason was often due to lack of records or deliberate secrecy, though some apparent contradictions are less easily explicable – Luscombe, for example, is called John in one part of Bean (p.824), Thomas in another (p.872) and 'G.' in the Register! I do not feel I have always yielded Ockham's Razor to such a Gordian knot particularly effectively, thus the preponderance of 'p-words' – perhaps, probably, possibly, putative. We were recently visited by an eminent scientist from Kunming, Xiao Tiaojiang, who has been working on genotyping camellia species. From this he can ascertain parentage, *including* whether the role is male or female: while this is still in its relative infancy, I hope that by the next Jubilee Edition some of the genealogies will be more accessible to cytology than they were to my research. In the end, of course, some secrets may never be yielded up and, besides, the flower's the thing.

## Looking towards the 20th century

In the 20th century the records are better though not perfect but the main problem is the sheer number of plays and players – dozens of hybridists facing hundreds of species and making thousands of plants in ever increasing dizzy complexity. And it is that which I shall deal with next time.

Towards the end of the 19th century it seemed to some as if not much remained to be discovered; at the beginning of the 20th it seemed as if the supply of new species would never stop. Sir Joseph Hooker, introducer of the first wave, correctly forecast the second when he prophesied in 1890, 'the genus will probably exceed all previous estimates the Chinese empire may contain more species than all the rest of the world beside' (quoted in B L Urquhart): in the second decade of the century, 312 new species were added, more than the total number described until 1900. To stem this flood Sir Isaac Bayley Balfour hurriedly erected his taxonomic dam: this was meant to be flexible and temporary but proved so popular with gardeners that it soon became codified – some would say ossified – into a system. We have now had the great revision of 1980 and another is in process: to 'lumpers' and 'splitters' alike I can do no better than quote one of Sir Joseph Hooker's first biographers, Leonard Huxley, on the subject, 'Man had not found what Nature indeed had denied, a common standard for differentiation between species, varieties and transitional forms; nor an independent basis for that abstraction, the specific type, so useful as a label, so dangerous as a determinant.'

Because the flow of plants has opened out into a flood-plain, it is hard to follow a single line, though several key species were used again and again. To *R. fortunei* and *R. griffithianum* were now added *R. discolor* and *R. decorum*, the former much used by my grandfather because of its late flowering; *R. calophytum* produced some fine early flowering hybrids. *R. thomsonii* remained popular for red and *R. campylocarpum* became so for yellow, as did the new arrivals *R. wardii* and *R. lacteum*; *R. williamsianum* was much used for smaller hybrids – 'none more lovely than it, but some making better plants for the average garden' (Bean; most of this section is drawn from Bean, by the way, a source far too under-used in the literature). *R. neri-iflorum*, *R. haematodes*, *R. forrestii* Repens Group and *R. sanguineum* subsp *didymum* produced most of the smaller reds and *R. dicroanthum* introduced orange (and passed on its double calyx). *R. elliottii* and *R. facetum (eriogynum)* were used for later-flowering reds but it is *R. griersonianum* which was king of its day – 155 hybrids and 48 awards in the 1969 *Handbook* Pt II, a record probably still only surpassed by *R. yakushimanum*, which came into its own after the Second World War. *R. auriculatum* was used for lateness.

The stream – to continue this over-used metaphor – had now divided into two clearly defined parts, lepidotes and elepidotes, with far more crosses, even proportionately, among the latter; Bean notes that lepidotes 'are less indulgent to the hybridiser . . . and seemingly unpredictable,' which he ascribed to their 'greater botanical diversity, and the prevalence of polyploidy' (cf. E K Janaki Ammal's article and chart in RYB 1950 ). Across the great divide, then, *R. augustinii* was much used for blue. *R. moupinense* produced some good smaller hybrids, as did the more tender Ciliicalyx-Alliance (*ciliatum, burmanicum, valentianum*); *R. fletcherianum* has had more use for dwarf yellows in recent years (I note *R. fletcherianum*, *R. thayerianum* and *R. websterianum* have all had their 'i's restored after an impassioned plea by Professor W Stearn at the Berlin conference – the 'i's had it, as it were!), as have other smaller species such

as *R. ludlowii* and *R. hanceanum* and *R. keiskei* (of the last two, especially Nanum Group and 'Yaku Fairy' respectively; I am told some believe Nanum may be a hybrid). Finally my favourites – *R. cinnabarinum* was crossed with *R. maddenii* and then back-crossed with *R. cinnabarinum* or Concatenans Group once or even twice; *R. cinnabarinum* (and Concatenans) was also crossed with *R. yunnanense*. 'Loderi' was of course the most popular hybrid used.

So there you have it, the main lineaments of inter-war crosses and indeed not only were surprisingly few species used surprisingly often but the older Himalayan introductions were of enduring importance – 'Naomi', 'Carita', 'Yvonne', 'Lady Chamberlain', 'Lady Rosebery' and 'Lady Berry' are all from Hooker introductions and *R. fortunei*.

It was to the Cornish gardens that many of these seeds first came; they and other great gardens helped fund the expeditions and to both patrons and explorers of all periods we owe a debt of gratitude . Two of the loveliest of all commemorate sad and horrible ends: Lady Dalhousie of *R. dalhousiae*, whose husband as Governor-General of India had been so helpful to Hooker, died of seasickness on the way home; Père Soulié, who first discovered *R. souliei*, was tortured to death in the Tibetan uprising of 1905. On a more cheerful note, in Lionel's case it is rather nice to think that where his great-grandfather had made a fortune from the transmission of specie, he spent one on the collection of species.

The main thing was and still is that it should be fun. J C Williams, the grand old man of his generation, advised Collingwood Ingram (considering his longevity perhaps the grand old man of his), 'Start hybridizing rhododendrons. It's the greatest fun. You get ten, fifteen, perhaps even twenty years of pleasurable anticipation, and only *one* day of disappointment – the day your seedlings open their first flowers!' (in Collingwood Ingram, RYB 1967).

And the same thing, though with rather more emphasis on a serious, scientific line of approach, was written by F C Puddle, 'I am personally convinced that indiscriminate matings are of little value, and it is only by a close study of pedigree and a scientific application of that knowledge that we can make real progress step by step towards our ideal. Even then we are speculating on possibilities, for hybridisation does not necessarily result in an equal mixture of the two parents, but rather a re-grouping of the characters derived from them. We rarely obtain our desires in one mating, so we go on from generation to generation ever seeking that elusive ideal, 'Perfection'.' (RYB 1933).

Or as Browning wrote,

'Ah, but a man's reach should
  exceed his grasp,
Or what's a heaven for?'

## Bibliography

BEAN, W J (1970) 8th edition. *Trees and Shrubs Hardy in the British Isles*, ed. Desmond Clarke; referred to throughout as 'Bean'. John Murray, London

BOWERS, C G (1960). *Rhododendrons and Azaleas*. Macmillan, New York

COX, P (1973). *Dwarf Rhododendrons*. London
(1985) *The Smaller Rhododendrons*. Batsford, London
(1990) rev.ed. *The Larger Rhododendron Species*. Batsford, London

COX, P & K (1988). *Encyclopedia of Rhododendron Hybrids*, Batsford, London – 'P & K Cox'

DAVIDIAN, H (1982-92). *The Rhododendron Species* Vols. I-III Batsford, London - 'Davidian'

VAN GELDEREN, D & VAN HOEY SMITH, J (1992). *Rhododendrons*. Batsford, London

HUXLEY, L (1918). *Life & Letters of Sir JD Hooker* Vols. I- II. London

KNELLER, M (1995). *The Book of the Rhododendron*

PHILLIPS, C E Lucas & BARBER, P (rev.ed.1979). *The Rothschild Rhododendrons*. Cassell, London

RUSSELL, J (1960). *Rhododendrons at Sunningdale*. Sunningdale Nurseries, Windlesham

SALLEY, H and GREER, H ( 2nd edition 1992). *Rhododendrons Hybrids,* Batsford, London – 'S&G'

STREET, F (1954). *Hardy Rhododendrons,* Wm Collins, London – 'F Street'
(1965).*Rhododendrons*, London – 'F Street'

STREET, F J (1987). *Rhododendrons Their Care and Cultivation* Century Hutchinson, London – 'J Street'

URQUHART, B L (1958). *The Rhododendron* Vol.I

WATSON, W (1912). *Rhododendrons and Azaleas,* in Present Day Gardening Series. London & Edinburgh

WILLSON, E J (1989). *Nurserymen to the World*

FLETCHER, H R (1958) The International Rhododendron Register, RHS, London – 'Register'
(1969). *The Rhododendron Handbook* Part II

(Hybrids). RHS, London

(1980). *The Rhododendron Handbook* (Species). RHS, London

BARTRUM, D, BERRISFORD, J, LA CROIX, I, KESSELL, M. all called *Rhododendrons and Azaleas*, WAKEFIELD, G. *Rhododendrons*, GALLE, F. *Azaleas*, LEACH, D. *Rhododendrons of the World* and TAPLEY, M. *Rhododendrons in New Zealand.*

*The Gardeners' Chronicle* vols.XI, XII, XV, XVIII, XXXV (1879, 1881, 1882, 1904)

*Journal of Horticulture and Cottage Gardener* Vol.21 (1871)

*Journal of the Royal Horticultural Society* Vols. 25, 65, 72, 76, 81, 83, 89 and *The Garden* Vols. 101, 112, 120 (1900- 1, 1940, 1947, 1951, 1956, 1958, 1964, 1976, 1987, 1995) – ' JRHS'

*The Rhododendron Society Notes*, Vols. I-III, 1916-31 – '*R.Soc.Notes*'

*Year Book of The Rhododendron Association*, 1929-39, *The Rhododendron Year Book* 1946-53, *The Rhododendron and Camellia Year Book* 1954-71, *Rhododendrons with Magnolias and Camellias,*1972-88/9 and *Rhododendrons with Camellias and Magnolias* 1990-95 all referred to throughout for simplification as 'RYB'

Private papers and correspondence at the Rothschild Archive, London, by kind permission of the Archivist – 'RAL'.

LIONEL DE ROTHSCHILD *is the son of Edmund and grandson of the older Lionel. He has grown up at Exbury and all the plants he writes about have been familiar to him from his earliest childhood. As well as writing on gardens he is a keen garden photographer*

# CHAPTER 11

# HYBRIDS IN THE UNITED STATES OF AMERICA

## PAT HALLIGAN

He was a big man, powerfully built, standing in his blue denims, braces and bow tie amid a myriad rhododendrons. It may have been his thick Norwegian accent that caught the attention or his enthusiasm for growing and breeding rhododendrons, but Halfdan Lem was a man whose passion was in the hunt: a treasure hunt of sorts, for the little gems that keep popping up among the multitude of seedlings in the garden of every hybridizer.

During World War II Lem corresponded with Fred Rose, a gardener of Townhill in England, and, because of the bombing raids, Rose sent Lem much rhododendron material to ensure its preservation. How lucky we are that Rose was in an area subject to German bombing! From one of Rose's seed came 'Anna', Lem's favourite parent and from 'Anna' came 'fine stuffs' as Lem would say – from just six seedlings of one cross came five unsatisfactory plants and . . . 'Lem's Cameo' (see figure 17) which he called

'Cameo' but had to affix his name because the name 'Cameo' had already been used.

With his fellow hybridizers in the Rum-Dum Club, Lem would engage in energetic debate on every aspect of rhododendrons. The club was an exclusive group with Bill Whitney, Lester Brandt, Hjalmer Larson, all professional growers and hybridizers, a tight-knit bunch who kept their secrets of growing and breeding close to their chests. And indeed why not since they were all selling seeds and seedlings to the general public? All, that is, except Lem who was only too happy to share his knowledge with others. He was a fair man and a friend recalls that when Lem was helping a young mother to select the one plant that she could afford on her budget, a group of well-known and well-heeled purchasers arrived to place what would amount to a large order. They expected him to drop everything and wait on them but Lem told them to wait because 'she deserves just as much consideration as anyone else'. And, in the spirit of fairness, if he was out of a required plant, he would always substitute a better plant than the one asked for without telling the customer. Lem would smile and say, 'I can't wait to see his face when he sees it bloom for the first time.'

In my experience Lem characterizes the type of person hybridizing today, full of wonder, eager to exchange views on rhododendrons with others and . . . a little bit quirky!

Lem passed away and his hybrids were left to another generation, but he passed on his enthusiasm and knowledge through innumerable letters to all manner of rhododendron lovers all over the world. Current members of the Northwest Hybridisers' Group can remember getting their first rhododendrons from Lem along with advice and, of course, that infectious enthusiasm.

**The Northwest**

Going back in time to the introduction of rhododendrons to the Northwest we see James Barto and Mrs A C U Berry as unsung heroes. Although few of their hybrids survive today, their aggressive introduction of new plants from England and from the pre-World War II plant explorers set the stage for future hybridizers. As Del James said, 'In all my visits to gardens in Oregon, Washington and California I have yet to see a garden that did not have plants from Barto.' After the war others such as Del James, Rudolph Henny

and Endre Ostbo took up his search for new material.

This new generation of rhododendron lovers found enough company to warrant some sort of club and so, in 1944, The American Rhododendron Society was founded in the very heart of rhododendron country. Soon rhododendron breeders such as Lester Brandt, Hjalmer Larson, Ted Van Veen, Roy Clark, Ben Lancaster, Robert Bovee and Bill Whitney were coming up with a rainbow of new plants. Most of these have been lost but a few of them are household names even today.

All was bliss in this mild and nurturing climate of the Northwest until the winter of 1950 when people were put on the alert. But it was not until that fateful night early in November 1955 that the full power of nature's might would be etched into every grower's consciousness. After a mild Indian Summer the temperature plummeted from a balmy 21°C (70°F) to a frigid −18°C (0°F) overnight. Death came with a white face and all those pampered beauties met a brown and inglorious end. It was a wake-up call to all horticulturists in the Northwest. No longer was it enough to come up with pretty plants; they had to be tough too. But the great flurry of hybridizing in the Northwest that had marked the late 1940s and early 1950s was slowly petering out. Some of the major hybridizers continued to produce new hybrids but few new people were there to take up the baton as the older ones faded away. Hybridization in the Northwest entered a period of hiatus in which only a few people were active. Not that these new hybridizers were insignificant. Great things came from the garden of Ned Broken-brough who worked extensively with Lem's hybrids and continues his work even today. Also Jack Lofthouse, salesman extra-ordinaire, who produced tremendous excitement among potential hybridizers. Other important figures include Joe Davis, Jim Elliott, Art Wright, Frank Mossman and Harold Greer.

In 1959 the FCC form of *Rhododendron yakushimanum* arrived in the North-west and before long everyone was 'yakking' everything in sight so that 'Yaku This' and 'Yaku That' started showing up on the plant registration lists. Funny thing though – all the plants looked the same! Nice, but all the same. Only now are we seeing second and third generation 'yak' hybrids starting to sport rich colours.

Warren Berg started a one-man intro-duction and hybridizing boom all on his own. An airline pilot, he was able to use his perks with the airline to introduce important new species forms, with which he hybridized, using especially *R. keiskei* 'Yaku Fairy' to produce many of the best new hybrids.

The seminal event which produced the second great wave of hybridizing in the Northwest was the inception in the late 1970s of the Northwest Hybridisers Group. For the first years Elsie Watson hosted those meetings. Breeders are differ-ent now since, instead of the closed group

of professionals of the 1940s and 1950s, we now see an open exchange of ideas and materials between breeders, insiders and beginners alike. Rhododendron breeding has been taken over by amateurs. Even the professional growers are amateur breeders and I think that this change in attitude has contributed enormously to the present day explosion of hybridizing in the Northwest. We are seeing tremendous new things from the gardens of Frank Fujioka, Clint Smith, Elsie Watson, Lloyd Newcomb, Dave Balint, Dan Bones, Roy Thompson, David Goheen and many others.

I too am a hybridizer and, like so many others, owe much to fellow breeders. To give just one example: two parents which have infused their blood into many of my plants are unnamed hybrids which Halfdan Lem gave to Lloyd and Eddie Newcomb. They subsequently gave them to me and I made good use of them. Hybridizing weaves a tangled web of both plant lineages and friends.

## Eastern States

Rhododendron hybridizing began in the United States before 1860 with Samuel Parsons of Flushing, New York, who pro-duced a number of *R. catawbiense* hybrids including 'Parson's Grandiflorum', 'Presi-dent Lincoln' and 'Abraham Lincoln' which, with his other hybrids, are bona fide antiques and deserve to be grown for their historical value alone. Besides, these hybrids are not bad plants and some are really tough survivors.

Many years passed and America's lack of interest in breeding rhododendrons was profound until Charles Dexter, a patrician of inexhaustible energy, came along. From among his crosses came 'Scintillation', for years the favourite hybrid in the East. After his death, even more remarkable was the flurry of activity on the part of Anthony Consolini, John Wister and many enthusiasts in the Sandwich Club to catalogue, test, introduce and further breed his creations.

By the 1930s several hybridizers were hard at work including Joseph Gable, an unsophisticated nurseryman in bib overalls, and Guy Nearing, a man for all seasons and survivor extraordinaire. Together they formed an unlikely collaboration resulting in 'Cadis' and the important parent 'Catalgla' by the former, and lepidote gems 'Mary Fleming' and 'Ramapo' by the latter: but they never did find the perfect red.

Tony Shamarello's parents brought their tradition in the nursery trade from sunny Italy to the bitter cold continental climate of Cleveland, Ohio. The killer winter of 1939 convinced Tony that hardier rhododendrons were needed and he started breeding rock-hardy plants. This objective has since been taken up by David Leach who has introduced a United Nations of hybrids. Joining the party were Weldon Delp, Lanny Pride and Edmund Mezitt. In the far reaches of Canada, Dick Steele and A W Smith have sought to push rhododendrons to the realms of the Northern Lights.

On the East Coast Gus Mehlquist has used his background in genetics to perform rhododendron magic, while Edmond Amateis showed what it really meant to produce a few good hybrids. Other honourable East Coasters, including Donald Hardgrove, Paul Vossberg and Warren Baldsiefen, have enriched many a garden with their creations. Hank Schannen, Nathaniel Hess, Dorothy Knippenberg and others are busily at work even as we read. Meanwhile Augie Kehr, Olin Holsomback and Russ and Velma Haag are leading the way deep in the heart of Dixie. All these names point to the fact that hybridizing in the East is truly vibrant with energy.

Azalea breeding was pioneered by B Y Morrison and Joseph Gable, soon to be followed by Fred Galle and Augie Kehr in the Southeast, Henry Skinner at the National Arboretum, Robert Gartrell in New Jersey, Peter Girard and Tony Shamarello in the Great Lakes region, and Polly Hill on the picturesque island of Martha's Vineyard. In the warmth of California Julius Nuccio and Howard Kerrigan have been creating evergreen azaleas especially suited to Mediterranean climes. Recently the geographic boundaries of azaleas have been pushed by Susan Moe and Harold Pellett in Minnesota and A W Smith in Canada.

## California

Because of the climate, hybridizing in

California has taken quite a different turn. Beneath the swaying palms subtropical rhododendrons waft their intoxicating perfume. First appreciating that scent in the 1950s and 1960s were Maurice Sumner, whose 'Mi Amor' and 'Owen Pearce' are still loved by *R. maddenii* growers, and Paul Bowman whose 'Else Frye' is one of my favourites. Soon, Jack Evans was coming up with great new things of his own, and when you add more recent Californian hybridizers, including Bill Moyles and others, you can find yourself surrounded by a distinctive and regional rhododendron flora.

Bob Scott carried on the work of the pioneers to produce *R. maddenii* hybrids in colours once considered unthinkable. Bob contracted multiple sclerosis and was unable to care for his plants. Paul Molinari once explained to me how he and Hadley Osborn were able to help their friend to continue breeding rhododendrons, despite his disability, by acting as his hands and feet. Such acts of co-operation and kindness are not uncommon among rhododendron lovers. Today Paul Molinari is acting as a one-man rhododendron clearing house for Californian hybrids.

From even further afield are the Vireyas and in California Peter Sullivan and Jack Evans began importing these brightly coloured tropicals in the 1960s. Peter Sullivan at the Strybing Arboretum bred Vireyas in earnest and through his generosity with both plant material and insight the baton was passed on to Bill Moynier of Los Angeles. Suddenly vividly coloured flowers began to appear from Middle Earth. Yes, they really do grow Vireyas outdoors in Los Angeles which is fortunate since you certainly will not have much luck growing regular rhododendrons there!

Bill Moyles conducts a special American Rhododendron Society seed exchange devoted to Vireyas and E White Smith of the Rhododendron Species Foundation publishes the journal *Vireya Vine*. These services link a small but dedicated coterie of Vireya breeders. Peter Schick and John Dulac have been key distributors of Vireya material from Australia and New Zealand while Dick Cavender, Bill Moyles and Jim Gerdemann have been busily creating new variations. (See Chapter 7).

Hybridizing in California illustrates just how diverse is rhododendron growing in the United States. We breed just about all types, from the lush beauties of the Northwest to the tough plants of the Northeast and from the subtropical *R. maddenii* hybrids and tropical Vireyas of California to the disease-resistant rhododendrons and azaleas of the Southeast. The great plains, the western deserts and the intermountain West remain to be colonized by rhododendrons, although individuals in unlikely places such as Oklahoma and Arizona are testing the possibilities. One area of breeding that has been lacking in the United States is the Section Choniastrum. We could take the example of Peter Valder of Australia and try these plants in Southern California and the Deep South. The plants are pretty weird so growing them should be an adventure. And is that not what breeding is all about?

**Acknowledgements**

I would like to thank Gwen Bell, Clint Smith, Bill Moyles and Austin Kennell for their help with this article.

PAT HALLIGAN *has a doctorate in plant ecology, hybridizes lepidote rhododendrons in Washington State and is active in the American Rhododendron Society. He is Chairman of their Ratings Committee*

# CHAPTER 12

# DECIDUOUS AZALEAS: THE HYBRIDS

# RENAUD DE KERCHOVE

Until recently azaleas were a separate genus, but they are now classified as a subgenus of *Rhododendron* called *Pentanthera* (see chapter 2).

The hardy deciduous azaleas were mostly derived from North American species *(R. calendulaceum, R. periclymenoides, R. prinophyllum, R. viscosum , R. canescens* and *R. speciosum* syn. *R. flammeum)*, introduced into Britain in the 18th or early 19th centuries, but also from one other species *(R. luteum*, the Pontiac azalea), introduced from the Caucasus in 1792. Two other asiatic species, not introduced until the mid-19th century, later played their part in the process. They are *R. molle* (1823), once known as *Azalea sinensis,* from China and *R. japonicum* (1861), once known as *A. mollis,* from Japan. This change of name has caused considerable confusion. In 1850, another North American species, *R. occidentale,* was also used by Veitch (UK) as a parent for a distinct group of hybrids.

The history of hybrid deciduous azaleas goes back to the early 19th century.

The first plants to be sold commercially were probably different forms of the wild species from North America and the Caucasus already mentioned.

## Ghent Azaleas

It appears that in Ghent Mortier, a baker by trade and a great plant enthusiast, had by 1825 started to cross the available North American species mentioned above with *R. luteum,* already available. His genius lay in retarding the flowering season of the early blooming species whose petals were susceptible to frost damage by crossing them with the later-flowering species. These hybrids were named 'Mortieri' by Sweet in 1831.

In 1834 Mortier sold his azaleas to Louis Verschaffelt of Roygem, who continued to cross the better cultivars In the *Annals of the Royal Agricultural and Botanical Society of Ghent* for 1846 Spae told the early history of the Mortieri azaleas and listed 12 cardinal varieties. In 1847 Morren added eight more. He claimed that the azalea nectar was poisonous,

*Louis Van Houtte, the great Belgian nurseryman. His catalogues are an invaluable source for research into the early deciduous azalea hybrids*

noting that some of Xenophon's troops had died after eating honey from *R. luteum*.

In 1849 Louis Van Houtte bought 25 of Mortier's cultivars from Verschaffelt, and later, in 1873, he bought another collection of six hardy azaleas from Louis Hellebuyck. In Van Houtte's opinion, Mortier, Verschaffelt and Hellebuyck, and one other, Van Cassel, were the most important hybridizers.

In 1855 Charles Lemaire published a list featuring 16 cultivars. They were pink with yellow tinges on the upper petals but none are known to have survived.

Ambroise Verschaffelt's catalogue of 1855 listed for the first time 11 double-flowered cultivars, including 'Bartholo Lazzari', 'Graf van Meran', and 'Narcissiflora', of which more later, acquired in Germany from J Rinz, who had been working on double-flowers since 1834. Some of the old German hybrids are still available. The first mention of 'Ghent' azaleas instead of 'Mortieri' appears in the same catalogue.

Meanwhile, in the middle of the 19th century, at Knap Hill in England, Anthony Waterer, father and son, began to use the Caucasian-American and East Asian species. None of their hybrids, except 'Nancy Waterer' (*R. molle* x *R. cal-*

*Ambroise Verschaffelt who bought Mortier's azaleas in
1834. In Van Houtte's opinion, one of the most
important azalea hybridizers*

*endulaceum*), was ever named. However it is still listed as a Ghent cultivar and is available (see below).

About this time, J R Gowen, the friend of Lord Carnarvon of Highclere Castle, was making the same crosses as Mortier had done. 'Altaclarense' (*sic.*), described in 1842, was a cross between *R. molle* and *R. viscosum* (syn. *R. viscosepalum*, pink-edged white flowers and yellow stamens). It has disappeared, but must have been close to 'Daviesii' dating from the same period, with the same parentage and still available. The cultivar now described as 'Altaclarense' (or more correctly, 'Altaclerense') is quite different, a soft yellow,

and does not fall into any recognized category. There is some doubt about the origin of another English cultivar, 'Unique', (*R. molle* x *R. calendulaceum*) still in commerce. Classified as a Ghent, it was in cultivation by 1864, and is variously attributed to Standish & Noble and to Anthony Waterer.

In The Netherlands, 'Hollandia', another cross between *R. luteum* and *R. japonicum*, was produced in 1902 by P M Koster.

The name 'Hardy Ghent' was proposed for the group in 1870 by Louis Van Houtte. The group was described as hardy to distinguish them from the *R. simsii* hybrids, the evergreen indica azaleas for indoor cultivation, which were the other great horticultural speciality of the Ghent region. He preferred this name to 'Azalea Americana'. Other pseudo-botanic names such as x *gandavense* were not generally acceptable for a range of hybrids stemming from such a large number of species. Both the Dutch and the Germans, however, always used the name 'Pontica azaleas'.

Recently more than 1,000 cultivars and 500 colour descriptions have been recorded by the Belgian, Albert De Raedt. It is probable that far too many seedlings were named in the 19th century.

In 1875 L Duval described the Ghent azaleas in these words: 'These beautiful plants have seen their star pale before the arrival of a newcomer, which possesses even more of the same qualities.' This newcomer was the group known as the Mollis azaleas (see below). Nevertheless, although the Mollis hybrids are earlier and have larger flowers appearing before the leaves, in my opinion their leggy habit after a number of years produces an ugly plant.

Between the two wars the cultivation of hardy Ghent azaleas was abandoned. In 1944 there was a concerted attempt at conservation in The Netherlands. The Botanical Garden Association in Boskoop made great efforts to trace Ghent cultivars, but succeeded in finding only 80 names corresponding with even fewer hybrids. Of these, 26 hybrids, comprising all possible colours and flowering periods, were selected. But by 1954 few Boskoop growers had more than 12 available, and  H J Grootendorst predicted an economic future for no more than perhaps 20 to 25.

In *The Garden,* Journal of The Royal Horticultural Society, November 1983, Archie Skinner, citing their elegance, perfume, autumn colour and charm, regretted the lack of present-day interest. He had 27 Ghent varieties in his collection at Sheffield Park in Sussex, formed for the National Council for the Conservation of Plants and Gardens (NCCPG). The interest of some Belgian gardeners was stimulated by this information and today more than 100 of the older hardy Ghents have been traced. One Belgian nurseryman (César Dekeyzer, of Lochristi) is prepared to propagate any old named cultivar offered to him.

**Mollis Azaleas**

The so-called Mollis azaleas are botanically speaking crosses between forms of *R. japonicum* and forms of *R. japonicum* x *R. molle.* They are also sometimes referred to as *R.* x *kosterianum.*

Louis Van Houtte, enterprising as ever, was the first to recognize the potential offered by these plants and he purchased in The Netherlands a number of cultivars which displayed considerable variation during the blooming season. In 1870 he selected and named about 20 cultivars, among which were 'Isabella Van Houtte', 'W. E. Gumbleton', 'Thérèse' (syn. 'Afterglow' or 'Pink Beauty'),

'Alphonse Lavallée', 'Comte de Gomer', all are still listed.

Oswald de Kerchove, President of the Royal Agricultural and Botanical Society of Ghent, contributed a brief history of deciduous azaleas and notes on their cultivation in the *Revue d'Horticulture Belge et Étrangère* (3. 1877). This contained an illustration of 'Comte de Gomer', a cultivar bearing bright pink flowers with orange flecks. It is still found in specialist catalogues (Esfeld, Wezelenburg).

Fred De Conink, of Ghent, had been the first to cross *R. japonicum* with *R. molle*, but in 1890 he sold all his stock to M Koster and Sons of Boskoop, in The Netherlands, where all future development took place. The first eight seedlings were marketed by Koster in 1892, including 'Hortulanus H. Witte', 'Hugo Koster' and 'Frans van der Bom' (all still available).

The Boskoop Tree and Plant Exhibition Association listed 45 cultivars, 26 Belgian and nine Dutch, but of these nine only 'J. C. van Tol' (1890) was still in cultivation in Boskoop in 1954. The origin of this hybrid merits special attention. Its parents are unknown but must consist of red and yellow species. Mendel's law applies to this hybrid, for when red is dominant, three-quarters of the progeny will be red and one-quarter yellow when selfed. The second generation reds gave two-thirds resembling the original 'J. C. van Tol'. This led M Koster and Sons to discover that by selective breeding they could produce progeny more or less uniform in colour, and therefore could market seedling azaleas true to colour. Many other growers also sold unnamed seeds and young plants simply as 'azaleas op kleur' (azaleas to colour).

In 1899 the Kersbergen brothers bought large quantities (perhaps 36,000) of Hoogendijk azaleas and even more from other Boskoop growers. They selected those of fine colour producing clusters of 14 large flowers. Around 30 of these plants were still in cultivation in 1954. Being strong-growing, easy to pack and transport, they supplanted the Belgian hybrids.

H J Grootendorst, in his *Rhododendron en Azaleas* (1954), lists some of the best examples of *Azalea mollis* as 'Christopher Wren' (large orange-yellow flowers), 'Hamlet' (deep salmon with red tints), and 'Winston Churchill' (deep red-orange). All are still listed.

Mollis azaleas mostly bloom in the first fortnight of May. They are not scented and have large, short-tubed flowers, the stamens of which do not project beyond the petals as do those of the hardy Ghents. They are strong-growing to begin with, easy to pack and transport but after a time their habit deteriorates.

### Rustica Azaleas

The Rustica azaleas (see figure 19) differed from the Ghent azaleas because of their double blooms, more compact form and early flowering season. They forced well, flowering before the leaves, and therefore found great favour with the public.

Charles Vuylsteke was the first to show these hybrids at the Ghent Floralies in 1888. He had established himself in Lochristi in 1882 and had a flourishing export business to England. H J Grootendorst has commented that Vuylsteke marketed many new hybrids produced by other breeders and the Rustica azaleas originated with Louis de Smet who had died in 1887. Vuylsteke did not know how De Smet came by these plants, but it is likely that they had *R. japonicum* blood. Of his 19 hybrids, some were so alike that only their flowering date distinguished them; five were white.

## Occidentale Azaleas

*Rhododendron occidentale* was first imported into Europe from western North America by William Lobb for James Veitch in 1850 (1851?). The species, perhaps the most beautiful of all in nature, first flowered in Britain in 1857. Anthony Waterer Senior crossed *R. occidentale* and *R. molle* in 1870 and called the plant *R.* 'Albicans'. It had almost white, green-speckled flowers, a strong perfume and flowered in June. According to Desmond Clarke, it appears to have been lost. The Occidentale hybrids now in commerce consist mainly of rather similar clones raised by M Koster and Sons by crossing *R. occidentale* with *R. japonicum* x *R. molle* azaleas in 1895. 'Delicatissima', 'Exquisita', 'Graciosa' and 'Superba' are all lovely with delicately coloured fragrant flowers in late May or early June.

### *Azalea viscosa*

Hybrids whose parents include *R. viscosum* are often grouped together under this name. 'Altaclerense', one of the first and a cross between *R. molle* and *R. viscosum*, can also be classed as a Ghent azalea, but as we have seen, it no longer exists.

Since 1938 B B C Felix of Boskoop has been crossing *R. viscosum* with *R. mollis* azaleas to obtain perfume with showy flowers. The research is still continuing. Flowering during the first fortnight of June, they are scented and of soft pink or creamy yellow hue.

### Azaleodendrons

This rather unattractive name was given to a new race of hybrids of the Ponticum series fertilized by pollen from azaleas. G van der Meulen was the first to use *R. japonicum* instead of *R. molle* as a pollinator using different rhododendron hybrids. He bequeathed his azaleodendrons to E Pynaert who exhibited six varieties at the 1892 Ghent Floralies. By general agreement the jury awarded the new creations a special silver medal. They were thought to be of major interest and E Pynaert named two of these new arrivals after a Dr Masters and Comte Oswald de Kerchove. Despite all the praise they received at the time, Grootendorst admitted in 1954 that as a class azaleodendrons had fallen into oblivion. It is not known why.

### Knap Hill and Exbury Azaleas

Closely allied to the Ghent azaleas are the

English so-called Knap Hill hybrids. As mentioned above, the Waterers did not name or sell their mid-century Ghent x *molle* hybrids, although their properties of size, richness of colour and later blooming were recognized in 1861 (*The Gardeners' Chronicle*, 1861, p531). But by 1900 their fame had spread in Britain. P D Williams of Lanarth, in particular, described their remarkable colours – brilliant scarlet, butter yellow and bright orange, including soft pink and white (*Rhododendron Society Notes*, II, 1924, p274). From 1921 onwards Lionel de Rothschild at Exbury began to experiment with the unnamed Knap Hill plants and he gained his first Award of Merit in 1934 with 'Hotspur'.

Further crosses have produced a splendid strain. Many have been named since, but they are usually supplied 'to colour'

All these hybrids named as being 'still available' are to be found in the *Rhododendron Handbook*, Part Two, 1964.

RENAUD DE KERCHOVE *is the great-grandson of Oswald de Kerchove and lives on the family estate at Beervelde in Belgium where he maintains a large and splendid collection of deciduous azaleas in which the Hardy Ghents receive special attention. To help maintain the domain he organizes two popular flower-shows every year*

# CHAPTER 13

# EVERGREEN AZALEAS:
# THE HYBRIDS

## JOZEF HEURSEL

The 'Japanese' evergreen azaleas are aptly named, since most of the original species used in breeding originated in that country. They belong to the subgenus *Tsutsutsia*. They arose in Japanese gardens several centuries ago and the parental species were mainly natives of Japan. They have been cultivated outdoors in Europe only since the beginning of the 20th century and their popularity is of recent date.

Hybrids now bred in Europe and the USA outnumber the old Japanese garden azaleas. These are mostly the large-flowered hybrids and it is hard to classify them as their parentage is in many cases no more than a miscellaneous assemblage of hybrids available to the breeder. The so-called Kurume group with small flowers are also now widely grown in the West and are of divers parentage, although they have a common history. They were originally bred for indoor decoration but since they were introduced to cultivation in 1919 by E H Wilson they have been grown as hardy plants for the garden.

*Rhododendron indicum,* the first evergreen azalea to reach Europe, was introduced into Holland in the 17th century. Called *Azalea indica* by Linnaeus, the name was for long used indiscriminately for all evergreen azaleas. The first species to be established in British gardens was the tender *R. simsii* (see figures 15 and 16) introduced by Captain Welbank. Others from China but of Japanese origin were the white *R. mucronatum* in 1819, followed by 'Phoeniceum' in 1824. William Smith of Norbiton in London raised seedlings in the mid-1830s when other better forms of *R. indicum* arrived. In the 1840s and 1850s these 'Indian azaleas' became very popular for greenhouse and indoor decoration and new examples were raised from the seed of the original introductions, many of which were themselves hybrids. They flowered in early May and were not forced as they are today. These old cultivars have long since been lost in Britain and by 1860 were eclipsed by the great race of Belgian 'Indians': by 1880 they had all but disappeared. Since then the great success story of the development of azaleas, both hardy and as tender pot plants, has continued in Belgium, Holland and Germany. Their greatest popularity has been as pot plants forced for the Christmas trade and over 100 million are grown and sold each year. The three forms of *R. simsii* found by Robert Fortune in a Shanghai nursery and sent to Standish & Noble in 1851 were probably influential in their parentage.

**Large-flowered azaleas**

The parents of the modern large-flowered evergreen azaleas are assumed to be three species (*R. indicum, R. scabrum* and *R. simsii*) and a fourth (*R. mucronatum*), never found in the wild but a regular inhabitant of Japanese and Chinese gardens. *R. indicum* L. (Sweet) is found on the islands of Honshu, Shikoku, Kyushu and Yakushima. It is late-flowering with narrow, leathery leaves and carmine blooms. It needs moisture, but cannot tolerate stagnant water. *R. mucronatum* G. Don (syn. *ledifolia*) was first imported from China into England by J Poole in 1819 and into Belgium in 1825. The most popularly cultivated type, 'Noordtiana', has white flowers and has played a key role in the development of winter-hardy plants. *R. scabrum* G. Don, from the Ryukyu Islands, with large, purple to red flowers, grows tall quickly, but is not hardy.

*Rhododendron simsii* Planch. (see figures 00), brought back from China in 1806 by Captain Welbank, is the most important of the four parents of the indoor evergreen azalea. It grows wild in many parts of China, as far west as Hubei, Sichuan and Yunnan. It also grows in Taiwan and Thailand. *R. simsii* was first cultivated in England in 1812, well before all other azaleas and was introduced into France in 1814, Belgium in 1818 and Germany at about the same time. However, in 1948 the National Arboretum in Washington, DC re-imported the form from the Nanking Botanic Garden and in 1979 the latter sent a plant of *R. simsii* to the Research Station for Ornamental Plant Growing in Melle, Belgium. Further variants of *R. simsii* were acquired for the Station's collection in 1989.

*Hybridizing in Europe*

Since 1820 all these plants were used for hybridizing in Belgium, Germany and France. In England the first breeder was William Smith of Norbiton (1830). Others were N de Cock who acquired the rootstock of 'Phoeniceum': this was used until the end of the 19th century. L Liebig won a first prize in Dresden in 1843 with 'Aurora'.

The Germans have been the most successful of the European breeders and can claim 47 per cent of existing cultivars. Belgium has 37 per cent, followed by the USA and Switzerland. Breeding in France, Australia and The Netherlands has been on a small scale. Belgium has the greatest number of breeders, but the Germans have had greater success owing, in the most part, to their skilful selection procedures.

The main objectives of breeding have been three: to reduce the cost of production; to spread the period during which azaleas will be in flower; and to make the flowers last longer. The German breeders excelled in the first of these aims by speeding up the time needed to produce azaleas of a certain size, that is 22cm (8′in). Julius Schaeme introduced a cultivar 'Paul Schäme' in 1890 that grew on its own roots and therefore did not need to be grafted. This cultivar was followed by others. In 1930 Reinhold Ambrosius introduced a carmine-red cultivar that grew even faster. With the success of 'Hellmut Vogel' introduced by Otto Stahnke in 1967, German breeders were able to abandon grafting completely. In Belgium also a mere six per cent of plants are now grafted.

In 1860 azaleas were flowering in April and efforts to advance the flowering time succeeded when Jozef Vervaene introduced the 'early' 'Vervaeneana' (1886) flowering in February or March. The major breakthrough for the ideal Christmas flower came with the Belgian 'Madame Petrick' (1901), even though this had to be grafted. 'Madame Petrick' had the additional advantage of producing abundant sports. But undoubtedly Otto Stahnke has been the most successful breeder. With 'Hellmut Vogel' he has advanced the flowering season by four months so that azaleas are now available for sale from 15 August to 15 May.

Giving buyers their money's worth is

certainly not a new concept: the first semi-double cultivar 'Madame van der Cruyssen', bred in 1867 by Eduard van der Cruyssen, enjoyed a huge success. Since double flowers are known to last longer than singles, this was a first step. 'Vervaeneana' featured large double flowers. 'Hellmut Vogel' had also improved longevity. To please the consumer, attractive colour-revealing buds have now become a quality feature and Otto Stahnke was again the breeder who introduced in 1972 the first cultivar, 'Friedheim Scherrer', with that feature. Other successful German breeders include Karl Glaser ('Aline', 1985) and Heinz Manten ('Memoria Theo Simon', 1986).

Vegetatively propagated plants like azaleas can suddenly produce variations, such as flowers of different shades, or other features – the shape of the plant or its leaves, frost resistance, or even greater or less vigour. Economically, the most important feature is, of course, the flower colour. Over the years new colours developed from sports have accounted for 50 per cent of new cultivars: 'Vervaeneana', 'Paul Schäme' (1890), 'Avenir' (1911, August Haerens) and 'Knut Erwén' (1934, 'Roger de Meyer') are examples. The last two are among Belgium's top selections of the 20th century. 'Hellmut Vogel' has produced more different sports than any other parent.

Most breeders have done their hybridizing with existing cultivars. The Research Station for Ornamental Plant

Growing in Melle under Dr ir. Jozef Heursel has focused on more fundamental research with azaleas from Japan (Hirado). This has produced the sweet-smelling azaleas 'Lara' and 'Mistral' (1984) and 'Mevrouw Marc van Eetvelde' (1992). Further research on colour inheritance is also going on, especially to find a yellow azalea. There is also scope for hybridization with other species of the *Tsutsutsi* genus.

### Hybridizing in Japan

Western, mainly *R. simsii*, hybrids were used to create potted plants. It is interesting to note that the same material used in Japan produced entirely different results, some as a result of selection and some to fulfil different key roles.

SATSUKI AZALEAS: The Japanese Satsuki azaleas are virtually *R. indicum* hybrids, although they owe something to *R. simsii* and *R. scabrum* and somewhat less to *R. simsii* var. *eriocarpum*. Satsuki azaleas are to Japan what the potted azaleas are to Europe. They first appeared 350 years ago and in 1692 no less than 162 cultivars were known. Commercial cultivation started around 1900. It was found that the volcanic soil known as 'tuff' or 'tufa', available throughout Japan, was a perfect growing medium for azaleas. A secondary revival in popularity occurred in 1925-41, and again in 1955 after World War II, when extremely large flowers were popular. Of two types cultivated, the Mie azalea

lends itself very well to being clipped in semi-spherical shapes to simulate rock formations. As a pot plant the Satsuki azalea is also well known in bonsai form. Nine hundred cultivars had been described by 1987 of which 60 were in commerce. The breeding centre of Satsuki is in Utsunomiya, Tochigi Prefecture.

Satsuki azaleas are single-flowered. The corolla size varies from large to small. The flowers are purple, lilac, carmine, red, pink and white and a typical plant may feature flowers with different colours, stripes, shaded sections and borders. Flowering is late, from mid-May to mid-June. In recent years, other breeders, such as B Morrison, of Glenn Dale, USA, have used Satsukis.

HIRADO AZALEAS: The mild, hot and moist climate of Japan's Hirado Island provided ideal conditions for hybridizing *R. scabrum,* coming as it did from the more southerly Ryukyu Islands in the Pacific. Hirado azaleas were first referred to in literature in 1712 when the island was the only part of Japan which, under the Daimyos (1616-1867), continued to trade with the West and was therefore prosperous. Hirado azaleas have large leaves and flowers and are much used in public places in Japan, but the European summers are too cold to permit flower buds to form.

### The Small-flowered Kurume Azaleas

It has been assumed that the small-flowered kurume-type azaleas originated from three species. The natural habitat of *R. kiusianum* Matkino is the island of Kyushu in southern Japan, hence its name. It grows on purely volcanic soil at an altitude of more than 1000m (3,280ft). The second species, *R. kaempferi* Planch., is found all over Japan in shady and mountainous slopes at less than 700m (2,300ft). The taxonomic status of the third species, *R. sataense* Nakai, has not yet been fully established and it is still classified as *R. kiusianum*. It is found on Takakuma mountain between 650m (2,130ft) and 800m (2,625ft). These three species have produced a major group of hybrids known as *R.* 'Obtusum' (Lindl.) Planch.

Between 700m (2,300ft) and 1000m (3,280ft) on the island of Kyushu *R. kiusianum* and *kaempferi* have hybridized naturally and the lower slopes are covered with transitional types. It was these that caught the eye of Ernest Wilson on his travels in the Kirishima crater area. Japanese breeders, and particularly M Sakamoto, had been breeding non-winterhardy hybrids near Kurume since about 1820. When Wilson visited K Akashi's nursery at Kurume in 1918 he picked out 50 of the most promising cultivars and sent two identical sets to Professor Charles Sargeant at the Arnold Arboretum, Boston. They arrived in April 1919 and became known as 'the Wilson Fifty'. Of these cultivars, 'Kirin' has undoubtedly become the most important. The plants were given English names which has subsequently caused great confusion.

### Hybridizing in Europe

These Japanese hybrids and species have been used by European breeders to produce azaleas to suit the tastes of the European customer. Commercial breeding started in Europe after 1920 when virtually all of 'the Wilson Fifty' cultivars were imported into the Netherlands by C B Van Nes and Sons and a London subsidiary of the Yokohama Nursery.

BELGIUM: The first Japanese azaleas to be brought into Belgium between 1901 and 1910 by Adolf Van Hecke (1874-1952) were 'Amoenum', 'Hatsugiri', 'Hinodegiri' and 'Yodogawa'. These plants had been brought back from Japan by Dutch bulb traders and were exchanged for Belgian potted plants. They were not grown commercially. In 1928 Flandria, a Bruges firm, who had imported some azaleas, including a few of 'the Wilson Fifty', exhibited three, 'Azuma-kagami', 'Kirin' and 'Kure-no-yuki', at the Floralies. One of Adolf Van Hecke's sons, Albert, exchanged some of the Van Hecke plants for these three cultivars. 'Kirin', which did particularly well, was sold to the Lam Brothers at Alphen aan de Rijn, in The Netherlands. It was an overwhelming success because it could be forced for the Christmas market. It was re-imported into Belgium then sold all over western Europe.

Other azaleas, like *R. indicum*, were also imported into Belgium through the Yokohama Nursery. Albert Van Hecke, on his return from Scotland, was able to persuade his father of the potentialities of spring-flowering Japanese azaleas for small gardens. Between 1932 and 1975 the Van Hecke family were breeding them, but it was one of the brothers, René (1912-73), who invested most time and effort into this research.

Only the cultivars 'Agnes' and 'Madame René Van Oost' remain to recall the work of another breeder, René Van Oost (1899-1975), well known for his Japanese azaleas.

One of the most influential breeders was an amateur, O F Wuyts (1892-1968), a Plant Protection Inspector. Starting in 1924, he crossed the material available at the time, such as 'Alice', 'Fedora'. 'Hinomayo', 'Palestrina' and the Arendsii hybrids from Germany, with the best of the *R. simsii* hybrids. Between 1944 and 1947 his selections were offered at the meetings of the Royal Syndical Chamber of Belgian Horticulture in Ghent. Unfortunately the names then provided have completely disappeared and it is therefore difficult to identify the successful ones. But nearly half of the current Belgian cultivars were from Wuyts. From 1960 onwards his selections were gradually introduced by T M Tollenaere (1898-1983) of Zaffelare and H De Meyer of Heusden.

Since 1963, I, in association with the Research Station for Ornamental Plant Growing at Melle, have been hybridizing using *R. simsii* cultivars. This work has culminated in three new cultivars:

'Directeur Van Slycken', 'Koli', and the winter-hardy 'Gilbert Mullie'.

GERMANY: Small-flowered Japanese azaleas were popular in the first decade of the 20th century, but were not sufficiently hardy for the climate of northern Germany.

Georg Arends of Wuppertal-Ronsdorf was one of the pioneers of breeding. His first ambition was to produce a hardy, small-flowered azalea similar to 'Hinodegiri'. To achieve this he crossed 'Benigiri', 'Hatsugiri' and 'Hinodegiri' with *R. indicum*, *R. kaempferi* and *R. mucronatum* 'Noordtiana'. He also wanted to produce plants resembling the indica type which would be sufficiently hardy to survive under light cover before being forced. His first results, known as the Arendsii azaleas, were exhibited in 1927 and were distributed under code numbers. They were not named until 1951. They are hardy, slow-growing and semi-deciduous, with a large leaf. The Aronensis seedlings produced by Georg and his son Werner were distributed commercially by G H Böhlje of Westerstede around 1960.

One of C Fleischmann of Wiesmoor's objectives was to develop cultivars whose young budding twigs formed in early autumn would be frost-resistant. He used both *R.* 'Obtusum' and *R. simsii* and succeeded with 'Multiflora' x *R. kiusianum*. He named the new race Diamond Azaleas. They flowered profusely and late, were both compact and hardy. W Thieme's

Brilliant azaleas ('Multiflora' x 'Vuyk's Scarlet') were closely related.

H Hachmann, Barmstedt, also aimed for hardy, compact cultivars. Other breeders were U Schumacher, W Nagel, G Mittendorf and E Pusch.

ENGLAND: Between 1935 and 1940 Lionel de Rothschild breeder of deciduous Exbury azaleas, bred some evergreens using *R. kaempferi* and, on one occasion, R. oldhamii. Some named cultivars are 'Eddy', 'Leo' and 'Bengal Fire'.

THE NETHERLANDS Dutch breeders have played a key role in ensuring that new plants are hardy. Major breeders have been H den Ouden & Son, Felix & Dijkhuis, W Hage & Co., W Koppeschaar, P Koster, C B Van Nes & Sons and A Vuyk. They were mainly active in the first half of the 20th century, after which breeding activity passed to the Research Station for Nursery Stock in Boskoop. Early forcing has been an aim. Attempts in the 1950s to introduce yellow flowers, using Mollis azaleas and a white-flowered Japanese azalea, have been disappointing.

Breeders in both Czechoslovakia and Switzerland have been active. Both extreme hardiness and early flowering have been objectives.

DR IR JOZEF HEURSEL *is Director of the Belgian Research Station for Ornamental Plant Growing. He has spent many years on breeding research, developing new azaleas and improving the production system for evergreen azaleas. He has travelled in South China and Japan*

# CHAPTER 14

# RHODODENDRONS IN BRITISH GARDENS: A SHORT HISTORY

## BRENT ELLIOTT

It would seem logical to divide the history of the rhododendron garden according to the chronological sequence of introductions: the American and Pontic period, the Himalayan period and the Chinese period. However, this is a history of garden style, not a history of rhododendrons themselves: other hands are dealing with the history of introductions and of hybridization. Tastes in garden-making do not automatically change on the introduction of a new plant; new introductions, if they are widely adopted, are taken up because they fit an existing taste, and there has often been a long time-lag between the introduction of a plant and its achievement of popularity. Furthermore, changes in taste are not always seen for what they are; it is all too easy, once a new taste has come to be taken for granted, to assume that the works of one's predecessors were the result of inadvertence, rather than a positive intention; over and over again, we can find writers condemning the works of the past generation as made 'without any

attention to colour', when what has really happened is a change in preferred colour combinations. Accordingly, I am going to divide the history of the rhododendron garden into the ages of the exotic specimen, of the American garden, of landscape colour, of the woodland garden, and of colour co-ordination.

A further caveat. Then as now, most literature on rhododendrons is devoted to a description of species and hybrids, or to lists of which rhododendrons are grown in a particular garden; there is little literature at any period that details how the plants were grouped, or what their intended visual effect was. The inevitable attrition resulting from frost and wind, hatchet and chainsaw, neglect and overgrowth, changing fashions and rhododendron fly, all make it difficult to speak with too much confidence of the appearance of rhododendron gardens in the 19th century, or in many cases, of more recent date. Also, I shall make no effort to update to a contemporary nomenclature the names of the rhododendrons and azaleas that occur in my quotations. Any reader who is interested in the history of rhododendrons will have learned to cope with this little difficulty.

### The Age of the Exotic Specimen

'The introduction of a useful or ornamental plant into our island is justly considered as one of the most important services that a person can render his country.' Henry Phillips (1823)

The earliest history of the rhododendron in this country is a history of plants in glasshouses and pots, and not immediately relevant to garden design. The first rhododendrons to be introduced came from Eurasian alpine climates, and successive editions of Miller's *Gardeners Dictionary*, while noting an increase in the number of available species, remain consistently gloomy about their successful cultivation in England. Attempts at cultivation in the open were few at first. Warmer-climate rhododendrons, when they began to arrive, also endured a probationary period before they were allowed into the pleasure grounds. Uncertainty over climatic tolerance led most gardeners to provide protected cultivation for any exotics from lower latitudes, and it was not until new introductions arrived in sufficiently numerous quantities, thanks to the Wardian case in the early 19th century, that gardeners could risk possibly fatal experiments to test their cultural requirements. Rhododendrons had a long and successful career as ornaments for the glasshouse collection – a story that does not concern us here.[1]

Enthusiasm for rhododendrons begins with the arrival of American species. Such enthusiasm was aroused by these immigrants from American bogs that they earned the label 'American plants', a term which included rhododendrons and azaleas as well as kalmias, magnolias, vacciniums, andromedas, and miscellaneous ericas; it came to be a general phrase for peat-loving plants. The word 'American' lingered in this context until the second half of the 19th century, long after American species had been relegated to a subordinate position by Asiatic ones; John Waterer continued to call his rhododendron exhibitions 'American exhibitions' into the 1870s. Other, less popular, terms were 'bog plants' and 'heath-mould plants'.[2]

The first nurseries of importance in rhododendron provision were those of Loddiges, and Lee and Kennedy, both in London (Hackney and Hammersmith respectively). It was from Lee and Kennedy that such early rhododendron gardens as Whiteknights built up their collections in the 1810s and 1820s, but by the 1830s Loddiges was taking the lead; by 1836 they were listing 28 varieties of *R. ponticum*, 73 Ghent azaleas, and several Highclere hybrids. For the most part, however, these plants were denizens of the glasshouse, and when introduced into the garden, tended to form part of collections arranged purely for botanical interest in sheltered enclaves. In 1828, John Claudius Loudon praised Whiteknights for the completeness of its rhododendron collection, but said that from the point of view of the 'beauties of landscape-gardening', 'nothing can be duller and more stupid, than the walled parallelogram containing the hot-houses and more rare plants, near the house at White Knights'. [3]

## The Age of the American Garden

Uvedale Price, the great promoter of the picturesque in landscape, warned against 'too distinct and splendid' colour in the garden, as tending to destroy the unity of the landscape; foregrounds were to be planted with dark green foliage, leading away into the blue distance through lighter colours. As long as such prejudices held sway, there was little scope for the introduction of rhododendrons into garden scenery.

Attitudes toward colour were changing in the 1820s, and not only among gardeners; this was the age when Constable and Turner were beginning to win their fight against the graded colour schemes of the 18th-century Academy and increase the tonal range of their paintings. John Claudius Loudon was only the most eminent of the gardeners who began to campaign for an increased use of colour in the garden, for the introduction of the flower garden as the chief element in the view from the house, and in particular for the presentation of broad masses of a single colour instead of the mixtures of colour that they found characteristic of the previous generation's planting.

Henry Phillips provides a good example of 1820s taste in transition: still basically a product of the age of Nash and Repton, unwilling to adopt the principle of solid masses, but nonetheless intent on increasing the colour content of the garden. In his advice on planting shrubberies, he recommended that the foremost (dwarfest) layer of planting could consist of contrasting groups of China asters, African marigolds, and Peruvian nasturtiums for autumn effect. 'The most beautiful shrubs should occupy the most conspicuous and prominent places. For instance, a projecting part of the plantation should be reserved for the purple rhododendron, the flaming azalea, and other bog plants.' [4]

Phillips also recommended the planting together of azaleas and rhododendrons; for those for whom this is the ultimate sin, it should perhaps be pointed out that he was writing at a time when the available choice of either was very limited, and the first Ghent azaleas had yet to reach the British market. Nonetheless, the terms in which he makes his recommendation are worth noting carefully:

'Clumps of the flame-coloured azalea should shine near those of the purple rhododendron, for as they both flower at the same season the contrast is as rich as a purple robe wrought with gold. It requires the nicest judgment to intermix even those plants which contrast or harmonise the best.'[5]

'Contrast or harmonize'; – this may seem to offer the gardener a wide latitude of effect, but it should not be assumed too readily that these words represent contrary approaches. In the first half of the 19th century, it was common to find 'contrast' and 'harmony' used synonymously. At a time when the analogy between harmony of colour and harmony in music was taken literally, it was argued that, just as adjacent notes on the piano make a discord when played together, so adjacent colours in the spectrum make a discord when juxtaposed. Red, yellow, and blue could make a harmonious colour scheme; red and orange could not. [6]

Phillips was by the mid-19th century a voice from the past; the mixture of rhododendrons and herbaceous plants, and the small scale of colour contrasts, were yielding to massing of colours on a larger scale, and to the first experiments in colour grouping of shrubs as well as of flowerbeds. The Leeds landscape gardener Joshua Major grouped shrubs by colour on an estate in Pontefract in the late 1820s, but no documentation has survived to show how the groups were arranged. [7]

The shrubbery, considered as a garden feature to be seen at a fairly close range, is one thing; the distant vista is quite another. Colour grouping would not make its way into the wider landscape until a later generation; but the initial impact of a patch of positive colour in the landscape was already appearing as a theme in the 1830s. James Mangles, in his *Floral Calendar* (1839), wrote of the effect of masses of rhododendrons on islands or accompanying lakes:

'Two of the most tastily disposed and ornamental gardens in England, are Lord Farnborough's, at Bromley, and Lord Carnarvon's, at Highclere; the principal feature of attraction in both these beautiful places is attained by a profusion of clumps, of American bog plants, besides gravel walks with long marginal belts on either side, profusely studded with Rhododendrons, Kalmias, Azaleas, Vacciniums, Andromedas, &c. &c.; and wherever a stream or lake is at hand, islands are judiciously introduced, and being thickly planted with these American shrubs, present in the summer one gorgeous mass of reflected floration, the splendour of the tints greatly enriched by the tremulous and varied shadows occasioned by the glistening of the waters, and the brilliancy of the carpeted surface above, reminding one of some of Claude Loraine's glowing sunsets.

At Lord Amherst's, at Montreal, near Sevenoaks, an oblong island has been made in the midst of an oval pond. It presents a perfectly matted surface of Rhododendrons, and every summer bursts out into one condensed mass of resplendent flowers, exhibiting in lieu of a common pond one of the most attractive objects in these beautiful grounds; and on a small scale, a good sample of *"capability"*.' [8]

By 1859, as George Lovell said, "American gardens"...have come to be considered as almost necessary features in the grounds of every country residence, large or small'. [9] Let us consider some of these earliest rhododendron gardens, and the rhetoric with which they were discussed.

At Kenwood was the first rhododendron collection to be described as a grove: 'quite a grove of Rhododendrons, which seem to grow with native luxuriance; many thousands are coming up round the old plants, from the self-sown seeds'. [10]

At Fonthill, William Beckford tried to create an impression of the 'mountainous regions of Catholic countries on the Continent', avoiding displays of modern plants; his American ground was 'disposed in groups and thickets, as if they had sprung up naturally, with glades of turf kept smoothly mown to admit of walking through among them, and examining their separate beauties'. This is the first report in the gardening press of a garden whose planting attempted to replicate an exotic landscape; such comparable examples as Penjerrick, where Anna Maria Fox accompanied the experiments on the acclimatization of plants with attempts to introduce cockatoos and monkeys into the forest, had to wait for a later date for press coverage. [11]

At Bagshot, *The Gardener's Magazine* in 1828 publicized 'an increasing arboretum' under direction of Andrew Toward, who I believe was the first head gardener to have a rhododendron hybrid named after him. The collections were already so abundant that thinning was in progress, and self-seeding was being observed in the peat-like soil. 'It seems to be a part of the plan of management at Bagshot, to distribute exotic trees over the margins of the native woods, and so, gradually, to give them a highly enriched and botanical character.' By 1842 a terrace walk had been raised alongside the American garden to serve as a viewing platform. [12]

At Keele Hall, Ralph Sneyd began planting early *R. arboreum* crosses about 1830; these groups of scarlet rhododendrons were later described as looking like 'little mountains, spangled and sparkling from top to bottom'. [13]

At Highclere, the first private garden to become famous for its rhododendron hybridization programme, *The Gardener's Magazine* in 1834 reported two large beds which contained 100 bushes of rhododendron hybrids; the planting strategy was 'to mass the varieties and species as much as possible together'. As the American garden developed to its eventual extent of 6.5ha (16 acres), the natural soil was removed to a depth of around 46cm (18in) and replaced by peat; rhododendrons were grouped in circles, ovals, and other curvilinear figures, with broad grass walks and trees between. In 1841 a feature was reported consisting of eight borders arranged to form a Catherine wheel, planted with new azaleas; this wheel was still to be seen in 1909, although the early rhododendron and azalea beds near the house were re-arranged in the 1850s. The Milford lake was fringed along its banks with rhododendrons and azaleas, as were the islands within it; further rhododendron beds flanked the major drives. What the colour effects were like is difficult to ascertain. In 1834, Highclere was commended for avoiding 'that surfeit of rich colours which we have heard some find fault with when criticising the London exhibitions'; in 1871, H Noel Humphreys compared the scene with a London rhododendron show, with a further comparison to the paintings of John Martin.[14]

Dysart House became famous for its American plants in the 1830s, but it was not until the 1850s that Robert Fish, head gardener at Putteridgebury and an important horticultural journalist, adduced it as a model for planning, with its rhododendrons 'thrown together in groups and bold, sweeping borders in grounds traversed with gracefully-curved walks, and these again bordered with broad, irregular margins of turf'. The significant lesson Fish drew from Dysart was the importance of segregating rhododendrons from herbaceous plants.

'There seemed to be no attempt to mingle flowers with the evergreens. What flowers would compete with these Rhododendrons in the height of their bloom? In the autumn, again, though cheerfully green, they would be sombre, contrasted with other things in the height of their beauty. The inference would seem to be – mingle not groups of these with groups of herbaceous flowers or bedding plants, but give them a garden for themselves.'[15]

The beginning of the 1840s brought the discovery of the self-seeding of *R. ponticum*, and the development of its use for covert planting. Some background is useful for setting the scene. As art, rather than nature, became the leading principle among gardeners, and the flower garden was seen as a challenge that was being successfully met, some gardeners cast their eyes further to the woodlands around the estate, and sought for ways of increasing their artistic content. The most radical attempts were made by men like Joseph Paxton at Chatsworth and Philip Frost at Dropmore, who enjoyed juxtaposing the wild and the highly cultivated, for example by planting the latest fuchsia cultivars in the woods and introducing clumps of bramble onto the manicured lawn. At Highclere in 1834, Loudon praised the contrast offered by a bank covered with sloes and juniper 'to the smooth polish of the pleasure-ground, and its groups of

*Philip Frost, head gardener at Dropmore, one of the first to use rhododendrons in a woodland setting*

rhododendrons and magnolias, below'.

While press coverage of this trend died down after the 1840s, it continued unabated; in the early 1860s the Covent Garden seedsman Peter Barr offered 'Paxtonian packets' of mixed annual seed for scattering in woodlands for a 'richly floriferous effect'. This trend culminated in 1870, with the publication of William Robinson's *Wild Garden.* [16]

Such was the climate of opinion when the discovery was noised abroad of the self-seeding capacity of *R. ponticum*. Hints had been made before 1840: in 1829 Jacob Rinz had reported from Fonthill about an abundance of self-sown rhododendrons.[17] However, it was in the first volume of *The Gardeners' Chronicle* (1841)

that the matter surfaced noisily. G S Mackenzie wrote in to report his discovery, to be answered by Philip Frost, head gardener at Dropmore, who airily pointed out his long experience of the fact that

'. . .where they are grown in woods they are sure to sow themselves by tens of thousands. In the woods here we have, by a little attention, thousands of self-sown seedling *Rhododendron ponticum*, growing on any kind of soil excepting stiff clay . . . *Rhododendron cataubiense* and its varieties are far more beautiful than *ponticum*, and therefore should be planted near walks and the margins of woods; it is also one of the best to cross the Nepaul kinds upon to obtain hardy varieties, which are mostly very beautiful. When in bloom, nothing can surpass the beauty of Rhododendrons in woods; last year the woods here were quite enchanting with them. It is very easy to fill woods with them, by sowing the seed broad-cast, where it is desirable to have them.'[18]

Shortly after, Donald Beaton, then head gardener at Shrubland Park in Suffolk, wrote that 'We intend soon to plant the *Rhododendron ponticum* extensively, as undergrowth in the plantations for ornament and for the use of the game.'[19]

Beaton's letter introduced a new note: underwood planting. Much attention was devoted to this topic in the early gardening press; for example, at Claremont, Charles McIntosh was praised for his creation of a laurel underwood 'by laying down the long straggling branches of the old plants, so that they now completely cover the surface . . . one of the most masterly things of the kind that has been done anywhere.'[20] By the 1860s the planting of *R. ponticum* for underwood and covert was widespread, and with it came a change of emphasis; the early reports of its wonderful ornamental quality faded away as it became commonplace. [21]

## Digression: Victorian Gardeners and the Rhododendron

The gardening press today is more likely to credit developments in the garden to the owner rather than to the gardeners in his employ, but in the second half of the 19th century gardening had a higher profile as a skilled profession. The gardening press began with men like J C Loudon campaigning for better salaries, living quarters, and education for gardeners; and by mid-century a number of gardeners had risen to public prominence. Of these the most notable was Joseph Paxton, who, having begun his career as an under-gardener in the Horticultural Society's garden at Chiswick, ended his days as a knight, a Member of Parliament, and a railway millionaire, with his career taking in such sidelines as architect, glasshouse designer, magazine editor, and company director, even while he retained his position as head gardener at Chatsworth. Not many gardeners could hope to emulate Paxton's meteoric rise in the social scale, but all could hope to be pulled a little distance in his wake, and by the second half of the century, celebrated gardeners were being head-hunted from estate to estate rather in the way football stars are today.[22]

The struggle to achieve professional status for the gardener was long and hard (and ironically the result was not long to endure, when you consider that gardening is today classed as a semi-skilled profession). Take the case of David Taylor Fish, later to become an advocate of colour planning in the wider landscape. He trained at Scone Castle, where 'the curriculum for apprentices was . . . a useful and an unvarying one. One year (the first),

*James Tegg, head gardener to several great estates including John Walter's Bear Wood. Men of his calibre were highly trained professionals and masters of many branches of horticulture*

fires and houses; the second, serve the kitchen; and the third, work in the flower garden.' Moving then to Putteridgebury, where his brother Robert was head gardener, he studied writing and drawing in addition to his gardening duties; he then went through a series of nurseries gaining additional experience, and a series of gardens in subordinate roles. Finally

'. . . came the offer of a head place. This offer proved my first great professional trial. From the summit of my

ideal I was brought suddenly down to the lowest level of everyday life by the offer of a situation at £30 per year, with board, and the half of a footman's room for lodging. Hardly had these terms escaped "Joe's" lips, when my indignation blazed forth, much to the good man's amazement. "Why," I asked, "couple the knowledge and culture of professional men with the rewards of a livery servant?".' [23]

Another example: James Tegg, who

became famous for a rhododendron garden, trained at Groom's nursery in Clapham, became known as a fruit grower and exhibitor while head gardener to Baron Hambro at Roehampton (in which capacity, just to note another skill in which gardeners were expected to be proficient, he designed the first bouquet presented to Queen Alexandra on her arrival in England), and then served a brief period as head gardener at Clumber Park, before taking up his most famous position at Bear Wood, the estate of John Walter, the proprietor of *The Times*. 'Of the many features added during Mr Tegg's charge was the planting of the Wellingtonia Avenue, the laying out of a new kitchen garden, the sunken hardy plant garden near the mansion, and the gradual extension of the pleasure grounds', including rhododendron and rock gardens. During all this time, while he continued his fame as a grower and exhibitor of fruits and vegetables, and added the role of estate forester to his role, he received press compliments like this:

'Mr Tegg deserves the highest credit for the admirable manner in which the grounds are kept. The visitor can walk along miles of pathway and not see a single weed; and the sward is so well kept, that scarcely a leaf could be seen lying upon its surface.'[24]

The head gardener was expected to be experienced not only in horticulture and botany; he needed to be able to turn his hand to surveying, garden design, flower arranging, building and engineering (especially in the glasshouse world) – and, of course, plant breeding. Interestingly, it is in the great rhododendron gardens that the status of head gardeners has remained highest in the 20th century (witness the Puddles at Bodnant), largely through their involvement with rhododendron hybridization. When we look back over the development of expertise in the cultivation of rhododendrons during the course of the 19th century, remember that it was primarily head gardeners who carried out the experiments and built up the resulting body of knowledge.

Much still needed to be learned about the culture of rhododendrons; at Whiteknights in 1835, it was reported that the rhododendron plantations had been 'burned up' in the drought because they had not been planted in the lowest part of the ground,[25] and the assumption that anything Asiatic needed greenhouse cultivation took a long time to die. This change of attitude was largely due to the Wardian case, the use of which began in the late 1820s by Loddiges' and other nurseries; the loss rate for plants plummeted, and as a result the ability of nurseries to supply large stocks increased. As gardeners found they had disposable quantities of new exotics, they began conducting systematic programmes of hardiness testing, for example leaving a certain quantity of plants out after the others had been brought back into the greenhouse to see what temperatures they could endure.

We can construct an approximate chronology of the education of Victorian gardeners in the ways of rhododendrons and azaleas.

**1820s-30s** Controversy over the botanical arrangement of the genus. Loudon had treated *Rhododendron* and *Azalea* as distinct genera in his *Hortus Britannicus*; in his *Arboretum*, he described Don's inclusion of *Azalea* in *Rhododendron* as 'however technically correct . . . injudicious in a practical point of view'.[26]

**1820s-40s** First age of hybridization, as Loddiges, Dean Herbert, and others begin crossing rhododendrons and azaleas; the climax of this first period of hybridization was Gowen's development of the Highclere hybrids, which began to be reported in 1831, and which, it was claimed, 'as far surpass the common rhododendrons as the new double Scotch roses do the old wild ones'.[27]

**1820s-50s** Experiments in hardiness, which by the 1850s were so successful that there was a general expectation the new Sikkim rhododendrons would be hardy. The 1850s to 1870s saw a dawning realization that rhododendrons in cultivation differed significantly from the wild state – comparing the plates of Hooker's *Rhododendrons of the Sikkim-Himalaya* with cultivated specimens of the same species not

only demonstrated their variability, but was frequently decided to be to the advantage of the British-grown plants[28]. The year 1859 saw not only a storm unmatched until 1987, but debilitating autumn frosts which provided a good test of hardiness, much discussed in the press for 1860.

**1830s-50s** Experiments on the grafting of rhododendrons, especially new exotics on stocks of *R. ponticum*. The years 1854-55 saw a debate on grafting in *The Gardeners' Chronicle*, the issue being whether grafting was suitable for garden, as opposed to greenhouse and exhibition, plants. The same period saw a fashion for growing rhododendrons as standards.

**1830s-50s** Realization that peat was not necessary for their cultivation. As early as 1835 *The Gardener's Magazine* reported on a 6.5m (21ft) *ponticum* being grown 'without bog earth' at Maeslaugh Castle,[29] but it was not until mid-century that the possibilities of peatless cultivation were extensively realized.

**1850s-60s** Discovery that rhododendrons were pollution-tolerant and therefore suitable for town planting. As a result, they became plants of major importance for municipal parks; W W Pettigrew, in 1928, published statistics about Philips Park in Manchester, where rhododendrons were one of the few trees or shrubs worth attempting to grow outdoors throughout the winter, and even they had an average

*Charles Noble, one of the great partnership of the Sun-
ningdale firm of Standish & Noble. The partnership
dissolved in 1854-5, Standish moving to Ascot while
Noble remained at Sunningdale until his retirement
in 1898.*

lifespan of only three years in the notoriously polluted atmosphere.[30]

As the railways began to carve their
way through Surrey, the focus changed
from the London-based Loddiges and Lee
to Knap Hill, the Goldworth nursery, and
later (from 1847) Standish & Noble at
Sunningdale. Here rhododendrons could
be seen growing as if in a garden setting,
and the displays of standard shrubs at
Waterer's were to become famous as pieces
of garden design by the 1870s. (Loudon
claimed, incidentally, that the reason so

many gentlemen started raising rhododendrons from seed in the 1830s was because
of the excessive prices of nursery-bought
stock.) [31]

The rise of rhododendron exhibitions
also played an important role, not only in
publicizing what was available, but in creating expectations of what rhododendrons
could look like in the garden. Waterer
started a long-running series of 'American
exhibitions' in 1849 at the Royal Botanic
Society's garden in Regent's Park, reports
on which became an annual feature of the
gardening press (to such an extent that a

report could sometimes be cribbed from a previous one – compare the 1862 and 1864 reports in *The Gardeners' Chronicle*). During the 1860s he started exhibiting at the RHS Garden in Kensington as well, and then branched out regionally, with a Manchester show in 1873 and shows in Cadogan and Russell Squares. The gardening press regularly issued cautions to the public about inferring garden effect from exhibition effect: the controversy about grafting rhododendrons was in large part a reflection of their use in the London exhibitions, and by the 1860s azaleas were reported as not coming true to colour under canvas.

In 1859 came what was effectively the first English treatise on rhododendron culture, in the form of a series of articles by George Lovell of Bagshot, summarizing his experience in the year of his death, in *The Gardeners' Chronicle*.[32]

## The Age of Landscape Colour

In the 1820s, Joshua Major had grouped shrubs by colour; in 1859 Thomas Appleby, who had been Major's foreman 30 years before, criticized the usual manner of grading plants by height in shrubberies (in which rhododendrons would appear along with box and spiraeas, in between tall shrubs, like thorns and laburnums, and dwarf shrubs in the front), and published proposals for borders grouped by colour. In his plan for a 12-row border, tall rhododendrons would occupy a row between laurustines and

sweet bays, while *R. ferrugineum* would fill a row between berberis and andromeda.[33]

The subject of colour planning in the wider landscape, which had occasionally been touched on in the 1830s, was brought into prominence by William Paul, the Waltham Cross nurseryman, with a series of articles on 'pictorial trees' in *The Gardeners' Chronicle* for 1864; here he recommended choosing trees and shrubs for landscape planting on the basis of colour grouping, whether by leaves, flowers, or bark. There was at first little response, but within a decade a number of other writers – James Bateman, Charles Lee, William Barron, D T Fish – had supported his proposals, and the 1870s saw landscape colour as a new field of activity among gardeners.[34]

This was a time when the flower garden colour schemes of the High Victorian period were being criticized by a younger generation of gardeners, like William Robinson, who turned against the massing of colours in the flower garden; the continuing proponents of massed colour, like D T Fish, began renewing the analogies of Loudon's age, and talking about the way in which nature masses colours – bluebell woods, hillsides covered with heath or furze, and so on. Not surprisingly, then, the gardening press of the period began to pay respectful attention to the effect of masses of rhododendrons, as at Bedgebury, where a writer in 1867 described the effect of an island of rhododendrons facing banks of wild heath: 'a

*Tittenhurst Park, Sunninghill, where formal beds of rhododendrons were brought into the parterre by Thomas Holloway in the 1850s and continued by T H Lowinsky in the 1920s*

mass of flowers to which our most highly cultivated flower-beds can bear no comparison'.[35]

In the garden, the immediate response was the planting of shrubs by masses, and the first garden noted for such planting was Waddesdon Manor, work on which began in 1874. Along the major drives were arranged triangular groups of shrubs, the points and bases of the triangles alternately coming to the front: rhododendrons and azaleas, berberis, philadelphus, lilacs, furze and broom

formed the masses.[36] This period was also the heyday of the 'subtropical garden', or garden devoted to foliage shape, and rhododendrons occasionally found employment here; Edward Luckhurst in 1876 described a portion of the grounds at Pencarrow where rhododendrons were mingled with gunneras and pampas grass – characteristic 'subtropical' plants – on a hillside leading to 'the crown and glory of the valley, a Rhododendron garden some two acres in extent'.[37]

An example will show how quickly

the introduction of exotic shrubs for land-scape colour became accepted. In 1880, William Paul published proposals for the management of Epping Forest, recently saved from development by the City of London. 'While preserving the general character of an English forest', he wrote,

'I would not altogether eschew those exotics which are thoroughly hardy, but rather seek to introduce such for the sake of grandeur and variety . . . Of shrubs of moderate and lowly growth the Rhododendron (*R. ponticum*) should specially abound. There are many spots in which it would thrive as well as in its native habitats, and the richness of its foliage in winter, and the gorgeousness of its blossoms in May and June, commend it to every observer.'

His suggestions provoked a reply urging caution on the introduction of exotics into a native woodland, but the caution was concerned only with conifers; no objection was provoked by the idea of multiplying rhododendrons.[38]

The traditional American garden played a decreasing role in these years. It occupied a sort of middle distance be-tween the principal flower garden and the wider landscape, but in the 1870s, atten-tion was shifting not only outward, to the informal landscape beyond the pleasure ground, but also to the immediate cur-tilage of the house, where a few pioneers

began replacing the familiar parterre with informal planting. At Tittenhurst Park, first Thomas Holloway and then T H Lowinsky brought formal beds of rhodo-dendrons into the parterre and its precincts; but this garden received little publicity until the 20th century, when its pioneering collection of flowering shrubs won it esteem.[39]

At Bear Wood, James Tegg created a flowering shrub garden, in which rhodo-dendrons, azaleas, and kalmias were the most important features, consisting of groups arranged informally on the lawn, characteristically composed of a centre of *R. ponticum* fringed by hardy hybrids. William Goldring, later a prominent garden designer who served his apprentice-ship by reporting on gardens for Robin-son's magazine *The Garden*, reported that:

'A noteworthy feature at Bearwood is the absence of all elaborate geometric designs, which are too often met with, defacing extensive lawns . . . Here there has been for several weeks past an uninterrupted display of flowering shrubs, which are planted in bold groups, with irregular natural-like out-lines.'

Another writer said that 'It is at places like Bearwood that the visitor realises something of the splendid decorative ser-vice the hardy Rhododendron renders in ornamental grounds, especially when seen as they are in such large masses.' While the gardens of the Mangles family at Hethersett and Littleworth Cross may have chronological priority over Bear Wood for bringing rhododendron groups into the precincts of the parterre, they did not receive publicity in the press, and it was Bear Wood that proved to be influential.[40]

The publication of William Robinson's *Wild Garden* in 1870 helped to popularize a term of uncontrollable ambiguity. Robinson eventually had to add a preface to later editions, specifying what he had meant by the phrase – not a wilderness, not a garden of native plants, but a labour-saving garden in which hardy exotics were encouraged to naturalize themselves. Surprisingly, in view of the self-seeding potential of *R. ponticum*, Robinson dealt only cursorily with the genus in that book, including it in a couple of lists (plants for bare areas, for fringing waterfalls) without further comment. His enthusiasm grew in the 1880s, however, and while the first edition of *The English Flower Garden* (1883) had little to say on the subject, his coverage increased in the second, and culminated in a statement which first appeared in the 6th edition (1898), 'The glory of spring in our pleasure grounds is the Rhododendrons'.

In a passage added in the 2nd edition of 1889, but which did not take its final form until the 5th edition of 1897, he advised gardeners to

'. . . show the habit and form of the plant. This does not mean that they

may not be grouped or massed just as before, but openings of all sizes should be left among them for light and shade, and for handsome herbaceous plants that die down in the winter, thus allowing the full light for half the year to evergreens.'

Since Robinson was also the author of a book on *The Subtropical Garden*, and an enthusiast for foliage and 'beautiful form', this emphasis on habit can be seen as another legacy of the subtropical movement. In the 3rd edition of 1893, he added a further warning that rhododendrons were 'often over-planted; that is to say, we are sure to see Rhododendrons in large and often inartistic and ugly masses in many country-places where no planting of any other kind worth speaking of is carried out'. (The words 'are sure to' and 'inartistic and ugly' were deleted beginning in the 8th edition; the latter phrase was replaced by the word 'lumpy'.)

The young Robinson, together with his contemporary William Wildsmith, head gardener at Heckfield Place, actively campaigned against colour schemes in the flower garden – to such an extent that the early articles of Gertrude Jekyll, proposing colour schemes for the border, were criticized in some quarters as a reversion to the standards of High Victorian bedding. I suspect that Robinson's growing enthusiasm for rhododendrons was fuelled in part by Jekyll, under whose influence he became ever more tolerant of colour schemes, so long as they were carried out in the herbaceous border, the rock garden or the wider landscape, and not in the principal parterre.

At Munstead Wood, Jekyll determined 'to group only in beautiful colour harmonies . . . to avoid overcrowding', and planted so that clumps of crimsons and purples would not be seen at the same time. Purples, she thought, grouped better in the shade, crimsons in sunlight. She divided rhododendrons into 'six classes of easy harmonies':

'1. Crimsons inclining to scarlet or blood-colour grouped with dark claret-colour and true pink.
2. Light scarlet rose colours inclining to salmon . . .
3. Rose colours inclining to amaranth.
4. Amaranths or magenta-crimsons.
5. Crimson or amaranth-purples.
6. Cool clear purples of the typical ponticum class, both dark and light, grouped with lilac-whites.'

Note that 'harmony' has now come to imply contiguity in the spectrum, rather than separation. As for azaleas: 'Any of them may be planted in company, for all their colours harmonise'. At one point in the garden, she created a sequence of azaleas leading up a hill: first whites, then pale yellows and pale pinks, then orange, copper, flame, and scarlet-crimson; then softening off with strong yellows, and dying away into the woodland with *Azalea*

*pontica*. These principles – spectrum-adjacent harmony, avoidance of immediate contrasts, and a colour series planned for recession into the distance – were Jekyll's general legacy for the succeeding 20th century. For the rhododendron grower, one lasting consequence of her principles was the admonition that 'Azaleas should never be planted among or even within sight of Rhododendrons'. Jekyll became the main source for this increasingly popular 20th-century rule.[41]

'Colour effects seem for all time to have claimed the attention of past and present planters', said a writer visiting Tortworth Court in 1914.[42] And colour selection has certainly proved to be the most contentious single issue in rhododendron planting during the present century.

### The Age of the Woodland Garden

Lord Armstrong's garden at Cragside was one of the most massive planting projects of the later 19th century: over 6,880 ha (17,000 acres) of bleak Northumbrian hillside transformed, beginning in 1864, into a thick coniferous and rhododendron forest. As early as 1880 *The Gardeners' Chronicle* referred to a collection of conifers and the carpeting of the ground with rhododendrons, kalmias, and heaths. By 1892 *The Gardener's Magazine* could describe 'impenetrable thickets' of hundreds of thousands of bushes, 'blooming so profusely as to light up the whole hillside with their varied colours'. As for these varied colours, one theme that the turn-of-

*Bodnant, N Wales, where, from 1908, Lord Aberconway planted Chinese rhododendrons in the existing woodland garden*

the-century articles emphasize is the combination of azaleas and rhododendrons: 'Varieties of Azalea mollis have also been freely employed, and it is of interest to note that they are quite at home, and bloom freely, their shades of orange and buff presenting a delightful contrast to the stronger tones of the rhododendrons.' The rhododendrons were 'enhanced by the groups of hardy Azaleas, which are even more brilliant than the Rhododendrons in spring, whilst their leaf tints in autumn are as rich as anything in the woodland'.

Cragside was hailed as 'one of the greatest examples of the planter's art during the present century'. Colour apart, Cragside brought a new note into the literature: the creation of a forest rather than a display collection.[43]

While none of the early articles makes any comparison with the landscapes described in Joseph Hooker's *Himalayan Journals*, it would not surprise me to learn that Hooker's work had helped to dictate the form this forest planting took. Comparison of British rhododendron gardens

*Minterne, Dorset, where Lord Digby also planted his rhodendendrons in already mature woodland. There were many other examples*

with Chinese and Himalayan scenery has been a minor theme of 20th-century discussions: George Forrest describing part of Rowallane as 'a bit of Yunnan', Frank Knight comparing the terrace gardens at Werrington Park to the areas from which Forrest collected (though that last may have been a sardonic comment on the state of overgrowth).[44]

Woodland gardens have been so often associated with rhododendrons that it has become a commonplace that it was the rhododendron which was the stimulus to their creation. On the contrary, the older the woodland garden, the less likely it is that it was planned specifically to accommodate rhododendrons; the tradition of woodland embellishment, discussed briefly earlier, continued through the 19th century, and provided a context in which rhododendrons only gradually became dominant. So, for gardens as famous in recent times for their rhododendrons as Abbotsbury, Bodnant, Borde Hill, and Westonbirt, early accounts of the garden mention rhododendrons in passing or not at all. Their absence from the early years of Bodnant is particularly ironic. The second Lord Aberconway recalled:

'We planted shrubs, but we did not plant Rhododendrons. My grandfather never planted Rhododendrons except some good old hardy hybrids, like 'Ascot Brilliant' which we still have. When I was 21 I remember discussing it with our Head Gardener, not MR. PUDDLE, but his predecessor. We discussed the possibility of planting some Himalayan Rhododendrons, and he said "Oh no, sir, they would never grow at Bodnant, don't try Himalayan Rhododendrons" . . . We should not always take advice. About 1908 VEITCH were selling Rhododendrons raised from WILSON'S collection in China of 1900, and I thought that we would try some of these Chinese Rhododendrons. I reflected that the Head Gardener could not say that they would not grow because he had never tried them. At the same time I thought that we would grow Himalayan Rhododendrons among them, and we have them mixed to-day. Of course the Chinese and Himalayan Rhododendrons were a great success, and although those grown in Cornwall grow twice as fast, they do very well in Wales.'[45]

The great influx of rhododendrons from China, brought by Wilson, Farrer, Forrest, Rock, and Ludlow and Sherriff, was accommodated in existing woodlands or coniferous gardens by Lord Digby at Minterne, the Aberconways at Bodnant, the Loders at Leonardslee and Wakehurst, Williams at Caerhays and Werrington, and others.[46] But the aesthetic of the woodland garden was already established by the time these gardens began to receive their new introductions, and the descriptions of these gardens in the early 20th-century press display a few characteristic themes:

**Massing** – whether special features like the massed azaleas around the stream at Leonardslee, or vague incantations like the following, about Tregrehan: 'Gardening assumes a new meaning when one sees the landscape painted with such a lavish hand, with great masses of colour and backgrounds of every varying tone of green'.[47]

**Highlights** – invocations of individual flowering trees becoming visible against a backdrop, as in the excellent phrase 'Flaring bushes of Rhododendron' used of effects at Bodnant.[48]

**Profusion and variety** – achieved by simple listing.

But discussions of these gardens tended to devote more attention to the enumeration of species and hybrids than to a discussion of planting principles. When the arrangement of plants was specifically discussed, it tended to be either according to geographical origin, as in part at Wakehurst and Leonardslee, or by series, as at Tower Court and Wisley.

Planting by series was already waning in popularity before the recent revision of the genus. At Wakehurst, after its transfer to Kew, a scheme to plant rhododendrons in their series was changed to planting in 'natural "cultural groups" '.[49] Nonetheless, two of the most important rhododendron gardens of the 20th century were arranged on this principle, and deserve some special attention; both were associated with John Barr Stevenson, who may be regarded as the foremost practitioner of planting by series.

At Tower Court, J B Stevenson created a series of avenues descending the ridge from his house, two of them lined with flowering cherries, one interplanted with Kurume azaleas, and the other with various series: 'These spread into the surrounding valleys, presenting in the spring a vista of most varied colouring, lapping in waves up to the terrace on which the house is built.'[50] At Wisley, the area called Battleston Hill, acquired in 1938, 0.5ha (1 acre) of which had already been put to use for Exbury trial hybrids, was developed after World War II with Stevenson's help. So many dead larches were removed that one side of the hill became quite sunny; some azalea series were planted in this open ground, and others where more shelter and shade were available. On the brow of the hill, *R. yakushimanum*, which created a sensation at Chelsea in 1947, was planted in open sun. 'No attempt being made to devise a colour scheme, the effect during a favourable spring is one blaze of

riotous colour.'

By the 1980s Battleston Hill was more likely to be criticized than praised in the press, and the storm of 1987 which devastated the area was greeted by audible relief in some quarters. Its replanting was not devoid of controversy: Christopher Lloyd attacked it in *Country Life* for the massed banks of azaleas.[51]

The long debate in the 19th century over the planting of rock gardens – should the rocks be considered as a picturesque feature, to be planted with conifers, ivy and other trailing plants, or as a place to grow exotic alpines? – was never completely resolved, but the proponents of alpines were the most vocal faction during the 20th century. Reginald Farrer was willing to give some small space to dwarf rhododendrons in *The English Rock Garden* (1919-20), but Sampson Clay omitted them altogether in his sequel *The Present-day Rock Garden* (1936). Some important rhododendron gardens had begun as rock gardens, from Rowallane, which as late as 1930 could be described in *New Flora and Sylva* as 'now as effective a bit of rock and Rhododendron gardening as one could wish to see', to the Lea Rhododendron Gardens, begun in 1935 in a disused quarry, and later adding alpine and scree beds as these became popular; but the Lea Gardens never attained the critical esteem that its predecessors had, and has always had an air of being looked down on for its very popularity with the public.[52]

## The Age of Colour Coordination

The recommendations of Jekyll for the avoidance of strong contrast and the grouping of related tints were taken up by the major garden designers and landscape architects of the postwar years, and gradually percolated down into the gardening columns of newspapers, where soft colours, harmony, and what in the world of interior decoration had come to be called 'colour coordination' became the accepted wisdom during the 1980s.

The invocation of Jekyll as an inspiration can be seen in the writings of Lionel de Rothschild in the 1930s:

'. . .the real art of gardening is not only to group plants to make a picture but also to see that colours mingle well. What has been done in herbaceous borders can just as well be done on a large scale in the woodland with Azaleas and Rhododendrons . . . Too many of the Rhododendron gardens of to-day have been planted with no eye to colour.'[53]

At Exbury, where work began in 1918, he created a dell 'where groups of mauves and pinks predominate – all the old favourites, all if you like false colours, but all blending beautifully together as there is nothing to clash'. (He was still prepared to allow such contrasts as purple and yellow – 'Purple Splendour' contrasting with the azaleodendron 'Galloper Light')[54]

One of the most influential designers of the postwar period was Sylvia Crowe, who consistently called for cool colours to be preferred in planting. 'The worst way to grow them is in a solid mass of mixed colours.' (The very phrase would have met with stunned incomprehension in the 19th century, when mixing and massing implied two opposing methods of grouping.)

'The salmon and orange pinks are the hardest to place and if used at all should be in small quantities grouped only with dark green or grey . . . In any large planting of rhododendrons, the cool colours should predominate, the white, blues, mauves and lilacs shading to the deep purples and clarets and the dark reds as accents. The strong pinks are better kept out of the picture.'

These views came to be widely accepted, and increasingly, where hotter colours were used, it was with an apologetic gesture toward the unregenerate taste of the general public. Take the recommendations of Lady Mary Howick:

'...pale pink or mauve, also yellow and white. But one cannot garden exclusively with pale colours . . . Some of the brilliant red rhododendrons are splendid and spectacular, especially if they can be isolated in their own green setting. The public certainly loves a good splash of colour, so one cannot do without it.'[55]

Jekyll's warning against associating rhododendrons and azaleas was repeated during the interwar years by gardeners like Lionel de Rothschild, who allowed that 'azaleas look very well against the dark green of Rhododendrons which have flowered earlier in the year.' After mid-century, it became an accepted tenet that they should not be planted together; Sylvia Crowe described the results as 'deplorable . . . for in the main the colours are incompatible', while Lawrence Banks gave as a rare exception to the rule 'a subtle combination of purple and mauve rhododendrons with the common yellow azalea'.[56]

The literature on colour coordination in the later 20th century has sought to dictate not only certain combinations, but also particular colours. Individual gardeners have always had their individual colour preferences: the 'bloody reds of Bodnant' (to use Eric Savill's phrase), and Hope Findlay's preference for yellow at Windsor Great Park. Blue became a fashionable colour for the flower-garden in the 1930s, and the same taste reached the rhododendron world, as at Colonsay and Tremeer, where mauve became the dominant colour. (At Colonsay, however, an element of strong contrast was maintained by a bank of orange-scarlet bushes.)[57] But the promotion of individual colours also led to a backlash against others. Christopher Lloyd recommended that:

'. . .some of the most popular and blatantly colourful azaleas should be judged by the same standards as the modern marigold – but more stringently, because the marigold may look reasonably appropriate in its formal garden setting, whereas the hotting up of an informal wood by azaleas is just a bit too much'.

J F A Gibson of Glenarn described his preference for species over most hybrids:

'The traditional Principal Boy in the Pantomime was a splendid creature, but he was usually short on subtlety. So it is with many elepidote hybrids and I would lay heavy blame on *griersonianum* with its shameless carryings-on with white and pink partners. Some of its crosses with red species are, of course, first rate, but I have yet to see one of its pink offspring which I personally can thole.'[58]

Russell Page expressed a nostalgia for what he thought were the monochrome shrubberies of the 18th and 19th centuries, 'invariably of native box and yew, later augmented by cherry laurel, Portuguese laurel, aucubas and skimmias' (he evidently had not read Henry Phillips), a happy situation which had been disrupted by the arrival of the rhododendron. 'Reticence and discipline' were to be the new attitude in garden-making; Page turned 'with relief to planting long quiet stretches of *R.* 'Sappho', *R. fastuosum flore pleno*, *R. catawbiense* or the simple and fragrant *R.*

*luteum'*. In terms of practical recommendations, the gardener was to avoid 'particoloured blight' and restrict himself to a palette of 'white, pale yellow, pale blue, rose and mauve. Bright reds and oranges and violets will throw these subtler harmonies out of key.' On a sufficiently large scale, he was prepared to allow the planting of groupings 'allied by their parentage and in all the modulations and variations of one colour' – so long as contrast was avoided.[59]

Against these trends in colour planning should be set a counter-emphasis on form. Robinson's insistence on keeping rhododendrons distinct enough to display their habit met with an increasingly favourable response in the 20th century. J G Millais promoted the planting of some species for their leaves alone, and J F A Gibson of Glenarn described the Falconeri and Grande series as 'such splendid pieces of garden furniture even when not in flower'.[60] The demand to keep larger-growing rhododendrons separate, rather than making them part of a group, was associated with Holford of Westonbirt, followed by the second Lord Aberconway and Eric Savill ('wider spacing . . . study a plant individually'), and has been heard with greater frequency as the century has progressed. Graham Thomas complained that 'Rhododendron plantings tend to be overcrowded. We have to go to High Beeches in West Sussex or to the landscaped expanses of Lochinch in South-west Scotland to see rhododendrons so well spaced

that we can enjoy their vast beauty.'[61] Later woodland gardens, such as the The High Beeches and the Savill Gardens in Windsor Great Park, placed greater emphasis on glades and a higher proportion of open space to woodland planting.[62]

The most significant instance of the pursuit of form was the work of Eric Savill and Hope Findlay in Windsor Great Park. Savill's work began in 1934, with the cutting of glades and grassy rides through a *R. ponticum* game covert; Findlay arrived in 1943, and the climax of their work was the creation of the Kurume Punch Bowl in the postwar years. 'In our judgement,' wrote Eric Savill, 'harmony of form is more important than that of colour and we are not perturbed if some of the strange mauves and puces find themselves immediately in front of the strongest reds, provided the former are derived from the Kurume . . .' – going so far as to proclaim colour-blindness a merit if it nipped the obsession with colour coordination in the bud. This was an extreme statement, however, and in the 1950s the Kurume Punch Bowl could be held up in other contexts as a model of one school of colouring:

'Colours were blended and distributed so that one colour would not predominate in any one area. The possibility of clashes was not considered to be a problem as it is a well-known fact that where one is mixing a wide range of colours, intermediate shades prevent the clashing of colours which would be intolerable if used in twos and threes . . .' [63]

This attitude to colour grouping, opposed to the colour coordination which was increasingly dominant, was held up for approval less and less as time passed, but the Savill Gardens continued to be invoked as a model for other qualities – those of form, or more specifically of three-dimensional scenic structure. In the early 1970s, Richard Bisgrove offered it as an example in a series of articles on garden planning directed at the amateur gardener with a small garden:

'In one area of the Garden wings of dark rhododendrons flank a broad central walk casting deep shadows against which primulas, azaleas, meconopsis and many other beautiful plants are displayed. Instead of being a flat panorama for the visitor walking up the side of the valley, the scene becomes three-dimensional, with successive groups of flowers receding into the distance. Had the rhododendrons been any closer the whole area would be in gloomy shadow; any further apart and they would be sporadic black lumps in a flat expanse of flowers. Clearly this type of effect is not easily achieved.' [64]

## Epilogue: the Age of Uncertainty

The hiatus in gardening caused by World War II often necessitated a radical new start. Many of the great rhododendron gardens had suffered, becoming neglected and overgrown. Lamellen, begun at the turn of the century, was neglected after 1941, and only brought back by Walter Magor in the 1960s, doing his pruning with his chainsaw. Gillian Carlyon took on the restoration of Tregrehan in 1945; two years later the restoration of H A Mangles' 1870s garden at Littleworth Cross began. Tregye had to wait until 1970 for Edward Needham to acquire it and begin restoration. At Arduaine, failure to thin the tree shelter had resulted in a large number of tall straggling bushes; reorganization of the garden began in 1971. But the phenomenon of gardens falling into neglect is a perennial one; at Eckford House, Benmore, neglect only set in in 1972, and by the end of the decade visitors from the Rhododendron Group were pronouncing the garden impenetrable. [65]

If one single change could be taken to indicate the uncertainties and reversals that have overtaken rhododendron gardening since World War II, it would be the changing reputation of *R. ponticum*. Once its ability to seed itself had been a source of delight; understandably, over-familiarity and the need to slash through *R. ponticum* undergrowth in restoring neglected gardens (one of the major themes of postwar renovation stories) went some way toward diminishing this sense of delight. Seedlings could still reward the gardener, however. Graham Stuart Thomas, perhaps the major inheritor in the mid-20th century of the tradition of Robinson and Jekyll, could praise *R. ponticum* as late as 1984 for its 'supreme value in the landscape; every plant is different and flowers a few days before or after the next, creating a blend rather than a blare.' [66]

As wild gardening slid gradually into a putatively ecological position, however, the attack on *R. ponticum* began. Immediately after World War II, the first wave of 'ecological' landscape theory still welcomed it, precisely because, like sycamore, it had naturalized and had therefore become part of the ecology. Witness Brenda Colvin: 'Rhododendron ponticum, for instance, the pale magenta one that grows so freely from self-sown seeds on light acid soils, has found a place along with heather and gorse, pine and birch on many a common.' [67] By the end of the 1960s, this attitude was becoming unrecognizable as an 'ecological' one; like sycamore, *R. ponticum* was now deemed worthy of extirpation because it competed too successfully with native plants, and the Forestry Commission was labelling it 'a noxious alien weed'.[68]

By the end of the 1960s, an increasing politicization of cultural attitudes was also apparent, affecting gardens as it did everything else. Russell Page had long ago quipped that 'rhododendron addicts form a large class in the upper strata of British gardeners' [69], and this class bias surfaced in the tabloid gardening press in the late 1970s and early 1980s: fulminations against the dominance of rhododendron

growers on the RHS, coupled with predictions that the future belonged to alpines, the democratic plants that could be grown by all.

Dwarf rhododendrons tended to be ignored in this rhetoric, however much actual writing on small garden planting brought them in. 'I do not believe this great genus is really appreciated by the public at large', wrote Lady Anne Palmer, echoing Lionel de Rothschild and other early promoters of dwarfs. 'There is a rhododendron for every garden, great and small.' [70] By the mid-1950s, Branklyn, Keillour, Knightshayes and Glendoick had created a tradition of arranging dwarf rhododendrons; in the first three, peat blocks formed the basis of planting, while at Glendoick, the Coxes experimented with a graded sequence of habits, starting with truly prostrate near the paths and increasing in size toward the centre of the beds.[71]

By the 1980s, the woodland gardens which had once been hailed as the great achievement of the 20th century were slipping rapidly into oblivion as far as garden historians were concerned. In 1960, Miles Hadfield's *Gardening in Britain* listed Hidcote, Bodnant, Sheffield Park, and Westonbirt as the great gardens of the century; in 1986, in Jane Brown's *The English Garden in our Time*, only Hidcote still held that position, to be accompanied by Rodmarton, Sissinghurst, Shute, and other gardens in a more formal tradition – the rest of Hadfield's list had disappeared (even Bodnant, surely one of the most important formal gardens in the country). Christopher Lloyd's quip in *The Well-tempered Garden* about 'a host of exotic but formless woodland "gardens" ' [72] expressed the new attitude succinctly: the plantsman's garden was to be considered a curiosity of horticultural history, not a work of art. I would not like to count the hours that the English Heritage Gardens Committee spent debating whether or when a 'plantsman's garden' qualified for inclusion in the Register of Historic Parks and Gardens.

As, around mid-20th century, landscape architects and garden historians discovered the merits of the 18th-century landscape park, they began to savage the rhododendron planting of the 19th and 20th centuries as inconsistent with the visual values of their preferred period, and the nod was given for the removal of landscape colour from historic landscapes where it was considered inappropriate to period. In 1948 Russell Page attacked the planting of rhododendrons at Stourhead, where in the 1920s a massive programme of replacing laurels, alders, ash, and *R. ponticum* with hybrid rhododendrons had been carried out: the 'whole mood of the composition [was] destroyed by enormous rounded masses of pink, crimson, scarlet and white rhododendrons'. In 1960 Brenda Colvin, in a letter to *The Times*, condemned the plantings for their destruction of the intended 18th-century effect, and the National Trust gradually implemented a policy of regrouping the rhododendrons so as to remove them from the precincts of the lake.[73]

The very idea of a rhododendron garden came under attack during the 1970s. Graham Stuart Thomas wondered whether it would one day be considered 'that, with its ease of cultivation and its magnetic attraction, the rhododendron has had an adverse effect on garden design in these islands'. Russell Page had already said that 'I have yet to see a well planted rhododendron garden'.[74]

But for sheer vituperation, nothing could surpass Germaine Greer in her 'Revolting garden' column in *Private Eye*, with her expressed revulsion for 'bloated heads of rubbery blooms of knicker-pink, dildo-cream and gingivitis-red'. Revising the history of the 20th-century garden, she claimed that:

'…the descendants of the great rhodo propagators deeply regret their ancestors' excesses. The R.H.S. swallowed the Rhododendron Association for the same motive that the whale swallowed Jonah, and is equally incommoded by the fact that it won't stay down.'

Greer herself remarked ruefully on the number of gardens open under the National Gardens Scheme that advertised displays of rhododendrons and azaleas; as usual, it is unwise to assume that the taste of the general public corresponds closely to the recommendations of critics and designers in the horticultural press.[75]

In the face of this apparent backlash against the rhododendron garden, what positive use for the plant can be discovered in the current horticultural press? I suspect that we are beginning to see the emergence into greater prominence of a trend that has been slowly growing during the 20th century: the use of rhododendrons as what have come to be called architectural plants. The insistence on form inherited, through meandering channels, from the subtropical movement of Robinson's young years, has also resulted in the use of rhododendron shelter planting to suggest walls and garden divisions, as at Achamore; of specimens as accompaniments to garden ornaments, as with the famous planting of *R. williamsianum* around a stone tank at Bodnant; of tubbed plants on terraces; of rhododendrons to frame a staircase, as at Glenveagh. The invocation of such architectural effects by Mary Forrest in *Rhododendrons 1990* suggests that this use of rhododendrons may still achieve greater prominence.[76]

But the traditional employment of rhododendrons in the woodland garden continues to furnish possibilities for innovative garden design. The last 20 years have seen the establishment of the former Sunningdale collection of rhododendrons in a new home, in Ray Wood at Castle Howard. The acclaim that has greeted James Russell's planting – for example, the use of bamboo as a windbreak, based on E H Wilson's description of finding rhododendrons against a backdrop of bamboos in China – suggests that there is still new life to be found in the old tradition.[77]

## NOTES

For simplicity the following abbreviations have been used:
*GM – The Gardener's Magazine;*
*GC – The Gardeners' Chronicle;*
*JRHS – The Garden or Journal of the Royal Horticultural Society*

[1] MAGOR, E W M. 'The beginnings of rhododendron growing and hybridization in Britain', *Rhododendrons 1986-7*, pp. 27-32; MILLS, L P. 'Rhododendrons: the early history of their introduction and cultivation', *Rhododendrons 1979-80*, pp. 6-20; KERKHOF-RUIJTER, C (1991). 'The introduction of the rhododendron in the British landscape', MA dissertation, Institute of Advanced Architectural Studies, University of York.
[2] O'NEILL, J (1979). 'From American to Peat Garden', *Country Life*, 30/8/79, 614-16; also (1831) *GM*, vol. 7, 251 for the expression 'heath-mould'.
[3] (1828) *GM* vol. 4, 176; see also vol. 9 (1833): 664-69.
[4] PHILLIPS, H (1823). *Sylva florifera*. 26-7, 33-4.
[5] Ibid. 202-7
[6] ELLIOTT, B (1986). *Victorian gardens*, 48-51, 87-90, 123-8;
(1993) 'A spectrum of colour theories', JRHS, **118**: 573-75.
[7] (1859) *Cottage Gardener*, **21**: 248-49.
[8] MANGLES, J (1839) *Floral Calendar*,.62.
[9] (1859) *GM*,.97.
[10] LOUDON, J C (1822). *Encyclopedia of Gardening*, 1226; (1841) *GC*, 471.
[11] Fonthill: *GM*, (1835). II:.443.
Penjerrick: CHALLINOR DAVIES, V. 'Penjerrick', *Rhododendrons 1980-81*, 26-31. See also *GC*, 1889 ii 749; 1901 i 309-10; and *The Garden*, 55 (1901), 70-1.
[12] (1828) *GM*, 4: 303, 433-37; (1829) *GM*, 5:

382; (1842) *GC,* 591-2.

[13] (1875) *GC,* i 622-3.

[14] (1834) *GM,* **10**: 245-9; (1841) *GC,* 400 [misnumbered 300]; (1858), *GC,* 575-6; (1872) JRHS, **1**: 613-4; (1909) *Journal of Horticulture,* **58** new series: 298-9.

[15] (1843) *GM,* **19**: 436-9, for a list of early hybrids at Dysart;
FISH, R (1856). *Cottage Gardener,* **16**: 256.

[16] ELLIOTT, B. *Victorian gardens, op.cit.,* pp.93-4.
(1834) *GM,* **10**: 248, for the remark about Highclere,.

[17] (1829) *GM,* **5**: 382.

[18] (1841) *GC,* 52 (Mackenzie), 85 (Frost)

[19] (1841) *GC,* 135

[20] (1834) *GM,* **10**: 325-30

[21] (1864) *GC,*.54, for rhododendron game cover at Enville.

[22] ELLIOTT, B. *Victorian gardens (op.cit.),*13-16.

[23] (1875) *GC,* i 655-6

[24] (1902) *GC,* i 184; *Garden,* 1902 i 170.

[25] (1835) *GM,* **II**: 502-3.

[26] LOUDON, (1838). *Arboretum et Fruticetum Britannicum,*.**2**: 1130.

[27] (1414) *Botanical Register,* **17**: 1414; (1831) *GM,* **7**: 135, 251; (1841) *GC,* 400 [misnumbered 300].

[28] (1859) *GC,* 97; (1871) *Journal of Horticulture,* **21**: 162-4; see also (1896) *GC,* ii 747-8, for a comparison between Hookers' plates and specimens at Heligan, reinforced by W Magor's comments in 'The garden at Heligan in Cornwall', *Rhododendrons 1982-83,* 1-3.

[29] (1835) *GM,* **11**: 361.

[30] (1863) *Florist*; (1869) *GC,* 663; (1928) *GC,* ii 308.

[31] (1829) *GM,* **5**: 571-2; (1834) *GM,* **10**: 258, 326, 331-2; (1871) *GC,* 169-70. Much work remains to be done on the history of the rhododendron nurseries; for a beginning, see RUSSELL, J P C (1947). 'Rhododendrons at the Sunningdale Nurseries', *Rhododendron Yearbook* 1947, 33-41; WATERER, G D (1985). 'The Knap Hill azaleas', *Rhododendrons 1985-6,* 26-35;

WILLSON, E J, *Nurserymen to the World* (1989)

[32] (1859) *GC,* 97, 144-5, 169, 193, 216-7, 264-5, 313-4, 360.

[33] (1859) *Cottage Gardener,* **21**: 248-9, 276.

[34] PAUL, W (1892).*Contributions to horticultural literature,* 219-79 (in which Paul's articles, published in *GC* between 1864-67, were reprinted; see also (1873) *Journal of Horticulture,* **25**: 212; (1873) *GC,* 1634-5; (1875) *GC,* i 716-7.

[35] ELLIOTT, B. *Victorian gardens, (op cit.)* 148-52.
Bedgebury: (1867) *Journal of Horticulture,* **13**: 253-5.

[36] ELLIOTT, B (1994). *Waddesdon Manor: the gardens,* and the references given therein.

[37] (1878) *Journal of Horticulture,* **34**: 69-71.

[38] (1880) *Journal of Horticulture,* **38**: 96-8, 182.

[39] (1906) *GM,* 253-6; (1934) *Country Life,* **75**: 267; (1935) 77: 273 (identical text); (1963) *GC,* ii 316-7.

[40] (1879) *The Garden,* **16**: 53-4; (1885) *GC,* i 798-9; (1891) i 667-8; (1894) ii 137-8; (1902) *Country Life,* **11**: 336-43.

[41] JEKYLL, G (1899). *Wood and Garden,* 64-70.

[42] (1914) *Journal of Horticulture,*.**68** new series: 272-3.

[43] (1880) *GC,* ii 325-6; (1892) *GM,* **35**: 397-8; (1900) *The Garden,* **58**: 271-2.

[44] ARMYTAGE-MOORE, H (1948). 'Rhododendrons at Rowallane', *Rhododendron Yearbook* 1948, 16-19; KNIGHT, FP (1966). 'Rhododendrons at Werrington Park' *Rhododendron Yearbook* 1966, 9-20.

[45] Abbotsbury: (1899) *GC,* ii 142-4: 'every conceivable variety of the Himalayan Rhododendron' grown in one secluded spot, otherwise no reference; contrast this with KELLY, J (1985) 'Abbotsbury Gardens', *Rhododendrons 1985-6,* 43-46.
Bodnant: (1950) *JRHS,* **75**: 261-9.
ABERCONWAY, 'The gardens at Bodnant'.
Borde Hill: (1902) *Country Life,* **12**: 840-5; contrast this with Clarke, RNS (1977) 'The Rhododendron species at Borde Hill', *Rhododendrons 1977,* 6-14.

Westonbirt: (1873) *Journal of Horticulture*, **25**: 81-4; contrast with FINDLAY, T Hope (1965). 'Rhododendrons at Westonbirt Arboretum', *Rhododendron Yearbook* 1965, 45-9.

[46] Minterne: (1902) *Country Life*, **11**: 528-33; DIGBY, Lord (1956). 'The history of the Minterne rhododendron garden', *Rhododendron Yearbook* 1956, 9-15.

Leonardslee: (1906) *GC*, ii 253-4, 272-3; SYNGE, PM (1955). 'Camellias and rhododendrons at Leonardslee', *Rhododendron Yearbook* 1955, pp.7-16.

Caerhays: WILLIAMS, C, (1949). 'Rhododendrons at Caerhays Castle', *Rhododendron Yearbook* 1949, 142-153; 'The age of rhododendrons at Caerhays', *Rhododendrons 1976*, 22-25.

[47] (1939) *GC*, ii 120.

[48] (1928) *GC*, i 156-8, 203.

[49] See various articles by SCHILLING, T: 'Rhododendrons at Wakehurst Place, the story so far', *Rhododendrons 1972*, 5-8; 'The Himalayan glade at Wakehurst Place', *Rhododendrons 1976*, 18-21; 'The Trans-asian heath garden at Wakehurst Place', *Rhododendrons 1992*, .20-23.

[50] (1930) *GC*, i 268; GOULD, N K & SYNGE, P M (1948). 'Rhododendrons at Tower Court', *Rhododendron Yearbook* 1948, 8-15.

[51] HANGER, F (1948). 'Rhododendrons at Wisley', *Rhododendron Yearbook* 1948, 20-34; (1953) *JRHS*, **73**: 122-7; LLOYD, C (1994). *Country Life*, **188**: 92.

[52] (1930) *New Flora and Sylva*, **2**: 171-9, 230-8; COLYER, J E (1978). 'Lea Rhododendron Gardens', *Rhododendrons 1978*, 18-21.

[53] ROTHSCHILD, L de (1940). 'Features of my garden – The home wood at Exbury', *JRHS*, **65**: 111-14; see also HANGER, F (1946) 'Exbury rhododendrons' *Rhododendron Yearbook 1946*, 5-18; and of course LUCAS-PHILLIPS, C E, & BARBER, P N (1979). *The Rothschild rhododendrons*, 2nd ed.

[54] ROTHSCHILD, L de (1940). *JRHS* (*op. cit.*).

[55] CROWE, S (1958). *Garden Design* 124-6; LEES-MILNE, A & VEREY, R (1980). *Englishwoman's Garden*, 76.

[56] ROTHSCHILD, L de (1953). 'The placing and planting of rhododendrons', *Rhododendron Yearbook* 1953, 9-32; CROWE, S. (*op.cit.*) 126; LEES-MILNE, A, &VEREY, R. (*op.cit.*) 29.

[57] SYNGE, P M (1970). 'Rhododendrons and camellias atTremeer', *Rhododendron Yearbook 1970*, 37-44.
(1955) 'Rhododendrons at Colonsay', *Rhododendron Yearbook 1955*, 24-30.

[58] LLOYD, C (1970). *The Well-tempered Garden*, 192-3; GIBSON, J F A (1967). 'The garden at Glenarn', *JRHS*, **92**: 341-7; see also CAMPBELL, Sir I (1983) 'Glenarn and the Gibson family', *Rhododendrons 1983-4*, 1-5.

[59] PAGE, R (1962). *Education of a Gardener*, 181-9.

[60] Millais, J G (1917). *Rhododendrons*, first series, 3; GIBSON, J F A (1967) *JRHS* (*op cit.*).

[61] SYNGE, P M (1954). 'Lord Aberconway and rhododendrons at Bodnant', *Rhododendron Yearbook 1954*, 7-11; SAVILL, E H (1954). 'The collection of rhododendron species at Windsor Great Park', *Rhododendron Yearbook 1954*, 17; THOMAS, G S (1984). *The art of planting*, 59; but see WILLIAMS, F J (1966). 'The garden at Caerhays', *JRHS*, **91**: 279-86, for a recommendation of thick planting and warnings about the fate of widely spaced specimens.

[62] BOSCAWEN, E & A (1974). 'The High Beeches', *Rhododendrons 1974*, 8-12; SAVILL, E (1950). 'The woodland gardens of Windsor Great Park', *Rhododendron Yearbook 1950*, 7-15.

[63] SAVILL, E. ibid., 12-13; see also ROPER, L 'The Kurume punch bowl at Windsor', *Rhododendron Yearbook 1956*, 22-27; and (1959) *The gardens in the Royal*

*Park at Windsor.*

64 BISGROVE, R (1973). 'Garden design', *JRHS*, **98**: 524-5.

65 Lamellan: 'An American looks at British rhododendron gardens', *Rhododendron Yearbook 1965*, 12-24.

Tregrehan: LAMB, C (1983). 'Tregrehan: the restoration of an old garden', *Rhododendrons 1983-4*, 25-9.

Littleworth Cross: GORDON, Lady A (1976). 'The restoration of the Mangles garden at Littleworth Cross, Surrey', *Rhododendrons 1976*, 13-17.

Tregye: NEEDHAM, E (1975). 'Tregye: rejuvenating a rhododendron garden in Cornwall', *Rhododendrons 1975*, 23-26.

Arduaine: CAMPBELL, Sir I (1966). 'The gardens at Arduaine', *Rhododendron Yearbook 1966*, 31-38; WRIGHT, E A T (1979). 'Arduaine revisited', *Rhododendrons 1979-80*, 27-34; and (1987) 'Arduaine today', *Rhododendrons 1987-8*, 25-9.

Eckford House: LOWES, K & HALL, A (1979). 'The garden at Eckford House, Benmore', *Rhododendrons 1979-80*, 47-54.

66 THOMAS, G S (1983). *Trees in the Landscape*, 88.

67 COLVIN, B (1948). *Land and Landscape*, 144.

68 ROBSON, M (1991). 'The ponticum problem', *Rhododendrons 1991*, 46-49.

69 PAGE, R (1969). (*op. cit.*), 189.

70 LEES-MILNE, A & VEREY, R (*op. cit.*), 99.

71 HICKSON, M (1974). 'Rhododendrons, magnolias and camellias of Knightshayes Gardens', *Rhododendrons 1974*, 18-20; COX, E H M & P A 'Rhododendrons at Glendoick', *Rhododendron*

*Yearbook 1968*, 5-16; COX, P (1976). 'The ideal dwarf shrub', *JRHS*, **101**: 144-7; GEORGE, A (1973). 'Choosing rhododendrons for a small garden', *JRHS*, **98**: 541-5.

72 LLOYD, C. *Well-tempered Garden* (*op.cit.*), 192.

73 WOODBRIDGE, K. 'The planting of ornamental shrubs at Stourhead: a history 1746 to 1946', *Garden History*, 4(i): 88-109, esp. pp.103-4; PAGE, R (1969). (*op. cit.*), 188; PAVORD, A (1995). 'Gardens' in NEWBY, H ed., *The National Trust – the next hundred years*; NATIONAL TRUST (1978). *The conservation of the garden at Stourhead.*

74 THOMAS, G S, *Art of Planting* (*op.cit.*), 59; PAGE, R (1979). 'English gardens from 1910 to the present day', in HARRIS, J ed., *The Garden*, 73.

75 *Private Eye*, no. 423 (3 March 1978), 8.

76 FORREST, M (1990). 'Rhododendrons in garden design', *Rhododendrons 1990*, 38-41.

77 RUSSELL, J (1981). 'Origins of the rhododendron collection at Castle Howard, North Yorkshire', *Rhododendrons 1981-82*, 29-30; LEMMON, K (1978). *The gardens of Britain: vol.5, Yorkshire and Humberside*, 62-4.

DR BRENT ELLIOTT, *Librarian and Archivist for the Royal Horticultural Society's Lindley Library, is author of* Victorian Gardens *(1986) and* The Country House Garden *(1995)*

# CHAPTER 15

# RHODODENDRON LOVERS IN THE BRITISH ISLES

## CYNTHIA POSTAN

It is clear that up to the mid-19th century the cultivation of rhododendrons was a hit and miss affair. Little was known about suitable growing conditions and quite hardy plants were often killed by being over-cosseted. James Bateman at Biddulph Grange, in his efforts to simulate a Himalayan 'ravine', failed utterly to achieve a satisfactory environment. And so it went on right up to the time when the Chinese rhododendrons arrived. The plants sent by the French missionaries to Franchet in Paris all died through ignorance.

However, after the Himalayan species had been established in the milder areas of the British Isles, the fortunate owners had a taste of things to come. Sir John Lemon of Carclew, 'one of the fathers of gardening in Cornwall', encouraged his friends to experiment with Joseph Hooker's species. Mary Forrest has shown how they gave gardeners experience in a favourable environment. James Veitch, the first nurseryman to grasp the potentiality of plants

from Western China, and Ernest Wilson, his collector, brought to this country in 1900 a large number of seeds of the new *Rhododendron* species. James Veitch invited John Charles Williams, (see figure 18) who had been growing rhododendrons in his garden at Caerhays since 1885, to experiment with Wilson's seeds; 25 sorts were bought from the first collection (these were planted out in 1905-6) and 15 from the second collection. A number of these introductions first flowered at Caerhays. It was no wonder that this garden became the focus of interest in the new species.

More new species came from George Forrest's expeditions in Yunnan, financed initially by another nurseryman, A K Bulley, but in 1905 and later, partly by J C Williams. Percival Dacre Williams, the cousin of J C Williams, whose garden at nearby Lanarth was equally favourable, was also growing rhododendrons. Other gardeners and friends began to follow this absorbing activity. One in particular,

Charles Eley, had from 1909 onwards been deeply engaged in raising the new flowering shrubs and trees from China. Unfortunately, he gardened in East Anglia, a harsher and dryer climate although this did not prevent him from trying to grow rhododendrons. The scene was thus set for a momentous coming together of gifted amateurs with the leisure and space required to pool their acquired knowledge.

## The Rhododendron Society

On a visit to Lanarth in 1915 Charles Eley had suggested to his friend, P D Williams, that they should form a group whose aim would be to share experience on a regular basis, but his suggestion was not then received with much enthusiasm. Later his scheme for an informal group of friends contributing regular notes to be privately circulated bore fruit. On his next visit, Mr John Guille Millais, of Compton Brow, Horsham, was present and PD Williams straightaway introduced Charles Eley as 'the Promoter', announcing abruptly – 'we are the Rhododendron Society and Charles Eley is the Honorary Secretary.' This momentous occasion and subsequent events are recounted by another friend and founder member, George Johnstone of

*Charles Eley of East Bergholt in Suffolk, the so-called 'promoter' of the Rhododendron Society. He was its honarary secretary and editor of the* Rhododendron Society Notes *from 1916 to 1931*

*George Johnstone of Trewithen in Cornwall. With his neighbours, J C Williams of Caerhays and P D Williams of Lanarth, he was a founding member of the Rhododendron Society and its unofficial historian*

Trewithen (*Rhododendron and Camellia Year Book,* No. 22, 1958, pp. 9-22), to which Charles Eley himself has added his own witty and self-deprecating memories (ibid, p. 22).

It is sad that 80 years have no connotation in the measurement of time to indicate their significance in man's progress, because 1916, the date of the foundation of the Rhododendron Society, was truly memorable for our chosen genus. Rhododendrons now grow all over the temperate world, honoured and nurtured by specialist societies in many countries, but in 1916 the British Society was the first such and became the channel for cooperation between four groups of people. Each was to play a vital part in the story. Pride of place must be given to botanists and collectors, for without William and Joseph Hooker the door might never have been opened. But nurserymen and private gardeners, representing commercial and amateur status, also played an essential part.

The Rhododendron Society was formed with the minimum of organization – a chairman (J C Williams) and a secretary (Charles Eley), both honorary posts – and few rules (of which no written record now exists). The founding fathers (J C Williams, P D Williams, J G Millais and Charles Eley) rapidly drew up a list of garden owners who were to be invited to join. These were: Major A Dorrien-Smith of Tresco, George Johnstone of Trewithen, Dame Alice Godman of South Lodge,

*John Guille Millais of Compton Brow, Horsham, was staying with PD Williams when Charles Eley unfolded his scheme for a society. He was one of its most energetic supporters and the author of the first book on hybrids*

Gerald Loder (Lord Wakehurst) of Wakehurst Place, Sir Edmund Loder of Leonardslee, Lieutenant Colonel Stephenson Clarke of Borde Hill (see figure 11), Edward Magor of Lamellen in Cornwall, Kenneth McDouall of Logan, Lieutenant Colonel Rogers of Riverhill in Kent, Sir John Ross-of-Bladensburg, in Northern Ireland, Sir John Llewellyn of Penllaergaer in Wales (died 1922), John Nix (died 1922) and Charles Nix of Tilgates in Surrey. Two more joined in 1916 – Sir Herbert Maxwell of Wigtownshire and H Armytage Moore of Rowallane in Northern Ireland. Four more in 1917 – the Earl of Stair, Lochinch, Sir John Stirling Maxwell of Pollok, near Glasgow, the Marquess of Headfort of Kilmacurragh in Ireland and Sir George Holford of Westonbirt (died 1926). Mrs Cuthbert of Beaufront Castle joined in 1919, Lionel de Rothschild and Eustace Wilding of Wexham Place in 1920 and Sir John Ramsden of Muncaster in 1922. Finally, Henry McLaren (later 2nd Lord Aberconway) of Bodnant in Wales and J B Stevenson of Tower Court joined in 1923, making 25 in all, although there were deaths during the early years.

Almost immediately the crucial decision was taken to elect as honorary members professional botanists from the two great Royal Botanic Gardens where so much of the work was being done – Professor (later Sir Isaac) Bayley Balfour, Regius Keeper of the Royal Botanic Garden, Edinburgh (RBGE), and W J Bean, Curator at the Royal Botanic Gardens, Kew (Kew); they were soon joined by the two great collectors, E H Wilson and George Forrest, and one eminent older gardener, Clara Mangles. These honorary members were elected for obvious reasons, but the list soon had to be enlarged again: Sir Frederick Moore, Director of the National Botanic Gardens, Glasnevin in Dublin, Sir David Prain, Director of Kew, and Professor Charles Sargent of the Arnold Arboretum in Boston. But the total number of ordinary and honorary members was always jealously controlled by election, at least partly because the information distributed to members was considered to be confidential until the illiberality of this policy was pointed out by Ernest Wilson.

The Society was immediately active, for all members were bound by the Rules to play a part. Each ordinary member, who by definition cultivated rhododendrons, had to submit every year a short piece describing what went on in his or her garden and what experience had been gained. These reports were published in a multi-volumed publication entitled *Rhododendron Society Notes* and edited by the Honorary Secretary, who carried on throughout his term of office a voluminous correspondence with his fellow members and others. A series of these letters received between 1922-24, preserved by his great-grandson, Rupert Eley, gives a vivid picture of the interests of garden owners in the 1920s. Sadly, few if any of

*J C Williams and George Johnstone comparing notes in the wood at Caerhays. They were frequent contributors to the* Rhododendron Society Notes *and played a crucial role in establishing the Chinese species in cultivation as well as contributing to the information needed to classify the flood of new species sent back by Forrest and Wilson*

Charles Eley's own letters have survived.

*The Rhododendron Society Notes*, published between 1916 and 1931 in three volumes and 15 annual parts, survive in the elegant edition printed for members (the copyright was purchased by the Pacific Rhododendron Society of America in 1976 and has been reproduced in a smaller-format facsimile) and they provide a feast of material about every aspect of species and hybrids, all of which broke new ground at the time. Much of what appeared in these *Notes* has formed the basis of today's received knowledge and practice. Some of the most memorable contributions were J C Williams' list of the species he grew at Caerhays and the reports of the two lectures given to members of the Society by Ernest ('Chinese') Wilson and George Forrest themselves in which they gave first-hand accounts of the natural conditions in which the species were growing.

By 1925 there was a feeling that not all members could sustain or provide a useful annual contribution and Mr Gerald Loder (afterwards Lord Wakehurst) reported on the various changes that might be contemplated. The most important of these was that, in spite of the strictly limited membership, other gardeners and interested parties had become aware of the Society's activities and benefits and were clamouring to be allowed to join. At this juncture it was decided to open ranks to admit whoever wished to join (subject to election), and to agree a

formal constitution with appropriate officers and a fixed subscription. The new body was to be known as the Rhododendron Association and was incorporated in 1928. All the functions of the Society, except one, were transferred to the Association and the Society itself became a purely private group who met at intervals to dine and to exchange views. Membership, however, remained fixed, and there was always keen competition for election whenever a vacancy occurred. It was not finally disbanded until 1951.

It must not be thought that this short account covers all the activities of the Rhododendron Society. But as these form a continuum with those of the Rhododendron Association, an account of them will be, with one exception, postponed until later. The exception, the first botanical monograph devoted to the genus *Rhododendron,* was so important that due credit must be given to the individuals whose brain-child it was.

The first formal botanical description of the species should be recognized as the 'lasting monument to the Rhododendron Society'. It should be remembered that in 1925 new species were still arriving from both Wilson's and Forrest's expeditions. Wilson had already introduced a large number of new species and Forrest was still sending back more.

These were hastily assigned at Edinburgh into what Sir Isaac Bayley Balfour always considered to be a temporary arrangement of series of species with similar characteristics. This story is told in Chapter 2 by Professor and Dr Philipson. However, the number available to gardeners was becoming confusing. The first attempt at making an orderly list came from Sir Isaac himself. His card index was presented after his death to the Society by J C Williams in 1923 and for ease of consultation was lodged in London. At the Society's Annual General Meeting in 1925 Sir Arthur Hill, the then Director of Kew, suggested drawing up an illustrated descriptive list of species. J Hutchinson, the Kew botanist, followed up this suggestion in greater detail. During the next two years three botanists compiled single-page botanical descriptions of each known species grouped into series. They were H F Tagg, RBGE (lepidotes), J Hutchinson, Kew (elepidotes) and Alfred Rehder, Arnold Arboreturm (azaleas). The crucial task of editing the work of these experts was put in the hands of J B Stevenson, a member of the Society since 1922 and later Treasurer of the Association. He has been described as a 'forceful character', and with his experience of building up his own species collection at Tower Court, he was well qualified to bring the project to a successful conclusion.

*The Species of Rhododendron* published by the Society in 1930 was the first attempt at a botanically reputable monograph on the genus and remained valid for many years – in fact probably until the appearance of Dr MacQueen Cowan's and Mr Davidian's revisions in the post-war

editions of the *Rhododendron and Camellia Year Book*. As a publishing venture it remained the sole responsibility of the Rhododendron Society who paid for all the costs of printing and distribution. This was a formidable undertaking for a Society with no funds beyond its 30-odd members' subscriptions, and so, a bank guarantee to cover printing costs was required. Even then, several of the more affluent and generous members were called upon to contribute privately. As each species was described individually in appropriate botanical terms *The Species of Rhododendron* must not be confused with the *Rhododendron Handbooks* for the use of gardeners referred to below. Thirty-eight de luxe copies were printed for the members of the Society and the authors, and a large number were printed for sale to the general public.

## The Rhododendron Association

The structure of the new Association set up in November 1928 remained unchanged until 1939 and the outbreak of World War II. The Constitution adopted was the model for that of the autonomous Rhododendron and Camellia Group revived in 1976 (see p.197). Officers elected were the President (Mr Lionel de Rothschild), the Vice-President (Admiral H Walker-Heneage-Vivian), the Honorary Treasurer (Mr J B Stevenson) and the Secretary (Mr Gurney Wilson). The latter was the only one to receive an honorarium. All these officers retained their positions until

1939. They were supported by an elected Council, E J Crosfield, the Marquess of Headfort, G W E Loder (Lord Wakehurst), the Hon. H D McLaren (2nd Lord Aberconway), F Gomer Waterer, E H Wilding, P D Williams. The Constitution governing membership and the conduct of business was printed in the first *Year Book* of the Association (1929). The subscription was set (and remained until 1945) at One Guinea (£1.1*s* 0*d*) The aims of the Association were brief: 'to encourage, improve and extend the study and cultivation of Rhododendrons by means of publications, the holding of Exhibitions and otherwise'.

The membership, now open to all, increased rapidly. By 1929 the numbers had already risen to 182, of which 13 were the original 25 founding members. There were six honorary members (including JC Williams, who held no office), two botanists (Professor W Wright Smith, RBGE, and W J Bean, Kew) and three plant collectors (George Forrest, Frank Kingdon-Ward, and Ernest H Wilson). Many ordinary members of the RHS joined and the full strength during the next decade hovered around the 350 mark and in the last years overtopped 400.

The new President brought with him the resources of his estate at Exbury and contacts in the wider world, both of which proved invaluable for managing the increased scope of activities. Indeed, the Association's success and international renown during its relatively short life was due in great part to the energy, generosity and dedication of this one man. Close collaboration also developed with the Royal Horticultural Society whose President, since 1931, the 2nd Lord Aberconway, was by good fortune another of the *Rhododronphilloi*. Together, these two friends made *Rhododendron* species and hybrids almost a British monopoly and a model for the gardening world overseas.

The day-to-day business of the Association brought with it a heavier burden for the secretary, and the Association was fortunate in the incumbent, Mr Gurney Wilson whose previous experience had been with *The Orchid Review*. He had much to offer the Association when it came to producing the famous Handbooks (see below). The Association also took over the organization of the annual Rhododendron Show, started by the Society in 1926.

The first important innovation was undoubtedly the new *Year Book,* edited by Lionel de Rothschild himself, offering members a different content from that of the old *Notes*. The main contents, apart from basic information such as the names of the officers, the constitution and the membership list, included some memorable articles on the characteristics of the species by Lionel de Rothschild and guidelines for would-be hybridizers based on his own experiences. In addition, it printed an up-to-date description of species in their series, compiled by W J Bean and J B Stevenson, and included new species as they were received and allocated by

*Lionel de Rothschild of Exbury Park, Southampton,
(1882-1942), President of the Rhododendron
Association from its beginning in 1928 until 1939.
His leadership and generosity were crucial factors in
promoting international interest in rhododendron
cultivation*

RBGE. It was, in the words of the President, compiled 'entirely from the garden point of view' and was 'of no interest to the botanist'. (The delightful addition of the anglicization of the Latin names was provided by E H Wilding from his book *The Names and Addresses of Rhododendrons).* But the format was the same as that of Part One of the *Rhododendron Handbook,* or 'Guide to the Rhododendron Species in General Cultivation', later published jointly in 1956 by the RHS and the Rhododendron Group. It also contained the first list of hybrids available from the principal nursery gardens. This became later Part Two of the *Rhododendron Handbook* and both parts will be referred to again later in the post-war section of this chapter (p. 197). Gardeners had never before had this information in such a compact form. It was also the first attempt at rating hardiness as well as the garden worth of hybrids. This last criterion did not always meet with the agreement of all members and to some extent was bound to reflect the personal taste of the assessors and the special climatic conditions of the British Isles.

What must be noted here is the part played by the secretary in putting together the material for the descriptions of the species and the names and parentage of the hybrids. The Association owed an enormous debt to Gurney Wilson. He used his experience of similar publications on the Orchidaceae, and more particularly that part dealing with hybrids. This method of presenting the material came to be known as the 'Stud Book' on the analogy of bloodstock breeding (see p. 197).

The first special 'Rhododendron' show also dated from this time. Held at the RHS Floral Hall, the show was organized by the Society on 26 April 1926 and subsequently by the Association who provided the judges and prize money. The first show was an unqualified success from the public's point of view, although its successor was affected, as many shows have been since then, by adverse weather in the weeks before. The Association received gate money from the attendance, but the Annual Accounts do not reveal that it contributed to the hire of the hall or to other expenses of the RHS so we must presume that it was part of the regular succession of shows staged by the RHS. However, what the accounts do tell us is that the shows, together with the printing and

distributing of the *Year Books*, were the main responsibility of, and a heavy drain on, the somewhat precarious resources of the Association. It was necessary more than once for an appeal to go out to members to contribute something extra. The appeal was never in vain, although the number of those who responded was smaller than the total membership.

However, the shows at Vincent Square have been a permanent fixture for the last 70 years and are still a great attraction. Many cups and medals have been presented over the years and are still keenly competed for. These include Challenge Cups for the best amateur and the best trade exhibits presented by Lionel de Rothschild; the Crosfield Cup for six hybrids raised by the exhibitor; the De Rothschild Cup for eight species; the Loder Cup for one hybrid truss; the McLaren Cup for one species truss; and the Roza Stevenson Cup for one hybrid spray. Awards to individuals still presented today include the Loder Rhododendron Cup presented by Lord Wakehurst in memory of Sir Edmund Loder, a founder member who died in 1920, to an individual who had contributed to horticulture; and the Alfred Waley Medal to a working gardener who has contributed to the cultivation of rhododendrons. Many of these awards date back to the 1920s and the old Rhododendron Society and had been transferred to the Association. Gold, silver gilt, silver and bronze medals with the Society's own *Rhododendronphilloi* logo were also awarded annually and are still treasured by the recipients.

There were many other innovations. One of the most original and influential for gardeners and nurserymen alike has been the Trials of new hybrids. The President generously offered space at Exbury in the early years. Plants from trade and amateurs alike were monitored regularly during the growing season by teams of experts, and those most suited for garden decoration were recommended to the RHS. The trials began in 1929 and continued until 1938 when they were transferred to the Society's garden at Wisley, as being more accessible for what had to be frequent visits. They were resumed after 1946 and continue up to the present day.

The trials were yet another example of the growing collaboration between RHS and Association and may have been one of the reasons why it was thought useful to have a mixed body representing both the RHS and the Association. Whatever the reason for the initial push, a Joint Committee began to meet in 1938 to regulate trials, consider awards to individual plants (the RHS had been making these for many years) and to judge the competitions at the specialist shows. It is today a Standing Committee of the RHS (known as the Rhododendron and Camellia Committee) with an equal representation, although it has no direct connection with the present Rhododendron Group. After 1945 it assumed even greater importance, as will be told later in this chapter.

**The RHS Group**

The Second World War of 1939 to 1945 inevitably caused a complete break in the activities of the 'Rhododendron' fraternity and the affairs of the Association went into hibernation for the duration.

When British gardens awoke from their slumber, things were, alas, never to be quite the same. Lionel de Rothschild, the Association's President, whose name had become practically synonymous with the Rhododendron Association, had died in 1942 aged only 60, and sadly none of his colleagues felt able to assume his mantle. His friendly rival in the hybrid business, Lord Aberconway, was committed to leading the RHS itself. Indeed, as I mentioned above, the Association's activities had in many respects become so closely entwined with the RHS that it seemed illogical to incur the extra expense of administration merely to maintain a separate identity when so many of the Association's concerns were already being managed by the Joint Committee. The sensible solution seemed to be to wind up the Association and to allow all members who so wished to register without subscription for membership of a 'Group, whose main interest would be rhododendrons'. Such membership would be open to all other RHS members at their will.

The Association was thus wound up and the assets were transferred to the RHS. The new Rhododendron Group was formed on the lines of the RHS Lily, Daffodil and Fruit Groups. In September

1945 a meeting of the Association passed a resolution to this effect. The existing Joint Committee, now a Standing Committee of the RHS, took over the adjudication of the shows and competitions; the awards and the supervision of the programmes. The *Year Book* also became the responsibility of the RHS through the Committee. An Editorial Board was set up to plan the dissemination of new information on classification, propagation, cultivation and hybridizing, hitherto the responsibility of the Association, by an RHS official team, in particular, Patrick Synge and N K Gould. The immediate result was the appearance in 1946 of the first of a series of 25 elegant, green-bound volumes, beautifully printed for those austere days, and lavishly illustrated, entitled *The Rhododendron Year Book*. The contents of the new *Year Books* far outstripped the old *Notes* of the Society or the cheaply produced Association's *Year Books*. The most cursory glance through the pages reveals articles by most of the acknowledged experts on every topic that a reader's fancy might light upon, many of which still make thoughtful reading today. The 1949 issue, Number 4, printed all the papers read at what must be counted as the first Rhododendron Conference ever to be held, attended by many friends from abroad, more especially the USA and Canada. It included a survey of the genus by Dr Mac-Queen Cowan, a paper on rhododendrons in the wild by Frank Kingdon-Ward and another on propagation by Mr Francis

Hanger, lately head gardener at Exbury. This kind of standard was maintained throughout the 25 years of its existence and make the series a permanent record worth consulting by botanists and horticulturists alike.

The same number also described a post-conference tour of nine major rhododendron gardens from Exbury, through Dorset to Cornwall and north west to Bodnant. This pattern for organized tours gradually became established, starting with one-day tours but eventually branching out into tours lasting up to a week. They were all organized by the Joint Committee's secretary, Robert Adams, and proved very popular, introducing a wider circle of gardeners to specialized rhododendron gardens. By 1966 they had become, with the annual shows, and the awards, important aspects of the Rhododendron Group's programme.

Membership was open to all RHS members and the numbers were about 300. The Committee already dealt with camellias and this genus was incorporated into the Group by order of RHS Council in 1957. *Year Book* No. 8 became the first *Rhododendron and Camellia Year Book*.

Of great importance was the publication of the material which had previously appeared in the Association's Year Books. Parts One and Two of *The Rhododendron Handbook* were first published in 1947. Part One – *Rhododendron Species in General Cultivation* - was the successor to the Association's *Year Books* for 1929 to 1939.

It made available to the general public a list of rhododendrons in their series; an alphabetical list of *Rhododendron* species (with synonyms); other species not in general cultivation; and, finally, lists of collectors' numbers from 1910 through to 1956. Revisions of Part One continued to be published until 1980. Part Two, *Rhododendron Hybrids,* the 'Stud Book', contained an alphabetical list of *Rhododendron* hybrids with their parentage and raisers (with dates). Another list gave the name and progeny of the different species. A third list gave names of hybrids usually available in the British Isles with stars for excellence and hardiness rating.

Unfortunately, these publications, particularly the *Year Books*, although sold at the lowest possible margin, were never to cover their costs, even though they were valuable contributions to horticultural knowledge. At the 1971 Annual General Meeting of the RHS, the President announced that the *Year Books* (including the Daffodil and Lily versions) were to be discontinued, as he admitted, entirely because of inflation and rising costs. The Treasurer also gave details of the gap between printing costs and sales. Looked at like this, the President pointed out that the main body of Fellows (as members were called in those days) were subsidizing a minority group and that this could not in equity be justified. In fact, it was the grave financial position of the RHS itself which turned the balance against the so-called 'minority interests'.

## The Autonomous Rhododendron, Camellia and Magnolia Group

Thus, once more the *Rhododendronphilloi* faced crisis, and this time it threatened to be terminal. A number of people on the Joint Rhododendron and Camellia Committee were not prepared to accept this fate and determined that the Group should not die. A quick dip into their pockets ensured that the 1972 number of the *Year Book* appeared on time. It did so in a slimmer, altogether different although cheerful, format, with the encouraging words of the Chairman, Sir Giles Loder: 'this modified edition can . . . keep readers up to date with recent introductions' and produce 'articles on how rhododendrons and camellias thrive, both at home and abroad'.

Mr Alan Hardy became the Honorary Editor whose responsibility it was to assemble the *Year Book's* contents, and it was largely due to him that the series continued to appear regularly each year and to fulfil its essential function as the flagship of the *Rhododendronphilloi*. At the RHS Elspeth Napier and James Platt gave him support in its production.

From 1973 to 1976 the *Year Books* were the only sign that the Rhododendron Group had survived. But in the background another generation of enthusiasts was equally determined that the Group should have a corporate existence. Early in 1976 a small committee of former members met to discuss taking over the administration from the RHS officials. A list of former members was circulated to know if they would be interested; 169 individuals replied in the affirmative and they became the nucleus of the new autonomous Group. For the first time since 1939 they were required to pay a subscription. For this £3.00 they were to receive the Year Book and a new bulletin. A committee was formed: after some early changes the Chairman was Walter Magor, the Honorary Secretary John Waugh Owens and the Treasurer David Farnes. Walter Magor also took over as Honorary Editor in 1974. The Bulletin was edited from 1978 until 1981 by Kenneth Lowes. He was later succeeded by Bruce Archibold, who in 1986 became Chairman of the Group, a post he still holds. In 1994 he was awarded the Loder Cup for services to horticulture in the field of rhododendrons.

Thus was the Rhododendron Group 'born again' and took charge of its own destiny. Although it never again controlled shows, competitions and trials, those who judged and sat on the relevant committees were inevitably also Group members. In this way close contact and sharing of responsibility with the RHS was maintained and still continues to the mutual advantage of both.

Since 1977 membership has increased to over 750, many members coming from overseas. Considerable activity now takes place within the regional branches (now numbering 10), who organize local lectures, shows and plant exchanges. This helps to mitigate the difficulties of visiting London, far away for many. But for the future, better liaison between the branches themselves and with the centre would certainly be to the Group's advantage. However, this is not history and does not concern us here.

CYNTHIA POSTAN *has been a member of the Rhododendron Group since the early 1950s and has edited the Year Book since 1988*

# CHAPTER 16

# RHODODENDRON LOVERS AROUND THE WORLD

## CYNTHIA POSTAN

Rhododendron lovers (or *Rhododendronphilloi*, as the British Rhododendron Society liked to call themselves) were not slow to discover the benefits of joining together to help each other. The British Society (including Scotland, Ireland and Wales) was the first to see the advantages in 1915 (see Chapter 15) and for a decade remained the only one. When, in 1928, as the Rhododendron Association, it widened its field to all comers, its advice and assistance were readily available to gardeners in other countries. Whether its existence was known in North-West Germany where a specialist nursery industry was establishing itself is not clear, for the German Rhododendron Society was formed in 1936, making it the second in time. It was not until the end of wartime restrictions that the next phase began. The USA and New Zealand vie for pole position here, both being formed in 1944, to be followed by Australia in 1954. Canada and Japan formed societies in 1972, the Swedes not long after, and in 1983 the Scottish Rhododendron Society broke

away from their English colleagues. Smaller groups exist, some national like the Sikkim Rhododendron Society and the Danish and, most recently of all, the Estonian Chapters of the American Rhododendron Society (ARS) and others regional, like the Rhododendron Group of the English Northern Horticultural Society. The last to be formed is the French Rhododendron and Companion Plants Group of the Société Nationale d'Horticulture de France. Total numbers of *Rhododendronphilloi* may now have reached between 7,000 and 8,000 worldwide. A formidable army.

As will be seen below, there are more similarities than disparities in their organization, and certain trends can be observed. In their early days, societies were hesitant in their aims: arranging for cultural instruction and distribution of plants at first, only later becoming aware of the possibilities of creating new hybrids and, more importantly, of learning about the original wild species. The creation of a species collection may, therefore, be taken as a sign of a Society's maturity.

Each Society is governed by what is possible in terms of climate and geography, but all have certain basic organizational problems. Among these are how to give widely separated gardeners access to others. The ARS quickly invented the 'Chapter', a device which enabled them to draw into the fold members from all the States of the Union as well as from other countries. Smaller national societies have created regional groups, in the case of New Zealand, autonomous. All, however, have to face up to financial realities and the difficulty of achieving all their desired aims.

The ultimate objective must be to create a viable international association. Tentative steps have been made in this direction and Ralph Sangster (Australia) has for many years worked hard to maintain links with the national societies through the International Rhododendron Union. There have been five official international conferences in various venues worldwide, drawing together experts to inform each other of botanical, scientific and horticultural progress. The conference literature has disseminated the resulting advances in useful knowledge. Apart from species and conservation collections, laboratory and garden research is going on in institutions too numerous to mention.

## The German Rhododendron Society (Deutsche Rhododendron Gesellschaft)

Founded in 1936, before the 1939-45 War, the German Rhododendron Society was the second oldest such society. However, in two major respects its origins were strikingly different from those of all the others. The Society had from the start a close relationship with a specialist garden under public control. The second difference was that its creators were not the owners of broad acres with the space and inclination to experiment with unknown species, as in Britain, nor yet were they prosperous amateurs with the desire to beautify relatively small gardens with their own hands, as on the Pacific coast of the USA and the countries of the Antipodes. They were men with an urban background. By a fortunate chance they had a flourishing commercial nursery industry near at hand.

The medieval Hanseatic port of Bremen had a wealthy merchant class who had for generations built themselves houses with large 'parks' on the outskirts of the city. Intensely patriotic, they had a tradition of generous public benefactions. Not far to the south, the town of Oldenburg was the centre of a lowlying region with a peaty soil, perfect conditions for growing ericaceous plants. These two factors were to prove a winning combination.

Although the first rhododendrons to be grown in North Germany were in the Schlossgarten of Oldenburg about the year 1800, the first nursery specialising in ericaceous plants was that founded in 1845 by G D Böhlje of nearby Westerstede. Some rhododendrons, such as *R. catawbiense* and *R. caucasicum,* had been introduced into Germany by the great firm of T J Seidel of Dresden (see Chapter 9), but in 1881 Böhlje brought many more from Boskoop in Holland. So successful was he that between the two World Wars at least 30 more nurseries were established in the area. The trade had always been in hardy rhododendrons because the severe North German winters do not permit species to survive in the open, and there was thus no incentive for German botanists and nurserymen to undertake plant collections.

The City of Bremen had had a Botanic Garden since 1905, founded by an oil millionaire, Franz Schütte. When he lost his fortune in the great German inflation, the garden was taken over by the City and was removed to the neighbourhood of the newly established Rhododendron Park, which also owed its origin to private benefactions and support from the City Fathers. The existence of these two flourishing public gardens and a successful nursery industry had a profound effect on the future of Rhododendron cultivation in this part of Germany and hence, inevitably, it led to the formation of a specialist Society.

The preparatory meeting took place on 18 October 1935 in the Council Chamber of the Bremen City Rathaus just when the organization to set up the present Rhododendron Park (on the site of an old private 'park') was going forward. This Park was always intended to be the home of rhododendrons and azaleas, together with other kindred plants. Bremen was considered to be a central situation for the development of horticulture, and a Society devoted to rhododendrons was an obvious accompaniment. The Rhododendron Park and the Deutsche Rhododendron Gesellschaft thus proceeded hand in hand.

The first President, Arnold v. Engelbrechten, was elected, and the Society was launched in May 1937 with the appearance of a small publication entitled *Rhododendron und Immergrüne Laubgehölze* (Rhododendron and Evergreen Shrubs) with contributions from Richard Homann, Dr H Sleumer, T J H Seidel and Camillo Schneider.

Since World War II the Rhododendron Park, and with it the Society, has entered a new and successful era. Enthusiasm for rhododendrons has increased enormously with the appearance of many new and exciting hybrids suitable for small gardens. Membership grew from 82 in 1951 to more than 600 five years later. By 1966 the number had risen to over 1,000 and about 80 per cent of the membership is now private gardeners, five per cent nurserymen and the rest scientists and institutions. Honorary Members included the former President Dr Nolting-Hauff, Herr G D Böhlje and Herr Dietrich Hobbie, both well-known nurserymen. The Society has branches in Essen and Munich, also members overseas in more than 17 countries.

The original aims of the Society were the same as those of other societies: to provide members with information about the cultivation of rhododendrons, to support research and to facilitate distribution. But the proximity of the Rhododendron Park has clearly been of the greatest advantage to the Society. New facilities such as the construction of the various glass and propagating houses have been partially financed by the Society. Study tours to other countries have been popular with between 55 and 85 members taking part. There is a flourishing Journal, *Immergrüne Blätter*, first published in 1962, and currently edited by Professor Dr Wolfgang Spethmann. There is close contact with the Institute for Fruit and Nursery Science of the University of Hannover, where fundamental research on rhododendrons is being carried out.

The present President of the Society is Herr Berndt-Adolf Crome, and the address of the Society is Marcusallee 60, 28359 Bremen.

**The American Rhododendron Society**

It was hardly a coincidence that the American Rhododendron Society had its beginnings in 1944. Prior to World War II, those addicted to rhododendron culture west of the Atlantic relied on contacts with members of the Rhododendron Association and with nurserymen in Britain or on the Continent. There had been a steady stream of information, seeds and plants to American growers and hybridizers. The war brought this all to an abrupt end, and prodded into action those enthusiasts who

felt especially deprived. The idea of an American Rhododendron group had been talked about – even seriously considered – in the 1930s, but the element of necessity was absent until the wartime scarcity provided it.

Two Americans, George Grace and John Henny, travelled up and down the north-west US coast in 1942 and 1943, talking to rhododendron growers, trying to kindle interest in a rhododendron society. A preliminary gathering of growers and collectors met on 29 May, 1944 at the home of ER Peterson in Portland, Oregon. At a second meeting on 20 June, John Henny was elected President and George Grace Secretary. An invitation was then mailed to all persons known to have an interest in the genus, announcing a public meeting for 7 July, 1944. 'A day to be remembered in horticultural history' was John Bacher's prediction. Thanks to publicity, membership applications were received from many states. The name the American Rhododendron Society was adopted in the autumn of 1944.

The members' dues of $5 a year helped finance the publication of a series of informative year books on Hybrids (1945), Species (1946), Stud Book (1947), Azaleas (1948), and Hybrids again in 1949. In that year the membership chose to focus the Society's efforts on the quarterly Bulletin, edited by Rudolph Henny.

Perhaps the greatest contribution to the growth of ARS membership came from the formation of local chapters in cities some distance away from the parent ARS organization at Portland. This enabled local groups to exchange information, seeds and plant materials. Their dues provided the income needed to finance the greatly improving quarterly Bulletin, as well as booklets on culture and other information.

By the 10th year the ARS had nearly 1000 members with chapters at Portland, Seattle, Tacoma, Eugene, Northern California, New York and Virginia (called Middle Atlantic). A plant-name registry was established (coordinated with the RHS), standards for plant ratings and awards were adopted, rules for flower shows were promulgated, two plant explorers (J F Rock and F Kingdon-Ward) were funded and their seed collections distributed. The Portland Chapter *was* the ARS for the first 10 years or so, and its leaders did double duty as chapter and national officers. In addition they oversaw the national test garden at Crystal Springs Lake Island, which was later turned over to the Chapter to manage. This 10-year incumbency by the Portland Chapter proved a disadvantage as it was almost 29 years before the Society was led by an easterner. A new by-law provided two vice-presidents, one from the Western and one from the Eastern region. (Membership was about equally divided between the two.)

John Henny presided over the Society for five years until 1949 when he was succeeded by C I Sersanous who served for almost 10 years until his death in 1958.

'He led the Society through its best years', said his successor, J Harold Clarke, who presided for five years.

By the 20th anniversary in 1964 there were 2,500 members, and 15 more chapters had been added (including Vancouver, BC). A salaried post of Executive Secretary and Editor was created following the unexpected death of the Editor, Rudolph Henny, in 1963. J Harold Clarke was appointed. As a result the Vice-President, Edward B Dunn, became the fourth ARS President. He also served a five-year term. Thereafter the President's term of office was two years. In the ensuing 30 years there have been 13 more presidents: the present incumbent is Herbert A Spady.

In 1965 the Rhododendron Species Foundation was incorporated independently of the ARS to provide a focus for the study and distribution of rhododendron species (see p. 205). A seed exchange initiated by Esther Berry in 1963 had by 1965 grown to be a major enterprise: 2,500 packets were sent out to 227 applicants. Twenty-two years later, seed from 36 states and 13 countries was listed and 12,000 packets were sold. The income provided support for the ARS budget and also helped to fund research projects.

Most of the plants enjoyed by ARS members in the early years were of European origin, but by the 1960s Americans themselves had begun to hybridize and their creations were finding hospitable reception across the country. Thanks to pioneering work in the Pacific Northwest, many fine new plants were introduced. In the eastern USA other breeders produced new hybrids for their less salubrious climate, but this story has been told in Chapter 11.

The quarterly Bulletin printed many articles from home and abroad and when, in 1982, it became a Journal and included research papers, it was recognized as an outstanding publication. There have been eight editors; the present Editor is Sonja Nelson.

The great expansion of chapters and membership had not been foreseen. The Board of Directors (six officers and 12 elected Directors) was increased when the new Chapter Presidents were made Directors. By 1974, with 38 Chapters, the Board with 56 members was unwieldy. Decisions of meetings held alternately on West and East coasts, tended to be inconsistent. New by-laws, approved in 1981, reduced the Board to 19. Chapters were grouped together geographically and were represented by a District Director. By 1994, the 50th anniversary of the Society, there were 72 Chapters, some of them overseas (represented by a Director at Large), and 5,600 members. Dues were $25. An Executive Director was responsible for the smooth running of this considerable organization. J Harold Clarke was the first of these officers and the only individual to have held all three offices of President, Editor and Executive Secretary. The present incumbent is Barbara Hall.

One outstanding achievement has been the creation of an endowed Research Foundation, proposed by August Kehr. Income from the invested endowment helps fund a small number of research projects each year, selected by the committee on research. One important benefit has been the discovery by Dr WC Anderson of the means of propagating rhododendrons by tissue culture.

Much of the work of the ARS is performed by its committees. Appointed by the President, they attend to the increasing number of functions and interests of the Society and its membership. A yearly meeting of the membership takes place at the National Convention, hosted by a chapter or district on alternate coasts each spring. Smaller district and regional meetings are held in the autumn on each coast.

**The Rhododendron Species Foundation**
While the ARS was organizing its members and stimulating the appetite of gardeners and hybridists, about 1961 a smaller but equally enthusiastic group were trying their hand at growing rhododendron species. They were disappointed to find that many so-called species grown from open-pollinated seed were turning out to be hybrids. The early post-war expeditions to China, the home of the most desirable species, had ceased and American specialists found themselves turning toward Britain to fulfil their demands for authenticated wild species.

On a visit to England at this point, Carl Phetteplace met Mrs Roza Stevenson, the widow of JB Stevenson of Tower Court, whose pioneer species collection had been moved to Windsor Great Park. Her fear that many fine species were in danger of being lost to cultivation struck a chord. Phetteplace's report set Dr and Mrs Milton Walker off on a similar trek to Windsor. There Sir Eric Savill and Mr Hope Findlay assured them that they could have any cuttings they wanted from Windsor and that they would help them to obtain cuttings from other British gardens where authenticated species (labelled by collectors' numbers) were growing.

The practical results for the US turned out to be a selection from various British gardens of the finest forms of species. Plant material was sent for propagation to the University of British Columbia, Vancouver, where Evelyn Jack and Nick Weesjes (later to be her husband) grew the plants on for two years.

Meanwhile, the Rhododendron Species Foundation had been incorporated in the state of Oregon, directors and officers chosen and by-laws adopted. Finances were extremely limited and Dr Walker's hope for a substantial endowment whose income would support the work of the Foundation was dashed. The Board opted to accept Dr Walker's generous offer to sell his home place to the Foundation for half its appraised market value and the bulk of the plants were brought there from Vancouver in 1964.

Unfortunately, the Foundation's finances failed to improve and in 1971 the plants had to move once more. As luck would have it, Percy Hadden (Jock) Bryden, lately Director of the Strybing Arboretum at Golden Gate Park in San Francisco had bought land near Salem, Oregon. As a member of the Species Foundation as well as the ARS he provided a new home for the species collection. New facilities were constructed to house the collection and to propagate plants for distribution to members and the nursery trade. Despite some freezing weather and more financial problems the collection prospered. So dramatically indeed that the new accessions outgrew the facilities and another move was imperative.

George Weyerhaeuser of Washington, was persuaded to grant the Foundation a permanent home at his firm's headquarters in Federal Way, Tacoma, Washington. Not only did he provide 9.7ha ( 24 acres), but he also constructed a perimeter fence, and built a greenhouse and lath house. He cleared the land, installed water and electricity as well as giving some financial assistance. The collection was moved to its final home in 1974.

In the last 20 years the collection, now known as The Rhododendron Species Botanical Garden, has seen great changes. Not only has it grown enormously, but its professional staff monitors the purity of the species, and the propagation facilities have expanded. The Foundation has a library, a corps of volunteers, a worldwide newsletter, educational programmes and visitors from around the world.

## New Zealand Rhododendron Association

The New Zealand Rhododendron Association can lay claim to be early in the race for the first national society. It was born at the Massey Agricultural College in Palmerston North on 10 August, 1944, while the War in the Far East was still being fought. Rhododendrons were grown in New Zealand from an early date (see Chapter 5). The climate is favourable almost everywhere from North to South Island, though conditions vary somewhat from warmer to cooler. Even so, the late Edgar Stead's garden at Ilam has been described as 'an inspiration and a cause for grievous envy'. However, six enthusiasts met at the Massey Agricultural College on that August day to adopt the provisional constitution and the inaugural meeting of the New Zealand Rhododendron Association was held on 4 October, 1944. Mr EF Stead was the first President and Dr J S Yeates the Secretary/Treasurer – a post he held for the next 21 years.

The aims were simply to encourage the cultivation, the study and the improvement of rhododendrons by such means as the Association should see fit. Members were to receive two plants each, propagated at Massey College, where the Botanical Department undertook to grow the Association's collection. These mostly came from Edgar Stead's garden at Ilam, but both seeds and plants from Britain (Edinburgh, Exbury and Bodnant among others) and the USA were imported as well as seeds from a late Kingdon-Ward expedition. For about 30 years this plant distribution was to provide members with plant material until commercial specialist nurseries began to fill the gap.

Administered by a council of officers and six members drawn from most districts of New Zealand, the activities of the NZRA have steadily grown. First, a typewritten newsletter kept members informed, then, from the mid-1970s the annual Bulletin was published, with colour pictures from 1981. The NZRA Registration Authority was set up in 1975 with Graham Smith as its first Registrar. Nearly 250 NZ cultivars have been registered with the International Registrar at the RHS Garden, Wisley.

In 1950 land was acquired by Mr W D Cook at Pukeiti Hill, Taranaki in North Island, for a national rhododendron collection, but for financial reasons it was run by a separate Trust: the Pukeiti Rhododendron Trust was incorporated on 31 October, 1951. However, in 1970 the NZRA collection, kept until that time at Massey College, became so congested that a plot of land at Kimbolton, near Palmerston North, was purchased as a new home for the collection. For some years this was maintained by the local Kimbolton Rhododendron Society. In 1989 a specially formed committee undertook to landscape the 4.9ha (12-acre) site and to create a garden that now attracts many visitors.

To fulfil the founders' aims, the

NZRA has been supporting research and the funding of interchanges with botanists and specialists from overseas. Of particular satisfaction has been the visits of botanists from the Kunming Botanic Institute in Yunnan SW China which has led to a permanent Agreement for Partnership between Pukeiti and Kunming. From this has come NZ planting, hunting and seed collecting expeditions of great value and interest to those participating and to members.

The widespread interest of rhododendron growers in the South Island far from Kimbolton and Pukeiti has stimulated the formation of local groups: Dunedin in 1970, South Canterbury in 1973 and Christchurch in 1976 – nine in all from Southland to Auckland. The groups are independent, but share some activities such as entertaining visiting lecturers every other year. Lastly, the National Collection, so much longed for, is at last being established, probably on several sites.

A membership of 1,000, its Kimbolton garden, its Bulletin and the annual conference are all proofs of New Zealand's leading role in the world-wide community of rhododendron lovers.

## The Australian Rhododendron Society

The Australian Rhododendron Society owes its origin to those members of the Ferny Creek Horticultural Society in Victoria who wished to study the genus *Rhododendron*. They formed a study group for that purpose in May 1954 and its success was such that they decided to call themselves the Australian Rhododendron Society (albeit remaining as a section of the FCHS) and to start the quarterly Journal of the Australian Society in 1959. Later in 1990 this became an annual, *The Rhododendron*. Its contents have always been of a consistently high quality.

The aims of the infant Society were anything but modest: its founders wished to extend their influence across Australia as well as within the State; to keep a Register of Australian raised cultivars; to build a library; to publish information; to develop the Australian Rhododendron Festival and to start a garden. At a general meeting on 12 February, 1960, 53 members of the original study group voted to form an autonomous Society which was the nucleus of the Australian Rhododendron Society as it is today.

Almost immediately the search was on to find a suitable site to develop a garden. The site, considered to be ideal was found at Olinda in the Dandenong Range. In August 1960, 40.5ha (100 acres) of the State Forest was set aside by the government of Victoria for the Australian Rhododendron Society to 'develop and maintain [a] garden without cost to the State'. Olinda is densely landscaped with rhododendrons and compatible plants and together with the Show Hall, glasshouses and other equipment it has been built and maintained by volunteers.

At one point in the 1970s the enthusiasm for the development of Olinda produced a nationwide membership of 750-800. Branches in other states were formed, each creating their own garden: at Wollongong on the steep Illawarra Escarpment in New South Wales; in the Mount Lofty section of the Royal Botanic Garden in Adelaide in Victoria.

The Society has formed strong links with the academic research at Melbourne University and it funds plant hunting expeditions, a periodic Baron von Mueller Memorial Lecture and international conferences.

There are great variations in climate, that of New South Wales being tropical and humid, while at Olinda frost and even occasional snow occur. The gardener's task of cultivating rhododendrons is thus quite formidable. Of all the Australian states Tasmania has the most ideal climate and soil conditions, and the Burnie (NW Tasmania) Branch has, in the last 10 years, established at Emu Valley what will probably be the best rhododendron garden in Australia.

The proximity of Papua New Guinea has created a permanent interest in the tropical Vireyas and has led to plant collecting and research into methods of cultivation and hybridization. This is perhaps the most interesting and distinctive avenue for Australian members to pursue, and certainly offers advantages which other national societies do not share. The second generation of members are full of fresh ideas and are more than ready to carry on the Society's ambitious objectives.

## The Rhododendron Society of Canada

For over 50 years a number of Canadian gardeners and some nurseries had been growing hardy rhododendrons in isolation, before a small group of devotees met in 1972 to form a society. They decided to retain a Canadian identity rather than become a part of the American Rhododendron Society to which several of them already belonged individually. As an encouragement and service to new members the executive arranged to provide a few introductory specimens and growing instructions. This led to the publication of a 32-page bulletin, usually circulated twice a year.

In the 1970s and early 80s the Society grew quickly to a membership above 400. Most members lived around Toronto, in Ontario's Niagara peninsula, near Halifax and in the southern part of British Columbia. Because these areas were far apart, three Regional organizations were formed – Toronto, Niagara and Atlantic. However, most members in British Columbia already belonged to the American Rhododendron Society.

Although total membership remained static, the regions became increasingly active, with auctions, group purchases and importations to help swell the numbers of plants in individual gardens. Each region held monthly meetings and lectures and held flower shows, while the Society held a major show and competition each year at either Toronto, Hamilton, St Catharines, Montreal, Halifax, St John's (Newfoundland) or Ann Arbor (Michigan).

With the successful introduction of cultivars able to withstand Canada's climate, two new activities have emerged as major interests. The first is hybridizing and propagation and hybridizers have focused on hardiness as their main goal, some use being made of our native species, *R. canadense* and *R. lapponicum* and a number of new crosses have been registered. The second activity has been the voluntary help given by members towards creating public rhododendron gardens. Several promise to become impressive collections in their respective regions.

The gradual shift towards home and public planting, hybridizing and propagation, has reduced the time available for administration and increased the cost of the bulletin. Twenty years' experience and greater cross-border exchanges have persuaded the Society to accept the ARS's invitation to become one of their districts while still retaining its identity as the Rhododendron Society of Canada. Its three regions have become chapters within the district. There was much soul-searching and some opposition to this decision, which, coupled with an increase in dues, has accounted for a decline in membership. But the increased facilities and excellent bulletins have stimulated renewed enthusiasm and optimism.

**The Japanese Rhododendron Society**

Founded in 1972, the Japanese Rhododendron Society has a present membership of about 1,000. The Society has 40 chapters established throughout the Japanese Archipelago, almost one in every prefecture. The aims of the Society, like many others, are to disseminate knowledge about rhododendrons through meetings, shows, research and publications.

The President's term of office is two years with the possibility of being re-elected for one more term. However, the office of Vice-President is a permanent one, and has been held for the last 20 years by Mr Hideo Suzuki, who is also the officer in charge of international liaison. There is a particular relationship with the RHS as Mr Suzuki is a Corresponding Member.

**The Swedish Rhododendron Society (Rhododendronsällskapet)**

The Swedish Rhododendron Society is a small society of about 650 members. The number is growing slowly but steadily. The majority of members live in Sweden, but there are others in the Scandinavian countries and also Iceland.

One of the founders of the society was Tor Nitzelius of the Gothenborg Botanical Garden, a specialist on rhododendrons who has made several travels to the Far East and had named *R. brachycarpum* subsp. *tigerstedtii,* one of the hardiest of the genus. There is a Chairman (currently Helge Persson), a Vice-Chairman and the usual officers, all of whom act on an honorary basis. For geographical reasons the country is divided into three regions or chapters – East, South and West (because of the severe climate there is no northern region). Each region has its own activities – courses, lectures, garden visits and other things which cannot be centralized – leaving for the centre the production of information (a quarterly Bulletin *Rhododendron Bladet* ), organization of travel, seed distribution and international contacts. Outstanding Swedish rhododendron gardens are the Gothenborg Botanical Garden and the garden of the late King Gustav Adolf at his summer palace, Sofiero, which he bequeathed to the city of Helsingborg. (His Majesty was a member of the British Rhododendron Association.)

The address of the Secretary is: Sven-Goran Alksgrand, Lonndalsv, 10, 450 33 Grundsund.

**The Scottish Rhododendron Society**
The Society was founded in 1983 by a small group of enthusiasts led by Ed Wright of Arduaine who felt there was a need to bring together those keen growers who were unable to attend the shows and meetings in London. From a small nucleus of experts and beginners the Society has grown in the last 11 years and in 1995 has a membership of about 220. It has benefited from the start from being a Chapter of the American Rhododendron Society (see p. 202). With its international organization, the ARS has provided many

facilities that would have been outside the scope of a small society. The advantages enjoyed by the SRS include the quarterly Journal of the ARS and participation in the Seed Exchange.

The Society's own activities include its Newsletter circulated three times a year and a major show, normally with over 500 entries in the Rhododendron section. It is held in a different part of Scotland each year. The Wright Brothers' garden at Arduaine might be considered as the launching pad of the SRS: it has now been presented to the National Trust for Scotland, but members of the SRS (and the ARS) have free entry in perpetuity.

Membership is open to all and has an international flavour. It includes many people from south of the Border as well as other parts of the globe. The affairs of the Society are run by a President, a Secretary/Treasurer and a board of Directors. The first President was Dr S Mackenna of Tarbert, who was followed by Hamish Gunn, Ed Wright and the present incumbent, Mervyn Kessell. The Society has had the confidence to stage the 1996 Annual Convention of the ARS at Oban in Argyll – the first ever to have been held outside the USA.

CYNTHIA POSTAN *has been a member of the RHS Rhododendron Group since the early 1950s and has edited their Year Book since 1988*

# NATIONAL
# SOCIETIES ADDRESSES

*American Rhododendron Society*
Barbara Hall, Executive Dir.
PO Box 1380,
Gloucester, VA 2306
USA

*American Species Foundation*
Donald E King, President,
PO Box 3798,
Federal Way,
WA 98063 3798
USA

*New Zealand Rhododendron Assoc Inc*
J D Sumter, President
PO Box 10
Milton
New Zealand

*Dunedin Rhododendron Group*
D Temple,
PO Box 5052,
Dunedin,
New Zealand

*Australian Rhododendron Society*
(has 4 branches – S. Australia, Tasmania,
Victoria, Illawarra)
Hon. Sec. LB Marsha,
PO Box 21, Olinda,

Victoria, 3788,
Australia

*NW Tasmanian Branch Inc*
(Neil Jordan),
PO Box 39,
Burnie,
Tasmania 7320

*Canadian Rhododendron Society*
Dr HG Hedges,
St. George,
Ontario,
Canada, NOE 1NO

*Danish Chapter of ARS*
Preben Escherich Holkjaer,
Lundegaardsvej 8,
Blovstrod, 3450 Allerod,
Denmark

*Swedish Rhododendron Society*
(Svenska Rhododendron Sallskapet)
Helge Persson,
Frejagatan 12,
S-43144 Mölndal,
Sweden

*Estonian Rhododendron Society*
Olev Abner,

Talinn Botanic Garden,
Kloostrimetsat 44
EE 0019 Talinn, Estonia

*German Rhododendron Society*
Berndt-Adolf Crome, President
2800 Bremen,
33 Marcus Allee.

Prof Dr W Spethmann,
Hon. Sec & Editor,
Institut für Obstbau und Baumschule,
Am Steinberg, Sarstedt. D3200,
W Germany

*Japanese Rhododendron Society*
Hideo Suzuki, RHS representative,
2-3-36 Sekuri-cho,

Kumegaya,
Saitame-ken 360,
Japan.

*Rhododendron & Companion Plants Group*
Société Nationale d' Horticulture de
France
Mons Philippe Demonsablon,
66 rue Denfert Rochereau, 92100,
Boulogne,
France

*Sikkim Rhododendron Society*
KC Pradahn, President
PB No. 25,
Gangtok,737103
Sikkim, India

# ACKNOWLEDGEMENTS

For the national societies: Clarence Barrett, USA; Peter Cameron, New Zealand; H G Hedges, Canada; Dr Lothar Heft, Germany; Mervyn Kessell, Scotland; Lionel B Marshall, Australia; Helge Persson, Sweden; Ralph Sangster, Australia; Hideo Suzuki, Japan.

For photographic research: Primrose Arnander (picture research); Florence Auckland; John Bodenham; Simon Bowes-Lyon; *Country Life* Picture Library; Peter Cox; Rupert Eley; the Exbury Estate; Michael Galsworthy; George Hooker, Ken Hulme (Ness Botanic Garden); Renaud de Kerchove de Denterghem; Lindley Library RHS; Raoul Millais; Tom Smit (Heligan); Ivor Stokes (Clyne Castle); Marilyn Ward (RBG Kew Library); Donald Waterer; John Wilks-Jones; Colin Will (Librarian, RBG Edinburgh); Julian Williams.

For personal communications and archives: Lord Aberconway; Robert E Adams; Melanie Aspey, The Rothschild Archive; Rupert Eley, Eley Archive; David Farnes; Derek and Christopher Fraser-Jenkins; Alan Hardy; Sir Giles Loder; John Waugh Owens; Charles Puddle; David Pycraft; H Sharp; Julian Williams.

For the index: Richard Padley.

The publishers wish to thank the following for their kind permission in allowing the reproduction of the photographs in this book:

Colour: Figure 1 Simon Bowes-Lyon; Figures 2, 5, 7 RBG Kew; Figure 3 Tom Smit; Figure 4 George Hooker; Figure 6 Peter Cox; Figure 8 A F Kersting; Figure 9 George Argent; Figure 10 Walter Schmalscheidt; Figure 11 *Country Life* Picture Library; Figures 12, 13, 14 Lionel de Rothschild; Figures 15, 16 J Heursel; Figure 17 John Bodenham; Figure 18 Cameracraft, Truro; Figure 19 Roel Jacobs, coll. Leon Declerq.

Black and white: pp.28, 44, 65 RBG Kew; pp. 30, 43, 99 (below), 100, 101 RBG Edinburgh; p. 56 George Hooker; pp. 63, 78, 169, 173, 174 *Country Life* Picture Library; pp. 74, 99 (above) University of Liverpool Botanic Garden, Ness; pp. 95, 162, 164, 167 RHS; pp. 110, 111 Walter Schmalscheidt; p.188 (left) Rupert Eley; pp. 188 (right), 191 Michael Galsworthy; p. 189 Raoul Millais; p. 195 Exbury Archives; p. 130 Donald Waterer. The end of chapter engravings are from J D Hooker's *Himalayan Journals* (RHS)

# INDEX

— ❦ —

Species Foundation
(USA), 205-07
*Rhododendron and
Camellia Yearbook,*
193
*Rhododendron Handbook,*
195, 198
*Rhododendron Hybrids,*
199
*Rhododendronphilloi,* 7
*Rhododendron Register*
1958, 50
*Rhododendron Society
Notes,* 190
*Rhododendron* species
and hybrids
*aberconwayi,* 82
Admiral Piet Hein, 127
*aequable,* 91
*afghanicum,* 16
*albiflorum,* 19, 31
*albrechtii,* 29, 34
Alexander, 112
Alice Mangles, 122
Alison Johnstone, 80
Altaclarense, (Alta-
clerense) 116, 120
Anna, 136
*anthopogon,* 16
subsp. *hypenanthum,*
16
*apoanum,* 88
Aprilis, 117
*arboreum,* 15, 16, 17,
71, 73, 114, 116, 119,
125, 128, 160
subsp. *delavayi,* 18
subsp. *zeylanicum,* 16,
76
*argenteum,* 25
*argyrophyllum,* 82
Ascot Brilliant, 120, 175
*augustinii,* 81, 131, 133

*aureum,* 19
*auriculatum,* 13, 133
Aurora, 124
*balfourianum,* 18
*barbatum,* 83, 125
hybrids of, 116
Barclayi, 124, 125
Beauty of Littleworth,
122
Betty, 125
Bianchi, 128
Blue Diamond, 82
Bluebird, 82
Blewbury, 82
Boddaertianum, 117,
128
Boule de Neige, 112
*brachycarpum*
subsp.*tigerstedtii,* 211
Bride, 120
Britannia, 127, 128
*brookeanum,* 89
*burmanicum,* 133
*calendulaceum,* 142
*calophytum,* 74, 132
subsp. *keleticum,* 17
*campanulatum,* 16, 73
hybrids of, 112, 116
*campylocarpum,* 16, 73,
119, 131, 132
subsp. *caloxanthum,*
83
*campylogynum,* 17, 18
*camtschaticum,*19, 24,31
*canescens,* 19, 142
Caractacus, 129
Carita, 133
Carlyon's Cross, 123
hybrids of, 116
*catawbiense,* 19, 109,
128, 162, 178, 202
hybrids of, 116, 118,
138

*caucasicum,* 114, 125,
202
*cephalanthum,* 14, 17,
18, 102
Cetewayo, 129
*championae,* 26
Chevalier Felix de
Sauvage, 128
Chionoides, 129
Christmas Cheer, 118
*ciliatum,* 56, 119, 133
hybrids of, 116
*cinnabarinum,* 65, 72,
80, 119, 133
subsp. *xanthocodon,*
102
*clementinae,* 74
*collettianum,* 16
Colehurst, 127
Coombe Royal, 123
Cornish Cross, 124,
125
Cornish Early Red, 116
Cornubia, 124, 125
Countess of Hadding-
ton, 126
Countess of Sefton, 127
*cowanianum,* 16
*crinigerum,* 103
Cunningham's White,
73, 113, 127
*cyanocarpum,* 18
Cynthia, (syn. Lord
Palmerston) 121, 131
*dalhousiae,* 16, 56, 80,
119, 133
var. *rhabdotum,* 75
Damaris, 82
*dauricum,* 13, 19, 23,
27, 31
hybrids of, 116
var. *atrovirens,* 110
*decorum,* 18, 132